audience

NO LONGER NEWSWORTHY

NO LONGER NEWSWORTHY

How the Mainstream Media Abandoned the Working Class

Christopher R. Martin

ILR Press
An imprint of Cornell University Press
Ithaca and London

First published 2019 by Cornell University Press

Printed in the United States of America

Library of Congress Cataloging-in-Publication Data

Names: Martin, Christopher R., author.
Title: No longer newsworthy : how the mainstream media abandoned
    the working class / Christopher Martin.
Description: Ithaca : ILR Press, an imprint of Cornell University Press,
    2019. | Includes bibliographical references and index.
Identifiers: LCCN 2018045179 (print) | LCCN 2018047961 (ebook) |
    ISBN 9781501735264 (pdf) | ISBN 9781501735271 (epub/mobi) |
    ISBN 9781501735257 | ISBN 9781501735257 (cloth ; alk. paper)
Subjects: LCSH: Working class—Press coverage—United States. |
    Industrial relations—Press coverage—United States. | Labor unions
    and mass media—United States. | Journalism—Social aspects—United
    States. | Journalism—Political aspects—United States.
Classification: LCC HD8066 (ebook) | LCC HD8066. M188 2019 (print) |
    DDC 070.4/493055620973—dc23
LC record available at https://lccn.loc.gov/2018045179

For Bettina, Olivia, and Sabine

Contents

NO LONGER NEWSWORTHY

Introduction

As Donald J. Trump gained political momentum leading up to the 2016 US presidential election, and even months after he became president, there was one vexing question that so many people in the news media wanted to know about his supporters:

> "Who are these people?" asked MSNBC's Joe Scarborough, *HuffPost* columnist Marty Kaplan, journalist Alexander Zaitchik, feminist author Kate Harding, and *Seattle Gay News*.
>
> "Who are they?" asked the *New Yorker*.
>
> "Who are Trump supporters?" asked *Forbes*.
>
> "Who are Trump's supporters and opponents?" asked *CBS News*.
>
> "Who are Donald Trump's supporters, really?" asked the *Atlantic*.
>
> "Who the fuck are these people?" asked *GQ*.
>
> "Who are these idiot Donald Trump supporters?" asked *Salon*.[1]

"These people"—whoever they were—became the subjects of the biggest political story in decades. But it was as if the collective mainstream news media didn't know where to begin. And they didn't. For the mainstream news media, the decades-growing chasm of economic inequality was just an inconvenient by-product of an economy they celebrated for its high-flying CEOs, ascendant brands, big mergers, and Wall Street wizardry.

For decades, politicians of both the Democrat and Republican parties seemed to have lost the words to speak about the working class, and they made only occasional halfhearted nods to working people's discontent ("retraining" has been a common refrain, as well as getting rid of job-killing taxes, regulations, and government safety net programs so "jobs" can trickle down from the class of job creators).[2] Entering this scene, Donald Trump did something significant: he actually invoked the term "working class." To be sure, Trump tossed in winking appeals to white supremacists and male chauvinists (and appeased traditional Republican factions of wealthy donors and evangelical Christians), but it was clear who was most highly valued in his base: white, working-class men, especially those with grievances stoked by an unhealthy diet of talk radio, Fox News, Russian-sponsored fake news, and his own outrageous lies.

Americans have seen the white, male worker deployed as the symbolic representation of the US working class with almost regular repetition in modern politics and news media reports of the past fifty years. There were Nixon's "hard hats" in 1970 and the "New American Majority" that reelected him in a landslide in 1972, the "Reagan Democrats" of the 1980s, the auto-workers riled up by Pat Buchanan and Ross Perot and taking their anger to the polls in 1992, and Joe the Plumber, John McCain's working-class mascot in 2008.[3] In fact, in this politicized celebration of the white, male, blue-collar worker as the quintessential US worker, women and people of color have been correspondingly defined as *not* working class and as *not* authentic US workers. Instead, they have been mainly ignored or treated as merely special interests of the Democratic Party.

To answer the Trump-era question of "Who *are* these people?" several books in 2016 and 2017 became the guides for the mainstream news media and their middle-class audience. Authors Arlie Russell Hochschild, Katherine J. Cramer, Joan C. Williams, and J. D. Vance took readers (assumed to not be part of the white working class) on an anthropological journey to demystify the world of this "other." The four books described these white "blue-collar" folks variously as "struggling," "resentful," "angry," and suffering from "extreme alienation."[4]

In *Strangers in Their Own Land,* the Berkeley sociologist Hochschild visited conservative working-class people in the Louisiana bayou region and found "distrustful, betrayed," and "humiliated and mad" people supplying the "kindling" for Trump's rise.[5] In *White Working Class: Overcoming Class Cluelessness in America,* Williams, professor at the University of California Hastings College of Law in San Francisco, explains that "the white working class has been insulted or ignored during precisely the period when their economic fortunes tanked."[6] In *The Politics of Resentment: Rural Consciousness in Wisconsin and the Rise of Scott Walker,* Wisconsin political scientist Cramer journeyed to the rural parts of her state, beyond the liberal confines of Madison, and found a "flyover" land, a place "that is often overlooked by journalists living on the coasts." Here, the residents had a "rural consciousness" that "encompasses a strong identity as a rural resident, resentment toward the cities, and a belief that rural communities are not given their fair share of resources or respect."[7] In *Hillbilly Elegy: A Memoir of a Family and Culture in Crisis,* Vance, now a principal of a leading Silicon Valley investment firm, returned to the Greater Appalachia culture and region of his family origins in Kentucky and Ohio and found a "hub of misery" where "the fortunes of working-class whites seem dimmest."[8]

When Trump won the presidential race, news organizations in the United States largely attributed it to these people. The *New York Times* said it most succinctly in a headline: "Why Trump Won: Working-Class Whites."[9]

With postelection perspective and—props to the news media—some outstanding reporting, we now also know that the confluence of a number of other factors led to Trump's victory, including an archaic Electoral College system that enables a loser of the popular vote to win; FBI director James Comey's reopening of questions regarding Hillary Clinton's e-mail server in the final days of the campaign; Trump's white-supremacist, immigrant-bashing, misogynistic campaign message; Clinton's unfocused campaign theme and lack of campaigning in the Midwest; the disingenuous "voter fraud" restrictions rammed through in fourteen states (especially Wisconsin) since 2014; the unprecedented amount of news coverage Trump received during the campaign, enabling him to spend far less than expected; and social media campaigning and fake news from domestic conservative sources and from Russia that benefited Trump's campaign.[10]

Yet the primary takeaway from the election is that the white working class made a difference in electing Trump president, and that group still remains the base of his support.[11] Although Trump has been quick to blast the mainstream news media as "fake news" whenever it does not serve his interests, he has greatly benefited from two problematic ways in which the news has recently and historically framed its coverage of the working class. First, the news media usually look at the working class only through the lens of a political news story, not through the lens of a labor or workplace story. Second, the news media typically consider the "working class" not in its entirety, but just in the stereotypical white male form, which nicely serves the purposes of divisive politicians who seek to exploit this image and divide working-class people on every other dimension: race, gender, sexual orientation, disability, and citizenship.

The Invisible Worker

The stars aligned in 2016 in lots of ways for Donald Trump. One important instance was the unexpected closing of the Carrier furnace assembly plant in Indianapolis. Those jobs were being moved to Mexico. If not for a viral video of the closing announcement (shot by one of the unionized workers), the news media's and Trump's attraction to the story as political symbolism of the struggling, angry, resentful, and alienated working class might not have occurred. Trump used the opportunity to score a "win" in the media as president-elect, and the Carrier workers became momentarily visible as the working class of the United States.

Most of the country's national news media easily slid into the same "working-class" narrative for the Carrier story (on which I'll elaborate in chapter 1). These were the people who elected Trump, we were told, and Trump returned the favor by saving their jobs. President-elect Trump had come, saved some Carrier jobs (good, but not as great as he sold it), and was gone. Most of the national news media quickly exited, too, as political topics turned to repealing the Affordable Care Act, tax "reform" with enormous breaks to the wealthy, and Trump's quixotic vision of building a "great, great wall on our southern border."[12] (Some news organizations did stick with the story of workers at Carrier and the nearby Rexnord ball bearing factory— another plant closing that Trump completely ignored—and I will discuss later how this is a good development for journalism.)

The news media presented Carrier workers as exemplars of the working class. Yet the whole of the working class is hardly ever presented or imagined by the US news media. This is a nation of people with all kinds of collars. Service-sector jobs account for 80.3 percent of US jobs; manufacturing, construction, and mining—the types of jobs Trump regularly cites for his economic objectives—make up only 12.6 percent, about the same percentage as health care and social assistance (part of the service sector), the fastest-growing employment category. People of all races, genders, and political persuasions inhabit the working class, and they exist as real people, not just occasionally visible and selectively cast props for presidential campaigns.[13]

But with few exceptions, America's working class is invisible, deemed no longer newsworthy.

Most Americans would not learn much about the working class from the news media. Moreover, most Americans would not know they are likely *in* the working class. By the broad measure of economist Michael Zweig, the working class constitutes 60 percent of America's 163 million worker labor force. In practical terms, Zweig defines the working class in a manner that sounds a lot like a broader electorate that has the potential to feel agitated: "The working class is made up of people who, when they go to work or when they act as citizens, have comparatively little power or authority."[14]

Some observers consider class in hierarchical terms based on income, typically starting with those in poverty at the bottom, with the working class just above it, followed by a large middle class, then perhaps an upper-middle class, and the wealthy. For example, Jesse Meyerson in the *Nation* wrote that "When I use the phrase 'working class' here, I mean 'in and adjacent to poverty.'" Nate Silver of *FiveThirtyEight* implicitly used the same income hierarchy, arguing that Trump's working-class support is a myth because his voters' median household income is higher than the national median. Joan Williams argued in *Time* that "class should not be determined by income alone," and I agree. She considers other markers of class, including education and family structures.[15] It might surprise some people to know that only a minority of Americans, 33.4 percent, have a bachelor's degree or higher. It might surprise even more people to know that 64 million American workers make less than $15 per hour.[16]

Entire books have been written about how socioeconomic class should be defined, so I will necessarily be brief on this matter.[17] But for the purposes of this book, I will opt for Zweig's definition of working class because the state of having "comparatively little power or authority" as workers and citizens is a condition that captures the lived experience of a vast majority of people. It was once far more common in the United States for workers who had little power or authority to join together into labor unions to give themselves a measure of strength. In doing so, they often attained what many would call a "middle-class" income and lifestyle. What made the difference was the labor union. Without it, they would again have little power or authority. With the long decline of labor unions, most workers and most citizens in the United States today live in a precarious condition.[18]

My concern in this book is about journalism's future as an inclusive social practice. Journalism critics Bill Kovach and Tom Rosenstiel offer a moral compass: "If we think of journalism as social cartography, the map should include news of all our communities, not just those with attractive demographics or strong appeal to advertisers."[19] Unfortunately, journalism's "map" for years has been exclusive, consigning working-class people and their communities to obscurity—a class-based redlining of the news audience.

Where Americans found themselves on Election Day in 2016 was certainly the culmination of long-term trends in politics, economics, and the labor movement. But we cannot overlook the role of the news media, too. More than fifty years ago, newspapers were the leading medium of journalism. They are still the leading source of original reporting today. Thus, the centrality of newspapers to journalism and America's democratic functioning is certain, then and now. But in the late 1960s, newspapers started on a course which has increasingly made "the less desirable customers"—the working class and people of color (often the same people)—invisible as workers and citizens in their communities.[20]

Newspaper companies' switch to a new business trajectory in the late 1960s and early 1970s changed the target news audience and altered the actual news narratives about the working class in US journalism. Moreover, it upset the status of labor unions and upended politics through the last third of the twentieth century and beyond. The news media's write-off of the working class set the conditions for the decline of labor news and the rise of a deeply partisan conservative media that hailed the abandoned white, working-class audience. (Working-class women and people of color had no similar emergent news media platform.) The right wing then attacked the upscale-focused mainstream news media as "elite" and ultimately as "the enemy of the people." Given this politicized media infrastructure, the "surprise" of a Donald Trump presidency seems much less of one.

On Wednesday, November 9, 2016, the morning after Trump's election, media critics Brooke Gladstone and Bob Garfield recorded their reaction in a podcast segment titled "Now What?" for their public radio program *On the Media* at WNYC. Appraising the performance of the news media and their own media criticism show during the presidential campaign, the two hosts each identified a shortcoming.

"We have to talk to people that we have discounted," Gladstone said. "With regard to the election, I think that we fell into the trap of everyone else. The focus was never on his supporters until the very end." Garfield agreed and responded with an additional criticism: "I think the bigger story that the press missed overall has been the quintessential slow boiling frog situation. And that is, that there's been a 30-some year campaign of big lies. Of demagogues in politics and in conservative media telling this ever-growing, more frustrated, more marginalized audience a number of things that are objectively untrue. I think that happened and kind of softened the target for an opportunist demagogue like Donald Trump."[21]

Both Gladstone and Garfield are mostly right. But in the news media's repeated focus on the shift of a relatively small block of white, male, working-class voters (who, to be clear, were just some of Trump's supporters: most of his "base" were regular Republican voters), they overlooked an even bigger group that is habitually discounted: the people who didn't vote, who in 2016 numbered more than 90 million Americans, 40 percent of the citizens who were eligible to vote. If "Did Not Vote" was a presidential candidate in 2016, its 90 million ballots would have easily beaten Clinton's 65.85 million votes and Trump's 62.98 million votes and swept the Electoral College.[22] Here is where the political story of a mostly invisible electorate reflects the story of a mostly invisible working class. Like the US electorate, the working class is far larger and more heterogeneous than it is portrayed in the news media.

What Actually Made America Great

It was 1952, and America was great. Unemployment was at 3.0 percent, the second-lowest year of any since World War II—only 1953 would be better.[23] The baby boom was on, housing starts and durable goods sales were up, exports led imports, states greatly increased their investment in education over the previous decade, high school graduation rates were climbing, wages were rising, and per capita federal debt had fallen since the war's end.[24]

Not everything was great. The unemployment rate for African Americans was roughly double the white rate (and continues to be so today). Women were only 33.4 percent of the workforce, only 20.7 percent of married women with children worked, and women (like racial minorities) had limited or no access to many jobs.[25] (Today, the employment situation for women is better, but a pay gap persists; women are paid 83 percent what men make. Black women and Hispanic women make even less, 65.1 and 59.3 percent, respectively, of what white men make. Black and Hispanic men also significantly trail white men in median hourly earnings.)[26] In 1952 the civil rights movement had not yet started, nor had the second wave of US feminism.

But those problems can be overlooked by people with a nostalgic eye and selective memory. The sprawling, mass-produced Levittown, New York, suburban community had just been completed in 1952, a hallmark of America's great era but also a reminder to those who looked more closely (only whites were permitted to buy houses there) of things not great. There were no civil rights guarantees yet in this America.[27] It was a white America in other ways, too: the 1950s was the last decade of the twentieth century in which Europe led all other continents in immigration to the United States.[28]

The year 1952 was part of the immediate post–World War II era that gave birth to Donald Trump's worldview. That time is the answer to the question of his red hat's slogan, "Make America Great Again." The "late '40s and '50s," were a time, Trump said, when "we were not pushed around, we were respected by everybody, we had just won a war, we were pretty much doing what we had to do."[29]

Steve Bannon, the right-wing Internet propagandist, Trump's former White House advisor and Svengali, and now deposed Breitbart chairman, contends that US greatness was ignited by "an enlightened form of capitalism" that emerged from its victory in World War II, which was a war between "Judeo-Christian West versus atheists," as Bannon oddly asserted in a speech at the Vatican in 2014. From this twisted interpretation of opposing forces in World War II, Bannon finds America's innate economic greatness and reason for its subsequent decline:

> That capitalism really generated tremendous wealth. And that wealth was really distributed among a middle class, a rising middle class, people who come from really working-class environments and created what we really call a Pax Americana. It was many, many years and decades of peace. And I believe we've come partly offtrack in the years since the fall of the Soviet Union and we're starting now in the 21st century, which I believe, strongly, is a crisis both of our church, a crisis of our faith, a crisis of the West, a crisis of capitalism.[30]

Like Bannon, Trump sees a good economy as one led by benevolent, paternal capitalists, preferably those made by a Judeo-Christian deity. Just like him. "I will be the greatest jobs president that God ever created," Trump pronounced more than once.[31]

Bannon and Trump imagine a new workers' paradise in the United States, where white male workers are again a rising middle class. (While Trump offered rhetorical greatness for those workers, his economic offer to black voters to support him sounded like it was straight out of the 1950s: "What the hell do you have to lose?"[32] His plans for women were equally retrograde, summed up with his ignominious comment that when you are a star like him, you can "Grab 'em by the pussy. You can do anything."[33]) Never in their description—one that is based on the economic successes of the 1940s, 1950s, and 1960s—do Bannon and Trump mention the crucial role of labor unions, the one institution that gave workers a voice and a measure of power in the economic system, and still can today.

Why is it that many seem to remember so much about when the US economy was "great," except for the most important details: that US workers fought for decades for respect and representation in the workplace and that the high wages of the 1950s, 1960s, and early 1970s existed because during this period from a quarter to more than a third of US workers were covered by contracts collectively negotiated by their labor unions? The benevolent leaders of "enlightened capitalism" then proceeded to rip through the last decades of the twentieth century with a war on labor unions, opposition to every increase of the minimum wage, and unprecedented levels of compensation to themselves. Then came this: declining union power, downsized and outsourced jobs, shrinking benefits, underfunded pensions, and managerial "flexibility" that has left workers in an ever-present state of insecurity.

The idea for this book started with an ordinary newspaper article from 1952. More than fifty years after the story was written, I was in Cleveland, at the Western Reserve Historical Library, looking through the collected papers of Anthony J. DiSantis, a labor reporter and columnist at the *Cleveland Plain Dealer* from 1942 to 1960. Yellowed, cut-out copies of DiSantis's articles had been carefully mounted in a scrapbook in part of his archives, and as I read a routine story about a strike by Greyhound Bus workers that he had written for the January 31, 1952, edition, something struck me as unusual.

The front-page story carried the headline "BUS UNION'S HEADS TALK TO STRIKERS; Workers Give In, Admit Them to Meeting; Hopes Ride on Session Today." The story, twenty paragraphs in all, jumped from the front page to page 5 and addressed the grievances of the striking workers and the attempts of the union leaders to talk with them. Aside from the estimate of the 25,000 stranded riders in paragraph three, there were no other mentions of the bus passengers until four short paragraphs near the end of the story.

The elements missing in this story were the unusual part: no headline or lead paragraph emphasizing affected passengers, no pictures of harried or exhausted commuters, and no comments from travelers angered by delays. The story simply ended with "Commuters who were able to get to Cleveland despite the strike made their return journey by hitch hiking or sharing rides with friends or availed themselves of added Cleveland Transit System bus service to the end of the line and then hitch hiked the rest of the way." That's it—some commuters were able to get to Cleveland on that day, and those who did found a way to get home. Thus, the article's central focus was on the details of the labor dispute and negotiations rather than the dispute's side effects on bus riders.

By contrast, consider more-contemporary accounts of strikes. In my earlier book, *Framed! Labor and the Corporate Media*, I looked at the major labor stories of the 1990s and found them to be typically structured around consumer themes. This kind of news story framing is evident in the coverage of another Greyhound bus worker strike—this one a national strike by Greyhound bus workers (represented by the Amalgamated Transit Union) in March 1990—thirty-eight years after DiSantis's 1952 Greyhound strike story.

Major newspaper reports on the 1990 strike all start immediately with consumer story frames. Headlines included "Passengers Stranded by Greyhound Strike" (*San Francisco Chronicle*), "Strike Hobbling Greyhound and Thousands of Its Riders" (*New York Times*), "Rough Road Ahead for Bus Riders" (*USA Today*), and "For Stranded Riders, a Hard Cold Floor" (*Washington Post*). Many of the stories included photos of travelers waiting in stations or trying to sleep on the floor or in chairs.

The lead paragraphs constructed stories emphasizing anger, inconvenience, exhaustion, and disruption of the innocence of small-town life:

> *Washington Post:* Hundreds of bleary-eyed passengers slouched in lines yesterday morning at the District's Greyhound bus station after spending the night on the cold floor or hard plastic chairs when drivers abruptly abandoned them to join the national strike.

> *Boston Globe:* Greyhound bus travelers in Boston did not waste time yesterday fuming about the nationwide strike of 6,300 bus drivers, as they headed in record numbers for South Station and Amtrak trains to Hartford, New York and points south.

> *St. Louis Post-Dispatch:* The first day of the strike by Greyhound bus drivers Friday left many communities without intercity service and delayed thousands of passengers, including elderly travelers and students on spring break, at bus terminals across the country.

New York Times: Nine thousand communities, most of them isolated rural towns and farming hamlets, were jolted today by the near-collapse of their only public transit system after drivers struck the Greyhound bus system in a wage dispute.

The Associated Press, which sends its stories to thousands of affiliate news organizations, also played up the consumer angle, with a story ("Caught in the Bus Strike") containing several vignettes from around the country. All of the passengers were upset about being stranded in locations short of their destination. But the most dramatic comment came from a man stuck in Indianapolis:

After spending the night on a hard floor in the Indianapolis bus station, Frank Rzepski of Philadelphia had little sympathy for the drivers.

"It's getting to the point where we're ready to go out there and fire one of the buses up, run over the strikers and say, 'See ya,'" he said.

What a contrast. In 1952 the effects of the strike on consumers were considered to be a given part of economic life. A transit strike? No big deal. You might have to walk, call a friend, or hitchhike. By 1990, the stories highlighted difficulties and indulged readers to identify with the anger and violent fantasies of consumers whose daily lives the striking workers had dared to interrupt. The implicit conclusion of these new narratives, as voiced by one of the other passengers quoted in the AP story, is "If you ask me, I think they should go back to work and let people go home."

Another kind of story could have been written about the Greyhound bus workers strike of 1990. The details for an alternative narrative featuring the workers' condition—the actual reason behind the strike—were readily available (all of the articles cited above carried bits of this kind of information). That narrative might have been a dramatic story about low-paid bus workers who conceded about 25 percent in pay and benefits throughout the previous decade versus the now-monopoly national bus service, back on its feet with ample profits and more than $1 billion in annual revenue, but giving workers only a 13 percent pay increase over three years in its ultimatum.

Yet none of the newspapers wrote that kind of story. Instead, from the 1970s onward, the mainstream media regularly stoked and aired grievances of consumers angry at labor unions. Ironically, the emerging conservative media would later use the same grievance-highlighting approach for its own stories against "liberal" media, Democratic politicians, and government in general.

A Working-Class Life

Readers sometimes expect a certain level of lived authenticity for permission to write authoritatively on the working class.

So for ethos and pathos, here is my brief story.[34] I grew up in a family in Central Ohio that was striving toward upper-middle-class status until my dad's alcoholism and my parents' divorce transported us into a working-class life after I turned nine. My dad died when I was fourteen. After the divorce my mom struggled with enormous burdens as a single parent raising three sons and a daughter. She returned back to work in mostly administrative assistant positions with low wages, few opportunities for advancement, and the routine sexism of the times. There was no history of union membership in my family. By the time I hit my senior year of high school, in 1980, President Reagan was blaming labor unions for all of the ills of the economy, and it seemed like a plausible explanation. I agreed with Reagan, initially. It took me a few years to actually understand what unions did and to realize my mistake. My two older brothers have labored in a succession of working-class jobs for their entire adult lives. I had a skill for academics and writing, and chose that path. I worked my way (painting houses, setting up and selling Christmas trees, painting house numbers on curbs, cleaning bed & breakfast guest rooms and bathrooms, teaching classes, and assisting in research) through three university degrees and paid off my government-supported loans. I was the second in my family to get a university degree, after my father. For a while as an undergraduate at Capital University in Columbus in the 1980s, I received survivor benefits from my late father's Social Security account. The payments certainly helped make ends meet in my family's household, for I still lived at home. However, Reagan phased out survivor benefits before I finished my first degree.

I worked with the state legislature in Ohio's historic statehouse for three years in the mid-1980s as a communications aide in the Senate Republican caucus. That bit of information always shocks people who know me now. In retrospect, it seems strange to me, too, but it was a valuable learning experience. One of the senators I worked with was Donald "Buz" Lukens. (John Kasich, later US representative and governor of Ohio, was a Legislative Service Commission fellow to Buz Lukens in 1975. I held the same assignment eleven years later.) In the Republican-led antidrug fervor of the 1980s, Lukens wanted all of his staff to take urine tests so he could proclaim that his people were drug-free. We all refused. Lukens later got reelected to Congress but didn't stay long after he was caught on hidden camera admitting to his sexual relations with a minor and trying to bribe accusers with government jobs.[35] He rebuffed calls for his resignation but got beaten in the primary election by John Boehner, already sporting a very dark tan as state representative on his way to become the US Speaker of the House. Lukens was later sentenced to prison for accepting bribes. Another state senator in my caucus, Robert Ney, also got elected to Congress. He is the guy who led the brief renaming of French Fries to "Freedom Fries" in the House cafeteria in Washington. This was meant to be a devastatingly symbolic blow to France for not supporting the 2003 invasion of Iraq. Ney was also a central figure in the Jack Abramoff lobbying scandal and served a prison sentence for corruption.[36] Although I remain fascinated by politics, a long career in service to people like these and their conservative policies looked soul-crushing to me.

I left for Massachusetts, where I attended Emerson College for two years to earn an M.A. in mass communication, something I could afford only with the help of government-supported academic loans. I then earned a Ph.D. in mass communication at the University of Michigan in Ann Arbor, where I first encountered a union. As a teaching assistant (TAs taught 40 percent of the courses at Michigan at that time), I joined the Graduate Employees' Organization at Michigan. It's still one of the best graduate employee unions in the country, and it sustained me with fair pay, a tuition waiver, and health care. I walked a picket line when UM (a very wealthy public institution) tried to downgrade our health care. Michigan is also where I began my research on labor issues in the early 1990s, and I met good people from the UAW, workers from the GM Willow Run plant, and the now-deceased veteran labor reporter Helen Fogel of the *Detroit Free Press*. I later met workers from A. E. Staley, Caterpillar, and Bridgestone/Firestone in Decatur, Illinois, who were on a tour of the Midwest as "Road Warriors" to gather support for their cause. Their predicament, a decade-long corporate assault on local labor unions, ripped apart the economic and social fabric of Decatur.[37]

Today I live in Iowa—perhaps the center of "flyover" America—and have been here for more than twenty years. The majority of my home state's voters opted for Donald Trump in 2016, but I live in one of the urban counties in Iowa (132,000 people counts as urban here) where he didn't win. My county also has the highest percentage of African Americans in the state. I make less money than my colleagues at larger universities, but my household income (which includes the income of my spouse, who is also a professor, and some publishing royalties) is enough to put us in the top 10 percent in income in the country, and that goes a long way in Iowa. I don't live in a gated community, but instead in a house by a public park in an old university neighborhood with students and people of nearly every socioeconomic class within a few blocks.

I teach at a public university, which makes me a public employee. I'm tenured in my academic position, which means after years of evaluation of my teaching, research, and service, I've earned the right to keep this position indefinitely but can be fired for just cause. Faculty members at my university, including me, work on average 52–54 hours a week. I'm white, male, heterosexual, married, and have two daughters. I believe that respect for everyone's holiday traditions doesn't ruin Christmas and that Fox News should stop suggesting otherwise. I believe that equal rights for GLBTQ citizens are fair and needed. I believe that black lives do matter and that African Americans and other people of color deserve far better treatment from the justice system, the education system, and every other cultural institution. I'm a feminist, which means I believe my wife, my daughters, and every other woman should have the same rights, opportunities, and job compensation in life that men are afforded. I never served in the military, but I did register (as required by law) for Selective Service in the 1980s, just in case the government declared war and needed to conscript me. I participate in a number of civic activities and serve on two community boards.

My younger sister is a high school teacher in Ohio and belongs to a union that Governor John Kasich tried to destroy in 2011, along with all other public employee unions, just like Governor Scott Walker did in Wisconsin.[38] (My younger sister also sometimes worked for Buz Lukens in the State Senate at one time as a page.) She had her "union awakening" as one of thousands protesting at the statehouse; the voters of Ohio eventually overturned the law in a referendum that union advocates put on the ballot.[39] My oldest brother works long hours in a tire warehouse that is not unionized. My other brother retired early on disability from chronic injuries suffered at a nonunion workplace. Fortunately, there is a worker's compensation system. He worked in one of the world's more difficult jobs—handling massive bulls so their genetically superior semen could be collected and sold to breeders. If a bull came at you, get out of the way, but don't hurt the bull—they are expensive, as he was often reminded. Nevertheless, he once had to smack a bull on the head with a shovel to keep it from goring one of his coworkers.

I belong to a union. For about five years, I was an academic department head—the boss and evaluator of about forty faculty and staff and supervisor of a $3 million annual budget—and I couldn't be part of the bargaining unit. As department head, I learned that administrators are not hand-tied by union rules (a common myth) but quite the opposite: a well-negotiated union contract improves the relationship between worker and management and makes for a lot less guesswork. I have since rejoined several hundred of my colleagues as a member of United Faculty, our local affiliate of the national AAUP (American Association of University Professors), founded in 1915.

As I was writing this book, Republicans used their new complete control of the Iowa House, Senate, and governor's office in 2017 to enact every item on the right-wing, Koch brothers–financed conservative agenda. No matter that majority public opinion did not agree with these positions, no matter that Republicans did not run on this agenda. Most significantly, they quickly undercut the state's public employee union bargaining system, effectively decimating contracts covering 184,000 public employees in Iowa.[40] When Governor Terry Branstad signed the law in February 2017, undoing a public employee collective-bargaining system that had worked well since it was signed by another Republican governor in 1974, one lobbyist was there to smile and shake his hand. That lobbyist was the Iowa director of Americans for Prosperity, the political advocacy group funded by Charles and David Koch that had provided the blueprint and political financing for undoing public employee unions in Wisconsin and other states.[41] We know this only because the lobbyist, Drew Klein, was nice enough to publicly tweet out the occasion of his special audience with the governor.

In that brief 2017 legislative session, Republicans in Iowa also outlawed counties from raising their minimum wage (another Americans for Prosperity priority), rolling back wages in the five counties that had already raised it above the state's meager $7.25-per-hour minimum wage. In Iowa a worker needs to earn $14.03 per hour to afford a two-bedroom apartment (at fair-market rent of $730 per month).[42] At Iowa's minimum wage, a full-time worker can generate only $377 a month for rent. Iowa's "pro-business" stance on the minimum wage is in the minority. Twenty-nine states have already raised their minimum wage above the federal minimum, which has been $7.25 since 2009.[43] (At least twenty-five other states have passed laws preempting cities and counties from raising their minimum wages above the state minimum.[44]) The Iowa legislature also cut workers' compensation

Drew Klein @Klein_Drew · Feb 17   ∨
Was honored to witness Governor Branstad sign this historic bill into law.
#ialegis #iagov #collectivebargaining @AFPIowa

◯ 43   ⇄ 9   ♡ 18   ✉

Figure I.1. Twitter post of Americans for Prosperity lobbyist Drew Klein, with Iowa governor
Terry Branstad, February 17, 2017

benefits. On the plus side, a bipartisan group of Iowa legislators passed a law
legalizing retail fireworks in the state. So much to celebrate.

At the federal level, one of Iowa's US senators is Chuck Grassley. He
wanted to get rid of the estate tax, which he and his fellow Republicans like
to cleverly call the "death tax." Whatever one calls it, the tax affects only individual estates worth more than $5.5 million. That touches very few people in
the United States and only the wealthiest personal farm estates in Iowa: a few
dozen each year, the *Des Moines Register* reported. But Grassley, a Republican
since 1980 who has long cultivated a "simple farmer" persona that belies
his multimillion-dollar wealth, persisted: "I think not having the estate tax
recognizes the people that are investing, as opposed to those that are just
spending every darn penny they have, whether it's on booze or women or
movies." A few weeks later, Grassley and his colleagues ultimately recog-
nized the good Americans—those who amass more than $5.5 million—and
doubled their estate tax exemption to $11.2 million.[45]

I like my job, although for decades I have worked long hours preparing
new classes, teaching, grading, advising, reading, writing, participating in
governance of the university, and doing outreach to the community. I have

some power over my own schedule, so if I need to pick up a daughter at 3 P.M., I can sometimes leave early and finish certain work later in the evening at home. If I want to teach a class on a new topic, there is a chance I can. If I want to write something that is both true and critical of the conservative media echo chamber, something that might anger conservative Republicans in the state legislature who built their careers on such propaganda, I can do it, even if my own university tries to distance itself from me (which it once did).[46] That's the ultimate value of tenure. But when the Republican state legislature treats both labor unions and university professors as their political enemies (what did we ever do to them except negotiate for a decent living, give their children a quality college education, build a great regional university, and enhance the state's economy?), it only reinforces my commitment to belong to a labor union. I'm also deeply committed to the practice of journalism. I teach journalism, and good journalists are my heroes.

Although the conditions of our lives and upbringing may lend authenticity to the stories we tell, those personal histories are not always a determining factor in the stories that *get* told. For journalism, the economic structure and target audience of the news organization have enormous influence on the focus and framing of its news stories about working people.

What Comes Next

This book is about what happened to US workers or, more specifically, what happened to the stories of those workers in the news media. How could it be that in a matter of a few decades, labor unions and the concerns of the working class went from being a normal, regular, respected part of journalism's coverage to an abnormal, misunderstood, and mostly invisible topic in the news media? Historian Jefferson Cowie, in his excellent history of the working class in the 1970s, found "class identity growing feeble as the decade wore on."[47] What was the contribution of journalism to undermining the working class and labor? More specifically, why did the mainstream news media change its approach and narrative frames about labor unions and the working class in the final third of the twentieth century?

From a broader view, what role did this journalistic transformation have in the later emergence of mostly white, working-class anger in the United States, the war on mainstream news media, the rise of radical conservative news media, and the surprising election of Donald Trump as a self-proclaimed working-class messiah? These questions will be addressed in the following chapters.

In chapter 1, I break down the news media coverage of president-elect Donald Trump's visit to the Carrier furnace assembly plant in Indianapolis. The plant became Trump's symbolic beachhead in his "plan" to save jobs only after the workers there pushed for months to gain national visibility to save their jobs from being shipped to Mexico. The news media emphasized stories of grateful white men whose jobs had been saved by the president-elect, playing into Trump's (and his conservative media's) public relations narrative. The news narrative conveniently ignored union workers who didn't fit into the Trumpian worldview. Only some news organizations continued to follow the story when Trump's promises to save jobs at Carrier fell short by hundreds of workers and the local union president called out Trump for lying. For the rest of the news media, it was a brief political story, and the Carrier workers again became invisible.

In chapter 2, I discuss the historical rise and decline of the labor beat at US newspapers, the one place where the topic of work was regularly covered. At one point in the twentieth century, the *New York Times* alone employed up to five labor reporters at a time. Although the United States has an even larger workforce today, the *Times* has just one labor reporter, and nationally there are only just a handful. How did this happen?

In chapter 3, I analyze how the US news media made a significant and devastating shift from targeting a mass audience to targeting an upscale audience beginning in the late 1960s. I draw on the newspapers' own advertisements to corporate advertisers in the longtime industry publication *Editor & Publisher*, which nicely illustrate this change in direction.

In chapter 4, I describe how this purposeful shift toward upscale audiences has led to an actual change in narratives about labor unions and workers in newspapers. Instead of being "with" the workers, the newspaper narratives began to go "against" the workers because they inflict inflationary damage and inconveniences on the newspapers' new upscale consumers. Moreover, as they let the labor beat wither, mainstream newspapers shifted their focus to reporting on upscale strivers with the new office "workplace" lifestyles column and with a new emphasis on personal finance reporting for America's budding individualist entrepreneurs. With the working class bereft of journalism that spoke to their lives, the emerging conservative news filled a gap, but only for the white working class they hailed. In the coming decades, conservative-aligned news media realized their ultimate political goals with a presidential candidate who embraced their method of stoking white, working-class grievances and trolling the mainstream media as elitist.

In chapter 5, I look at the idea of political voice. I chart how the shift in journalism's positions about labor unions and the working class relates to the shift in focus of the Democrat and Republican parties in the late 1960s and early 1970s and the concept of the "Silent Majority" encouraged by the Republican Party. As the media and politicians talked less about class, and the working class lost their voice, they found it again in the nascent Tea Party and Occupy Wall Street movements, which had similar origins but wildly divergent solutions. I also look at the case of Iowa's shift in political voice in the 2016 presidential election.

In chapter 6, I more deeply analyze one outgrowth of the shift in journalism and politics: the rise of the concept of "job killers." Conservative politicians have successfully coined the term "job killer" for the laws and policies that impede corporate autonomy and unchecked profit taking. Ironically, these laws (e.g., raising the minimum wage, health care reform, workplace safety rules) are designed to aid the working class. Yet the term is often uncritically repeated by journalists. The durability of "job killers" as a public concept speaks to a major failure of the press.

Finally, in chapter 7, I conclude with how journalism might, from another perspective, rethink the nature of America's "job killers." The chapter also features the story of the financial industry's intentional sabotage of workers and how the news media response amounted to "let them eat cake"—literally, in the case of Hostess Brands—and how the mainstream news covered recent teacher strikes. I also identify where journalism can improve its coverage, erase the redlining of the working class, and make workers newsworthy and visible again.

Chapter 1

Trump, Carrier, and the Invisible Worker

Three weeks after his surprising victory on Election Day, November 8, 2016, Donald Trump had what might be eventually known as the best day of his presidency. And with his swearing-in ceremony still weeks away, he wasn't officially even president yet.

On November 29, Trump confidently tweeted hints of a dramatic conclusion to reports that he had been in discussion with executives at Carrier Corporation in Indiana to save hundreds of jobs that were scheduled to be exported to a new assembly facility in Mexico: "I will be going to Indiana on Thursday to make a major announcement concerning Carrier A.C. staying in Indianapolis. Great deal for workers!"

That Thursday, December 1, Trump arrived in Indianapolis. The video, which was frequently replayed in TV news stories, shows him among more than twenty men in suits, striding triumphantly through the Carrier furnace assembly floor with his black overcoat and too-long red tie, talking briefly with United Technologies (UTC) CEO Gregory Hayes and followed by other men in suits, including Bob McDonough, president of Carrier, which is a division of UTC. Trump was also joined in the tour by vice president-elect (and still Indiana governor) Mike Pence, and both occasionally gestured with finger pointing (I acknowledge your presence!) and thumbs up to assembly workers outside of the frame. Then, later, Mike Pence announced "a man of action, a man of his word, and the president-elect of the United States of America, Donald Trump." Trump took the platform in front of a white backdrop dotted with oval blue Carrier logos and announced he was saving a lot of jobs: "Actually the number's over 1,100 people, which is so great, which is so great."

Most of the nation's news organizations praised Trump for this huge win, even before he actually made the announcement and full details were known.

On November 29, Breitbart, which was already in the bag for Trump, wrote that "Donald Trump isn't even president yet and he's already winning for American workers."[1]

The *New York Post,* also in the bag for Trump, led its story with "Make America work again. President-elect Donald Trump and Vice-President-elect Mike Pence struck a deal with Carrier on Monday, saving 'close to 1,000' jobs in Indiana by preventing the air-conditioning company from moving its production lines to Mexico. . . . Trump made bringing factory jobs back to the United States and revitalizing America's working class a staple of his campaign."[2]

But other news organizations, even the nonconservative ones that Donald Trump persistently berated in speeches and tweets, scored this as a victory, with Trump realizing a key campaign promise.

For example, early in the morning on November 30, CNN anchor Christine Romans, reporting on Trump's tweet and his coming appearance, said that "terms of the Carrier deal were not released, but there are already questions and critics." Yet that didn't prevent her from immediately concluding with "what is clear: this was a negotiation, this is a *big win* for Donald Trump. He is making good on his promise to stop companies from shipping jobs overseas."[3]

The *Washington Post* came to the same conclusion: "President-elect Donald Trump scored a victory Tuesday night when Carrier, an Indiana-based manufacturing company that had announced plans to move at least 1,400 jobs to Mexico, said it would keep 1,000 jobs in the state."[4]

The *Christian Science Monitor* had questions about the deal but reported "at first blush—and certainly for the workers involved—the Carrier news was a stunning piece of good news."[5]

Kristen Welker, for NBC's *Today Show,* in a live report on December 1 before Trump's announcement, began with "Here in Indiana, president-elect Donald Trump is going to be touting his first big win, as you say keeping more than a thousand jobs here at this company, Carrier AC, from leaving the country. . . . [cut to her voice-over] Donald Trump trying to show that even as president-elect, he can put the art of the deal into practice."[6]

Here's What President Trump Will Do

The drama of the Carrier plant closing started with a viral video. A mobile phone video from one of the workers attending Carrier's February 10, 2016, jobs announcement soon gained more than four million social media views and was picked up by several news media organizations. Chris Nelson, president of the heating and ventilation company Carrier Residential and Commercial Systems North America, spoke to hundreds of workers and was amazingly bureaucratic and fully lacking in empathy. "Relocating our operations to Monterrey will allow us to maintain high levels of product quality at competitive prices, and continue to serve the extremely price-sensitive marketplace. I want to be clear, this is strictly a business decision," he said to shouts, boos, and derisive laughter.[7] Nelson told the workers multiple times to "quiet down."

Any mindful presidential politician could see there was turmoil and anxiety over work in the middle of the United States. February 2016 was a busy month in the presidential primary season. However, most candidates said nothing about Carrier's decision to send 1,400 jobs in Indianapolis to Mexico. But Donald Trump, America's self-proclaimed blue-collar billionaire, did say something.[8] The Carrier closing was tailor-made for how he was positioning his candidacy, and his conservative media allies responded by properly setting the table so he could eat up his competition on the jobs issue.

On February 12, Breitbart.com turned the Carrier story into an exclusive featuring only Trump. With Steve Bannon as the executive chair of Breitbart News (he would not become the chief executive of Trump's campaign until August 17 of that year), the story heralded Trump as the savior of blue-collar manufacturing jobs; the Breitbart headline read "Exclusive—Donald Trump on Ford, Carrier, Shipping Jobs to Mexico: 'I'm the Only One Who Understands What's Going On.'"[9] The first sentence of the story made Breitbart's promotional objective clear: "Donald Trump, the billionaire and national GOP presidential frontrunner who just won the New Hampshire primary and is polling ahead of the field in South Carolina, is seizing a major political opportunity with the news that Ford and Carrier are shipping thousands of US jobs to Mexico."

The conservative, Rupert Murdoch–owned *New York Post* expanded the reach of the story with the posting of a 43-second excerpt of the viral video the same day, with the title "Stomach-turning moment 1,400 workers lost their jobs" and a brief caption.[10] *CNNMoney* also posted the story on February 12, with a more substantial story and the headline "Carrier workers' rage over move to Mexico caught on video."[11]

At 7:01 A.M. the next day, Trump linked to the *New York Post* headline and video and tweeted a message consistent with the blue-collar messiah angle of the Breitbart exclusive: "I am the only one who can fix this. Very sad. Will not happen under my watch! #MakeAmericaGreatAgain."

February 13 was an important date: a CBS Republican primary debate with the remaining six GOP candidates was planned for that evening in South Carolina. No other candidate mentioned the Carrier closing except Trump, who had already primed the mainstream news media with his Breitbart story, *Post* video, and tweet.

Trump continued to make the exported Carrier jobs (along with Ford and Nabisco's similar export of jobs to Mexico) the central economic parable of his campaign. He again cited Carrier in the next Republican primary debate, on February 26 in Houston. Then, a few days later at a rally in Louisville on March 1, Trump revealed his economic strategy—actually, a chatty scenario, but this is as precise as it got with Trump—to keep Carrier and other manufacturing jobs in the United States if he would become president:

> Here's what President Trump will do. . . . I think you're going to love it even though it really isn't presidential. I will call the head of Carrier. And I will say "I hope you enjoy your new building. I hope you enjoy your stay in Mexico. But you've just left the United States. There's no more taxes that you're gonna pay. There's no more jobs that you're gonna produce. Fourteen hundred great people have been left out in the lurch. Here's the story, folks. Every single air conditioning unit that you build and send across our border, you're going to pay a 35 percent tax on that unit." [cheers] . . . I'm working for you. True. True. So here's what's gonna happen. Within 24 hours, I'll get a call, the head of Carrier, and he'll say, "Mr. President, we've decided to stay in the United States." All right, that's what's gonna happen. [cheers] A hundred percent, by the way. A hundred percent.[12]

Trump continued referencing Carrier at a rally in Syracuse in April, at a stop in Indianapolis in April ("Believe me, if I were in office right now, Carrier would not be leaving Indiana, that I can tell you, that I can tell you."),[13] and in the September 26 general election debate against Hillary Clinton.

Trump's campaign identified a major rift in the US economy, and in the words of Breitbart, he indeed was actively "seizing a major political opportunity." Although unemployment levels had been declining and Wall Street was back in the money, good-wage factory jobs had been leaching out of the United States for years. And then on Tuesday, November 8, 2016, Trump, who had hammered away at this major political opportunity, eked out an Electoral College victory with the help of several midwestern states and became the president-elect.

When President-Elect Trump Is Reminded of What He Said

That might have been the end of the Carrier story for Trump, if not for a really good piece of accountability journalism. In a November 14 report, *NBC Nightly News* broadcast a story about the Carrier plant, returning to the site of which Trump had often spoken but never once visited during the primary or the general election campaign. How were the Carrier workers doing? All of the workers were still scheduled to lose their jobs to $3-per-hour workers in Monterrey, and they still weren't happy about it. Trump, who as a candidate said "Here's what President Trump will do" about Carrier, was now the PEOTUS, president-elect of the United States. And, fortunately for the workers, president-elect Donald Trump, who reportedly gets most of his news from television, saw the report that evening.[14]

NBC Nightly News anchor Lester Holt introduced the package and handed off to reporter Kevin Tibbles.

> **TIBBLES VOICE-OVER:** When Carrier Air Conditioning told its 1,400 employees that it was shutting down . . .
> **CHYRON TEXT AT BOTTOM OF SCREEN:** "PRESSURE ON TRUMP TO KEEP JOBS PROMISE"
> **VIDEO:** clip of mobile phone viral video that shows loud response to the closing announcement
> **TIBBLES VOICE-OVER:** . . . it became a focal point for Donald Trump in the election.
> **VIDEO** (Trump speaking at rally): We're bringing jobs back to our country; we're not going to let Carrier leave . . .

TIBBLES VOICE-OVER (still photo of Carrier workers protesting for jobs earlier in the year): Many at Carrier are now counting on him to keep his promise.

VIDEO (unidentified African American male Carrier worker): Put your money where your mouth is. It's just as simple as that.

TIBBLES VOICE-OVER (footage of workers and customers in bar interior): Across from the plant, Sully's Bar and Grill, where workers after their shift say they have high expectations for the president-elect.

VIDEO (unidentified white male Carrier worker): We want you to do what you said you were going to do. We're gonna hold you accountable.

TIBBLES (ON CAMERA): Just down the road another blow to American jobs, the Rexnord plant—it makes ball bearings. It, too, is now moving to Mexico. Three hundred and fifty jobs lost.

The story then provides a sound bite from Donald Grimes, University of Michigan (it's not clear what he does, but a later check confirms he is a senior research specialist at the University of Michigan's Institute for Research on Labor, Employment, and the Economy), who says that US manufacturing will continue to be relocated to "lower-cost countries" and "that's just a fact of life." Tibbles notes in a voice-over that Carrier is "trying to ease the workers' transition" with three years' advance notice and funding for education and retraining. The story continues:

TIBBLES VOICE-OVER: Some Carrier workers see politics at play.

VIDEO (African American female worker; identified as LATISHA WILLIAMS/CARRIER EMPLOYEE): They just say whatever needs to be said to get people's vote, especially in a time like this when we're all losing our jobs."

VIDEO (of earlier white male worker, now identified as T. J. BRAY/CARRIER EMPLOYEE): If he can come here and save these fourteen hundred jobs here tomorrow, I'll gladly vote for him again.

TIBBLES VOICE-OVER (video of gambling machine and billiards in bar): Many of these American workers say they took a gamble on Trump and are now hoping the payoff means winning back their jobs. Kevin Tibbles, NBC News, Indianapolis.

Figure 1.1. Carrier worker T. J. Bray on *NBC News*, November 14, 2016

The three Carrier workers that day at Sully's Bar and Grill across the street from Carrier all called Trump to account. But T. J. Bray (also the communications representative for United Steelworkers Local 1999), who was on camera twice, said the one thing that seemed to pique Trump's attention: he supported Trump. In Trump's memory, Bray was always all-in for Trump, and that's what mattered most. In fact, in an August 23 *CNNMoney* report that Trump apparently did not see, Bray criticized Trump's shallow promises of jobs and said that "this guy's an entertainer. He's a clown."[15] But in Trump's mind, Bray was the prototypical Midwestern working-class Trump supporter.

Although Trump denied he ever made a promise explicitly for Carrier (he did), he was willing to negotiate on behalf of Carrier because there were Trump supporters there, and the public relations optics must have looked good. "So now because of him, whoever that guy was," Trump said in his speech at the Carrier plant. Interestingly, Trump said nothing of the other two workers featured in the NBC story.

In his candidacy announcement in June 2015, Trump said "I will be the greatest jobs president that God ever created," a claim he repeated several times through the campaign.[16] Now, as president-elect, he had a chance to prove himself. Shortly after the NBC report questioning his commitment to the Carrier workers, the Trump-Pence team held secret discussions with Carrier's corporate parent, UTC. Then Trump began to build drama that something was afoot with a series of tweets. Once he announced that he would be going to Indiana on December 1, Fox News worked as his advance unit to spread news of the "Great deal for workers" soon to be visited upon the Hoosier state.

The (White, Male) Working Class Boards the Fox News Trump Train

On November 30, anticipating the good news of Trump's announcement the next day, Fox News anchor Megyn Kelly interviewed two white, male Carrier workers, Paul Roell, a seventeen-year employee and team leader, and T. J. Bray, a fourteen-year employee who had appeared in the November 14 NBC report. As in most Carrier stories, Kelly showed the viral video of the plant closing announcement, and she asked both men how they felt and how the situation affected their families. Then she asked the question that the Fox News organization wanted to highlight: as Carrier workers (it's not necessary for Kelly to say the obvious adjectives: white, male), are they Trump supporters or not?

Figure 1.2. Fox News host Megyn Kelly with Carrier workers Paul Roell and T. J. Bray, November 30, 2016

KELLY: When Donald Trump, 'cause he made this an issue when he was on the campaign trail, when he was saying he was coming after Carrier, uh, did you guys support him, were you Trump supporters before November 8?

BRAY: Uh, I was not a huge Trump supporter. I didn't really know how to take Mr. Trump. But I'm glad that he actually lived up to a promise and stuck with it, and I'll gladly throw some support to him. And if I get a chance to shake his hand [Kelly, in split screen, nods with a slight smile here] tomorrow to thank him for saving my job, I'll gladly do that.

KELLY: How 'bout you, Paul? How did you feel about him then and now?

ROELL: I supported him the whole time. Even in the beginning when everybody said he wasn't serious about running as a candidate. And when he was going for the Republican nomination, nobody thought he would get it. His own party was against him. When he got the candidacy to be the nominee for the Republicans, everybody still said he wasn't going to get the election. He did it. Three weeks after he gets elected, he makes the announcement—he done what he said he was going to do with Carrier [Kelly talks over final word].[17]

Kelly's network colleague, conservative pundit Sean Hannity, continued the hosannas to Trump in another November 30 report on Fox. Hannity introduced Robin Maynard, a white male who was a twenty-four-year Carrier employee. After asking Maynard his reaction to both the closing announcement and then Trump's more recent announcement to preserve jobs, Hannity then celebrated Trump as a unique savior and prompted Maynard to give thanks:

HANNITY: What do you say specifically? I can't really think of another instance off the top of my head where a president or a president-elect picks up the phone and says, "Don't send these jobs to Mexico. Keep them here. We're going to lower the corporate tax rate. We have other incentives that we're going to be making for all corporations." What do you have to say to president-elect Trump, vice president-elect Pence?[18]

MAYNARD: I would like to personally thank them, shake their hands tomorrow, and just tell them thank you for going to bat

Figure 1.3. Fox News host Sean Hannity with Carrier worker Robin Maynard, November 30, 2016

for the blue-collar workers and us little guys down here that—
you know, in saving our jobs and keeping them here in America
and not sending them to Mexico or somewhere else out of the
country, and just really appreciate them taking time out of their
busy schedule and out of their holiday time, Thanksgiving, to
start working on this, and then to put it into action a couple days
later to end up having a—you know . . .

Hannity concluded by both pandering to his guest and getting the facts
wrong about what Maynard's factory makes:

> **HANNITY:** All right, Robin, I'm—I'll tell you what. Next air con-
> ditioner I buy, promise—because I'm glad we're making them
> here—is going to be a Carrier. That's my promise to you, OK?
> **MAYNARD:** OK. Thank you, sir.
> **HANNITY:** All the best, sir. Thank you.[19]

Fox Business News also did a Carrier employee interview on November 30. Host Adam Shapiro interviewed Robin Maynard, the same subject
of Hannity's interview. Like Hannity, Shapiro prompted the Carrier worker
to give thanks to Trump:

> **SHAPIRO:** What would you say to president-elect Trump and to vice president-elect Pence about this deal? Because we're going to learn the details tomorrow. It looks as if there are some tax incentives to keep them there. But at the end of the day, one thousand people stay on the job. Isn't that the key?

Maynard again offered his sincere thanks.[20]

No one could have been more giddy about Trump's "big win" than Steve Doocy of the *Fox & Friends* show, one of Trump's favorite programs.[21] Early in the morning on December 1, before Trump's announcement at Carrier, Doocy interviewed another white male, Rick Link, a fifteen-year Carrier employee, to drive home the point that Trump is indeed the ascendant blue-collar president, leading the white working class into the Republican fold.[22] Link's interview was perfect fodder for Fox: so good, in fact, that he was back on with Doocy the next morning. About halfway through the interview on December 2, Doocy asked this question:

> **DOOCY:** I gotta ask you about this, for the folks who didn't see the interview with you yesterday, you're a lifelong Democrat. Uh, you told us yesterday that for the most part, the Carrier plant, a lot of Democrats. It's a union job as well. There were a number of people in attendance yesterday who may not have voted for Donald Trump, but Donald Trump saved their jobs yesterday, didn't they?
>
> **LINK:** Yes, he did. He did. Some of those naysayers before were all excited and was [*sic*] hoping to shake his hand. It kinda tickled me [Doocy giggles] for the plain fact that I got so much crap from people because I was voting for Trump. And now, you know, he came to Indy, he's president-elect, he's gonna save our jobs, and now they are all like Trump, Trump, Trump [Doocy giggles again]. You know, it's a little vindicating, and I get to snicker and laugh at these people now. So, overall, I'm pretty happy with everything that happened.
>
> **DOOCY [smiling and head nodding]:** Yeah, they didn't vote for Donald Trump, but now they are on the Trump train.

A minute later, Doocy wrapped up:

> **DOOCY:** All right. Well, Rick Link has a job, has a career, thanks to Donald Trump and company.[23]

Figure 1.4. *Fox & Friends* host Steve Doocy with Carrier worker Rick Link, December 2, 2016

Other reporters covered the same narrative, including Dean Reynolds at CBS, who interviewed Paul Roell and his wife. NBC's Kristen Welker's package showed a clip of T. J. Bray's November 14 NBC interview; an unidentified but happy white, male worker at Carrier wearing a red Trump "Make America Great Again" cap; and white worker John Feltner at Rexnord Bearings, a factory just about a mile away from the Carrier plant that announced in October 2016 that it would also ship its 300 jobs to Mexico, an announcement that had received no attention from Trump. ABC's December 1 report by Tom Llamas also interviewed Feltner at Rexnord.[24]

Who Counts as American Workers?

Viewers and readers of most national television and newspaper reports of the 1,400 workers affected by the Carrier closing might be surprised to learn this: the Carrier factory workers are roughly 60 percent black and 40 percent white, and the workforce is about half men and half women.[25] The eleven-member Local 1999 Executive Board has eight African American members and three white members. Two of the Executive Board members are women. The person who made the viral video of the Carrier announcement that brought so much attention to the dire situation of the Local 1999 workers was Lakeisha Austin, an African American woman. The diversity of the Carrier workforce was hiding in plain sight: in the viral video of workers

at the Carrier announcement, in the subsequent rallies in the streets of Indianapolis, in the background on the floor of the factory the day Donald Trump
showed up, and on Local 1999's website.

Only the *New York Times* ventured to poke holes into the myth that Carrier was a bastion of white, male workers. Nelson D. Schwartz, who wrote
several excellent stories on the Carrier situation, wrote this on the eve of
Trump's visit to the Indianapolis factory:

> In the popular imagination, the Indianapolis factory where 1,400 Carrier
> workers build furnaces and fan coils looks like a scene out of "The Deer
> Hunter" or "Norma Rae." Blue-collar guys walking through the plant
> gate, lunch pail in hand, or white women barely getting by after years on
> the line.
>
> But the reality at the Carrier plant that Mr. Trump will visit on Thursday
> is very different.[26]

The main photo for this *Times* story, featuring two African American women
workers at Carrier, Carol Bigbee and Arnita Gray, was a rare depiction in the
national news.

Steve Bannon, then Trump's campaign chief executive officer, later chief
strategist, and erstwhile executive chair of Breitbart News, liked to call
Trump supporters "working-class hobbits."[27] It's worth noting, considering
the racist content that frequents Breitbart, and how much of the news media
represented Carrier workers, that all of the fictional hobbits are white.[28] And
that was the view of real Carrier workers from Fox News and most other
network and cable news programs: they were cast in the role of white, male,
working-class hobbits from Middle America, a place to the news media that
might as well have been Middle-earth.

There were some better reports on the Carrier story. As noted earlier, Nel-
son D. Schwartz wrote several good pieces for the *New York Times*. Cristina
Alesci did a more than seven-minute video story about Carrier and the global
economy on August 23, 2016, for *CNNMoney* that included an interview with
Bray, Chuck Jones (Local 1999's white president), and Robert James (Local
1999's African American vice president). Kevin Tibbles, who reported the
November 14 NBC News package that called Trump to account, also did a
November 30 follow-up that quoted James and Bray. CNN's Martin Savidge
resisted the "white, male, working-class" narrative in a November 30 report
and interviewed two African American women, Ciera Turner and Margaret
Wilkerson, and an African American man, Edward Conway, all who were

at the same Sully's Bar and Grill visited by other journalists. Savidge also interviewed Chuck Jones. Bryan Gruley and Rick Clough of *Bloomberg Businessweek* wrote an excellent postmortem analysis in March 2017 with the story titled "Remember When Trump Said He Saved 1,100 Jobs at a Carrier Plant? Well, Globalization Doesn't Give a Damn."[29] The most consistent and extensive new coverage was local, with the *Indianapolis Star* and ABC affiliate WRTV (which sent reporter Rafael Sanchez to Monterrey, Mexico; made a five-part documentary series on the closing's effects on the full diversity of the plant's workers; and developed a comprehensive time line) among the best.[30]

When Donald Trump Addressed the Workers He Almost Forgot (and Then Forgot the Other Workers)

On December 1, 2016, Trump finally took a trip to Indiana and walked through the factory of the furnace assembly plant. On the speaking platform, after being introduced by Mike Pence, Trump explained to the hand-selected guests and the news media how he knew he needed to make things right and bring economic justice to the Carrier workers of United Steelworkers Local 1999. Trump's speech is the climax of one of his campaign's signature themes and of the long efforts of the Local 1999 workers to make themselves and their situation visible to the entire country. Because so much of what Trump says is at odds with his earlier statements of how he would save the Carrier jobs, I quote it at length:

> TRUMP: I want to thank Greg Hayes of United Technologies, because when I called him he was right there. I wish I could have made the call when they were doing their original decision, but it worked out just as well, other than I would have liked to have had an answer a year and a half ago.
>
> We had a tremendous love affair with the state of Indiana. Because if you remember during the primaries, this was going to be the firewall. This was where they were going to stop Trump, right? And that didn't work out too well.
>
> And it was a firewall—for me it was a firewall. And we won by 16 points, and the election we just won by 20 points—almost 20 points. [light applause]
>
> And that was some victory. That's pretty—that's pretty great. And I just love the people, incredible people.

Figure 1.5. Donald Trump and Mike Pence walk through the Indianapolis Carrier plant, December 1, 2016; still from *Voice of America News* report, July 21, 2017

So, I got involved because of the love affair I've had. This has been a very special state to us. And I'll never forget, about a week ago I was watching the nightly news. I won't say which one, because I don't want to give them credit, because I don't like them much, I'll be honest. [laughter]

I don't like them. Not even a little bit.

But they were doing a story on Carrier, and I say, "Wow, that's something. I want to see that."

And they had a gentleman, worker, great guy, handsome guy, he was on, and it was like he didn't even know they were leaving. He said something to the effect, "No, we're not leaving, because Donald Trump promised us that we're not leaving," and I never thought I made that promise. Not with Carrier. I made it for everybody else. I didn't make it really for Carrier.

And I said, "What's he saying?" And he was such a believer, and he was such a great guy. He said, "I've been with Donald Trump from the beginning, and he made the statement that Carrier's not going anywhere, they're not leaving."

And I'm saying to myself, "Man."

And then they played my statement, and I said, "Carrier will never leave." But that was a euphemism. I was talking about Carrier like all other companies from here on in. Because they made the decision a year and a half ago.

But he believed that that was—and I could understand it. I actually said—I didn't make it—when they played that, I said, "I did make it, but I didn't mean it quite that way."

So now because of him, whoever that guy was—is he in the room, by any chance? That's your son? Stand up, you did a good job. [applause]

You did a great job, right? That's fantastic. And I love your shirt. Oh, wow. Oh. Ha ha. [laughter]

Put it on, cameras, go ahead. Put it on. [the worker remains off-camera.]

Well, your son is great. And he meant that, didn't he? He really meant it.

At first I said, "I wonder if he's being sarcastic, because this ship has sailed." And then I said—it was 6:30 in the evening, and I said, "Boy, the first thing I'm going to do is go there and—say do call the head of Carrier?" who's a great guy, but I've always learned I've got to call the top, and I heard about Greg Hayes. He's a great executive.

You know, I don't know if you know, United Technologies is one of the top fifty companies in the United States, and one of the top companies anywhere in the world. They make many other things other than air conditioners, believe me. Their list of companies is incredible.

So I called Greg Hayes. I heard of him, but I never met him. And he picked up the phone, "Mr. President-elect, sir, how are you?" It's wonderful to win. You know that. Think if I lost he wouldn't have returned my call. I don't know if—where is Greg?

I don't know, would you—if I lost and called you I don't think you would have called. I would have tried for you, but I think it would have been tougher, right? What do you think, Greg?

Yes, he's sort of nodding "yes, you're right." [laughter]

But I called Greg and I said, "It's really important, we have to do something. Because you have a lot of people leaving and you have to understand, we can't allow this to happen anymore with our country. So many jobs are leaving and going to other countries. Not just Mexico, many, many countries. And China is making so much of our product that we're closing up a lot of plants."

And I mean, I wrote down some numbers that are incredible, but the numbers of manufacturing jobs that are lost, especially in the Rust Belt—and the Rust Belt is so incredible. But we're losing companies, it's—it's unbelievable, one after another, just one after another.

So I said, "Greg, you've got to help us out here. We got to sit down. We got to do something." And I said, "Because we just can't let it happen."

Anyway, he was incredible. And he said, "I understand." And I said, "I wish I made this call a year and a half ago, it would have been a lot easier call."

Only because of your son, OK, believe me? Your son, whoever the hell your son is, these people owe him a lot. And I just went through—he's out in the factory. I thought they were all going to be in this room. This room's not big enough.

Yes, I know. I don't know who arranged that one. Because I had—we just visited a thousand people in the factory that are going wild, in the plant.

But I will tell you that United Technologies and Carrier stepped it up and now they're keeping—actually the number's over 1,100 people, which is so great, which is so great. [applause]

And I see the people. I shook hands with a lot of the people. They're right behind us working. I guess, what is it, you're so—you're making so many air conditioners you didn't want to even have them come off for a half hour. He's a ruthless boss. [laughter] He's ruthless. But that's OK.

You know, I did say one thing to the Carrier folks and to the United Technologies folks. I said, the goodwill that you have engendered by doing this, all over the world, frankly, but within our country, you watch how fast you're going to make it up. Because so many people are going to be buying Carrier air conditioners. You know, we've had such help here.

After highlighting the Carrier case in his campaign appearances and debates for almost a year, Trump's resulting speech is an extraordinary record of his commitment to the working class and his approach to the economy. There are eight points worth clarifying:

1. Trump apparently wasn't planning to do a thing for Carrier workers until he saw the *NBC Nightly News* report on November 14. Astonishingly, Trump admitted this in his speech, treating the plant closing like merely an entertaining anecdote. "I never thought I made that promise. Not with Carrier. I made it for everybody else. I didn't

make it really for Carrier . . . that was a euphemism. I was talking about Carrier like all other companies from here on in. Because they made the decision a year and a half ago." (For the record, it was 8 months and 29 days from the February 10, 2016, Carrier announcement to the November 8, 2016, election of Trump, about one-half of the "year and a half" period he repeatedly claimed had elapsed since the Carrier decision.)

2. Unlike his earlier campaign boasting, Trump called Greg Hayes and asked him to save workers' jobs, not the other way around.

3. Unlike his earlier campaign boasting, Trump didn't threaten UTC with a 35 percent import duty on every unit made in Mexico but instead gave a general promise to lower the business tax for corporations and cut unspecified regulations (not disclosed in the speech or anywhere else) and arranged $7 million in Indiana tax breaks specifically for Carrier. Perhaps Trump threatened to disrupt UTC's $5.6 billion in government accounts (mostly through its Pratt & Whitney aircraft components), as some news reports surmised? UTC's Greg Hayes denied that there was any mention of government contracts or any "quid pro quo."[31]

4. For almost a year, Trump had been referring to the Indianapolis plant as a maker of air conditioners. However, the Indianapolis plant makes furnaces. Yet Trump repeated the same error multiple times in his big speech. (Some news media reports made the same mistake.) Chuck Jones, the president of Local 1999, later said that he couldn't believe it: "In the primary, Trump kept saying Carrier produced air conditioners. They make those in Tennessee." Then came Trump's major announcement at the factory. "On the floor, he watched them making furnaces. Still he says air conditioning!" Jones said. "If you're such a brilliant man, you should know what the hell you are talking about."[32]

5. Of the 1,400 Carrier workers concerned about their jobs, the most important worker that day for Trump was the one he referenced in his speech—"a gentleman, worker, great guy, handsome guy"—the guy who Trump saw on the November 14 NBC news report who still wanted Trump to save their jobs. Yet in his personal appearance Trump completely whiffed recognizing that worker. At one point in his speech, Trump says "So now because of him, whoever that guy was—is he in the room, by any chance? That's your son? Stand up, you did a good job."

"That guy" in the NBC report was Bray, who was sitting right in the front row, where the Trump campaign had requested him to sit. Yet Trump couldn't recognize him and apparently had no plans to bring him up on the stage. Instead, another employee misidentified the worker. As a local television station later reported, "A woman who works at Carrier said that it was her son . . . except it was not. Bray, sitting where he was directed, just watched as the situation unfolded." The report said Bray "did manage to snap off a few pictures along the rope line, but his moment was gone."[33] Interesting fact from Trump's own seven-point list on "How to Impress Anyone in Business": "Remember people's names and small details about them." It is telling that Trump prepared for Hayes but not for Bray.[34]

6. The labor union, Local 1999, was completely shut out of the negotiations regarding saving any jobs. Trump said nothing about the union in his speech.

7. Trump continually ignored other jobs that were being shipped from Indiana to Mexico at the same time. On February 10, 2016, Carrier announced that it would be closing its furnace manufacturing plant on the west side of Indianapolis and moving jobs to Monterrey, Mexico, eliminating 1,400 jobs. Simultaneously, United Technologies Electronic Controls (UTEC) announced that it would move its microprocessor controls operations for the HVAC and refrigeration industries in Huntington (about 95 miles northeast of Indianapolis) to Mexico as well, eliminating another 700 jobs. UTEC workers are represented by the International Brotherhood of Electrical Workers (IBEW). In October 2016, Rexnord Bearings, just about a mile away from the Carrier plant, announced it would ship its 300 jobs to Mexico, too. Those workers are also members of the United Steelworkers Local 1999. So, in total, at that time at least 2,400 manufacturing jobs were announced to be shipped from Indiana to Mexico in 2016. Trump focused only on the Carrier jobs in Indianapolis.

8. Trump's biggest mistake was on the point that mattered the most to the workers: he exaggerated (or lied about) the number of jobs that would be saved at Carrier. President-elect Trump's deal with UTC fell far short of the 1,100 he ballyhooed—or, in his further exaggeration, "actually the number's over 1,100 people, which is so great, which is so great." Later, Trump added "And by the way, that

number is going to go up very substantially as they expand this area, this plant. So the 1,100 is going to be a minimum number." Trump's "expand this area, this plant" is a more misleading exaggeration. The $16 million UTC pledged to invest in the Indianapolis factory was, according to Greg Hayes, for automation, which will likely lead to *fewer* workers in the future.[35] In fact, after negotiating with Trump and Pence, UTC saved just 730 jobs of the Local 1999 workers, plus 70 salaried positions. In sum, 550 Carrier workers lost their jobs. (In the other two factories, all 700 UTEC workers lost their jobs, as did all 300 of the Rexnord workers.) Local 1999 President Chuck Jones told Indianapolis NBC affiliate WTHR on December 5 that they weren't provided any information on jobs when Trump made his announcement the week before. "We didn't know the breakdown before because no one would give us any information," Jones said. "Now what we're losing is 550 member jobs." WHTR asked: "So how did the president-elect get to that 1,100 number last week?" The answer: "Trump was including 350 research and development jobs that were never going to move to Mexico in the first place. Those were jobs that Carrier said all along would stay in Indianapolis."[36] Of course, when Trump and UTC both failed to share any precise data with the Local 1999 or the news media in advance of Trump's December 1 announcement, there was no way to fact-check the deception that day. According to Jones, "People were sitting there thinking that they were saved, only to find out next day that they lost their jobs."[37]

WTHR contacted Pence's staff asking for clarification on the numbers, and they flat-out lied: "In response, Pence spokesperson Matthew Lloyd said, 'More than 1,000 jobs for hardworking Hoosiers were going to leave Indiana for Mexico. Those jobs are now staying right here in Indiana thanks to the efforts of President-elect Trump and Vice President-elect Pence.'"[38]

The news coverage of Trump's speech was an extraordinary record of the news media's inability to understand these issues. Much of the national news media wanted to tell Trump's less complicated story, no matter the facts: that the (white, male) working class put Trump in the White House, and now Trump was putting them back to work, just as he promised.[39]

When Donald Trump Gets Called a Liar by the Leader of the Carrier Workers

Trump's "win" in Indianapolis was the prelude to his Victory Tour rallies in Ohio and a number of other states where he had earned Electoral College victories. Although the Victory Tour arenas had low attendance, Trump's efforts in Indianapolis, particularly as portrayed by the news media, seemed to have a positive effect on the US public.

A survey conducted on December 2–5, 2016—just after Trump's announcement at Carrier in Indianapolis—by Hart Research Associates and Public Opinion Strategies found that "more than half of Independents and a quarter of Democrats said they are comfortable and prepared to support Trump as president. An overwhelming 56 percent of those respondents said the top item on his economic agenda should be keeping jobs in the U.S."

One of the pollsters from Public Opinion Strategies linked Trump's favorable numbers to the Carrier agreement. According to CNBC, "Republican pollster Micah Roberts said the results indicate Trump's push to keep jobs on US soil, like his recent deal with Indiana-based air conditioner company Carrier, extends his appeal beyond the coalition of voters who helped him win the election. 'Americans see it as him being potentially a strong advocate for the worker,' said Roberts, who is vice president at Public Opinion Strategies."[40] The other partner in the survey, Democratic pollster Jay Campbell of Hart Research Associates, "warned the group could lose hope if Trump fails to deliver on his jobs promises."

In fact, the good news was fleeting. Just as the survey finished in the field, it became public that Trump had fudged the numbers and had delivered on only part of the jobs promised to Carrier workers. In a December 6 story in the *Washington Post*, Local 1999 President Chuck Jones criticized Trump for getting up in front of workers assembled at Carrier on December 1 and telling them 1,100 jobs were saved, when only 730 of the production jobs were saved, along with 70 salaried jobs. "But he got up there, and for whatever reason, lied his a-- off," Jones told the *Post*.

The next day, December 7, the thin-skinned president-elect sounded off with two retaliatory tweets:

> If United Steelworkers 1999 was any good, they would have kept those jobs in Indiana. Spend more time working—less time talking. Reduce dues.
>
> Chuck Jones, who is President of the United Steelworkers 1999, has done a terrible job representing workers. No wonder companies flee country!

No matter that Trump never previously cited the union at all in his reasons for Carrier sending jobs to Mexico. And no matter that Mike Pence tweeted this statement from the Indiana governor's office on March 2, 2016: "Appreciate the chance to meet with Chuck Jones & hardworking men of Local 1999 about our efforts to save Carrier jobs."

Republican National Committee chief strategist (and soon-to-be Trump spokesperson) Sean Spicer pushed back on the truth, too, in order to salvage Trump's version of the narrative. On Fox News (of course), Spicer again repeated the wrong numbers—"a thousand jobs"—and accused Jones of being "a union boss that goes out and fabricates how the story went down for no reason. He should be grateful for Mr. Trump and Governor Pence's efforts to help save those jobs." Spicer concluded, "I think Mr. Trump is never going to sit back and let someone take a shot falsely at him without him responding."[41]

On December 8 the *Washington Post* gave Jones a chance to write a response to Trump. The piece was titled "I'm the Union Leader Donald Trump Attacked. I'm Tired of Being Lied to about Our Jobs."[42]

The Missing Story of Inequality between Workers and Their Corporation

If Donald Trump thought Jones and the union did nothing to save the Carrier jobs, he wasn't paying attention, nor was he talking to his vice president-elect, who was still the governor of Indiana and who had presided over the planned closing of the plant.

Jones and Local 1999 offered huge concessions to Carrier in a bid to keep the jobs: "We came up with $23 million in savings, but the Carrier brass said that wasn't enough. They could save $65 million by moving to Mexico. We couldn't match that unless we were willing to cut wages to $5/hour and cut all benefits."[43]

And the concessions offered by workers weren't the first concessions. Before the United Steelworkers began to represent Carrier workers in 1998, the workers had accepted a dual wage structure earlier in the decade that still existed in subsequent contracts at Carrier.[44] All newly hired workers were on the lower pay tier. Thus, in 2016 a worker in the starting production associate position at Carrier would earn $16.05 on the lower-tier pay schedule, $4.45 less than the regular higher-tier pay for that same position.[45]

The United Steelworkers Local 1999 did more to keep those jobs in Indiana. They rallied at the Carrier plant and at the Indiana statehouse. They did mailings to Carrier and Bryant distributors (UTC owns both heating/air-conditioning brands), and they protested at a party for Bryant distributors. They sent union representatives to the UTC stockholders meeting. They sent two groups of Local 1999 union workers to Capitol Hill to lobby Congress. They used social media and did as many regular media interviews as possible. They offered huge concessions to UTC, but not enough to compete with $3-per-hour pay in Mexico. As Chuck Jones wrote, "The Union did any and everything we could possibly do to get UTC to change their mind and keep these jobs here."[46]

With fewer labor reporters than you can count on one hand, the national news media rarely cover such stories. The Carrier closing would have been just a local story except for the fact that it occurred in a presidential election season and at least two candidates started talking about it. Donald Trump mentioned the Carrier closing several times but never visited the workers. Bernie Sanders visited the workers and spoke in their defense at the statehouse rally on April 29, 2016.[47] Local 1999 later endorsed Sanders. After Trump won the presidency, Jones said that "I and others agreed that we needed to stay on Trump because he used the situation at Carrier as part of his platform and he benefited from it in the form of votes, and we wanted him to keep his campaign promises."[48]

Carrier's Indianapolis plant was well run and highly profitable before that February 10, 2016, announcement.[49] Yet UTC knew it could squeeze even more profit out of making furnaces. On a call with investors exactly one month after the Carrier plant closing announcement, Bob McDonough, president of the UTC Climate, Controls & Security division that includes Carrier, hinted at exporting more jobs to low-wage countries: "We've shifted an abundant part of our manufacturing footprint to relatively lower-cost countries, about two-thirds. Still there's some opportunity there." His salary in 2016 was $6.4 million.[50]

UTC Chairman and CEO Greg Hayes was compensated even better, earning $13.4 million in salary, stock, and stock options in 2016.[51] The CEO he replaced, Louis Chenevert, who quickly retired after the UTC board "was reportedly unhappy with Chenevert after he took a side trip to Taiwan during a business trip to check on the construction of his yacht," left UTC with a golden parachute of $195 million in stock options and pension benefits.[52] In 2016, on $57.2 billion in sales, UTC earned $5.1 billion in profit.[53] In a chatty conversation with CNBC's Jim Cramer, Hayes revealed that his corporation holds $27 billion of its earnings overseas, to avoid paying US taxes on it. In that same conversation, Hayes referred to the viral video of the Indianapolis plant closing as "a little bit of bad luck" and "unfortunate." He wasn't talking about the workers in Indianapolis. He meant his own predicament because of all the public attention.[54]

Under the Cloak of Invisibility

The workers of United Steelworkers 1999 tried hard to make themselves visible. And, like in most cases of profitable factories being shut down because work can be done more cheaply elsewhere, the workers gained little but local news media attention.

It was only because of "a little bit of bad luck" that the story became bigger and happened to align with the campaign of Donald Trump. The plant closing—in the politically valuable state of Indiana and with a serendipitous viral video that showed the heartbreak of the plant-closing announcement—became an iconic example for Trump. Yet, from his own comments, Trump seemed willing to forget the Carrier workers after his election. Only the workers' own persistence—and a timely television news story—brought Trump around to try to pressure UTC into saving (some of) the jobs.

The national news organizations that covered the Carrier story did so mainly from a political perspective. These Carrier workers were the white, male, working-class, blue-collar, Middle America breadwinners who were Trump's voter base. That was certainly the editorial objective of Fox News, the *New York Post,* and Breitbart, but it was also largely the narrative picked up by the other national news media. The news media's general focus on white, male Carrier workers as subjects denied the fact that the Carrier workforce was far more diverse in terms of gender, race, and politics than the role they were given in the story (as white, male ardent Trump supporters). In the Trumpian economic populism, the white, male Carrier workers the news media featured, to the exclusion of others, suggested which Americans have jobs worth saving. (To be clear, we should not begrudge white, male workers jobs. But everyone who wants a good-paying job deserves one, not just people who fit the demographic profile of presumed political supporters.)

Only some of the news organizations that covered Trump's Carrier announcement followed up on the fact that Trump misrepresented the number of jobs saved and called the union president a liar when he dared to tell the truth about it. By that time, most national news media had gone home.[55] Some news media noted that Trump's ad hoc solution for saving manufacturing jobs—presidential-level deals for each troubled plant—wasn't sustainable; in fact, Trump moved on to the much easier habit of taking personal credit for any corporation creating jobs.[56] Yet no media outlet troubled readers and viewers with a more comprehensive solution to the problem: legislation. Among the proposals introduced in 2017:

- END OUTSOURCING ACT (S. 234), sponsored by US Senator Joe Donnelly (D-Indiana). This bill would amend the WARN (Worker Adjustment and Retraining Notification) Act to require employers to affirmatively disclose all outsourcing prior to plant closing and mass layoffs, and for the Department of Labor to publish a list of all employers outsourcing jobs. It also would amend the tax code to deny deductions to outsourcing employers, to recapture tax credits that outsourcing employers had previously received, and to grant a tax credit of up to 20 percent of expenses for companies that insource jobs from overseas to increase their number of full-time US employees.
- BRING JOBS HOME ACT (S. 247), sponsored by US Senator Debbie Stabenow (D-Michigan). Like the related End Outsourcing Act, this bill would grant a tax credit of up to 20 percent of expenses for companies that insource jobs from overseas to increase their number of full-time US employees and deny deductions for companies that outsource employers.
- OVERSEAS OUTSOURCING ACCOUNTABILITY ACT (H.R. 357), sponsored by US Representative Cheri Bustos (D-Illinois). This bill requested what seemed plainly evident after the Carrier episode: it would require the president to develop a comprehensive strategy to stop the outsourcing of US jobs and report progress back to Congress at least every two years.
- CLOSE TAX LOOPHOLES THAT OUTSOURCE AMERICAN JOBS ACT (H.R. 5145), sponsored by US Representative Rosa DeLauro (D-Connecticut). This would eliminate lower tax rates for foreign profits.
- STOP OUTSOURCING AND CREATE AMERICAN JOBS ACT OF 2017 (H.R. 3217), sponsored by US Representative Jerry McNerney (D-California). This would increase penalties for tax-evasion practices in tax-haven countries. It also establishes a preference in the awarding of federal contracts to companies that have not engaged in outsourcing.

The fact that many of the sponsors and cosponsors of these legislative proposals represent states and districts stricken by corporate outsourcing should have made the bills even more relevant and worthy of debate. The fact that the Carrier Local 1999 workers went to Washington, D.C., in July 2016 to lobby in favor of the Bring Jobs Home Act and its companion bills makes the legislative proposals even more newsworthy.[57] The fact that all of the sponsors and cosponsors were in the minority Democratic Party certainly affected the progress of the legislation, but this should never mean that journalists should ignore the merits of the arguments.

Local outlets such as the *Indianapolis Star* and WRTV stuck with the Carrier story into 2017 to follow the fate of other Indiana workers whose jobs were exported.[58] At the national level, Indianapolis became a touchstone political story, a place to find displaced workers and have them reassess their opinion of Trump. *Bloomberg Businessweek, Time,* the *New York Times,* the *Washington Post, In These Times,* the *Nation,* and CNN all followed up substantially with in-depth reporting in 2017 and 2018.[59] In a way, they were all trying to answer the same "who *are* these people" question—who are these white Middle Americans who supported Trump, and do they still support him? Although the stories of the workers were vivid and heartbreaking (Farah Stockman's in-depth profile of forty-three-year-old Rexnord steelworker Shannon Mulcahy for the *New York Times* is particularly poignant, as Mulcahy's job was extended a little longer only because she trained the low-wage workers who would be taking over her job in Mexico), the reporting often fell short on interrogating the larger economy.

Most news reports viewed displacement by outsourcing as a commonsense economic inevitability. The stories framed the usually white workers as pitiable characters, casualties of a global economy over which they could have no control. Stockman's engaging story also subtly communicates the values of the news media's upscale audience. Mulcahy's daughter Nicole received enough scholarship awards to attend Purdue University, but Mulcahy's prospects looked bleak. "It was as if Nicole were floating away on a life raft, while Shannon stayed behind on a sinking ship," Stockman wrote.[60] Nicole's story is indeed a triumphant one, but if college is the only way to succeed, where does that leave the Carrier and Rexnord workers and the 66.6 percent of US adults who don't have a bachelor's degree or higher? That's what most of the news reports never addressed.

Sarah Jaffe's story for the *Nation* offers a model of how tell personal stories of the working class and provide solutions to their economic predicament. Jaffe first acknowledged that the anger over economic oppression "isn't unique to white, male workers" but affects black, Latino, and women workers as well.[61] After telling the stories of several steelworkers in

Indianapolis, she introduced system-wide solutions that could change the outlook for all facing displacement. A tax structure that removes incentive for short-term profit, denying government contracts and imposing tax penalties for offshoring jobs, better global trade rules for labor and the environment, worker-owned cooperatives as an alternative to shareholder-owned corporations, a universal basic income, and laws to restore unions and their bargaining power are all ideas Jaffe covered that could be part of the journalistic discussion. The alternative is to just chronicle the demise of the entire working class.

Although Trump tweeted "No more!" to shipping jobs away, the Rexnord jobs followed many of the Carrier jobs to Mexico. And there were even more Indiana manufacturing jobs literally going south, *Bloomberg Businessweek* reported: "Elsewhere in the state, auto parts supplier CTS Corp. in Elkhart is sending production to Asia and Mexico, cutting 230 jobs. Welbilt Inc. closed its Sellersburg beverage systems factory in January and sent production to Mexico, eliminating more than 70 jobs. Harman Professional Solutions shifted some operations in Elkhart to Mexico, killing 125 jobs."[62]

These were more of the invisible workers.[63]

Chapter 2

The Rise and Fall of Labor Reporting

Today, the labor beat (sometimes called the workplace beat) in local and national news in the United States is almost nonexistent. A conference gathering of labor/workplace beat reporters from the country's leading newspapers could fit into a single booth at an Applebee's.

The trajectory of labor reporting in US newspapers looked much more promising in the nineteenth century, as it developed along with the rise of professional journalism. In the early nineteenth century, newspapers and magazines gave "scant attention" to labor events such as strikes, for strikes themselves were rare.[1] This began to change, starting in the late 1820s, as the US economy expanded beyond its agrarian roots and as newspapers entered into the "penny press" era of wider distribution and more popular content in the 1830s.

Regular reporter assignments to a labor beat emerged in the 1870s. Little is known about the earliest labor reporters; in the late nineteenth century, newspaper writers rarely had bylines, so their work is not easily identified.[2] In the early twentieth century, as journalism adopted more professional standards, bylines became more common, and labor reporters became more knowable.

Still, there is some documentation of the first US labor reporters of the nineteenth century. *Editor & Publisher,* the leading newspaper trade industry journal of the twentieth century, was launched in 1901. *E&P*—as its title might suggest—was generally supportive of the business interests of the industry. But the first year of the journal included a sympathetic piece on unions and labor reporters.[3] The writer, Arthur S. Brunswick, once a labor reporter at the *New York Daily News,* provided a rare commentary on the state of labor news, which had been a regular part of newspapers for only a few decades: "Twenty or twenty-five years or so ago, when trade unions and strikes followed each other in rapid and regular succession, the late George Bartholomew, managing editor of the *New York Daily News,* conceived the idea of 'bunching' all labor items together, and out of that custom grew the labor column and the labor department. The man also who came to cover labor news as a regular assignment then began to be known as the labor reporter. The late Harry Levy, of the *News,* claimed to have been the first regular labor reporter."[4]

Thus, working from Brunswick's estimation, by approximately 1875–1880 the *New York Daily News* had established a regular labor beat. At that time, the *Daily News* boasted on its front-page nameplate that it had "The Largest Circulation of any Daily Paper in the United States," an average of 100,262 each day of publication, although it soon would be surpassed in circulation by Joseph Pulitzer's *New York World* and William Randolph Hearst's *New York Journal.*[5] Alexander Benjamin Finkelstein Mamreov, another labor reporting pioneer, worked at the *New York Times* from 1876 until 1900, when he died suddenly at age forty-nine.[6] Within the next five to ten years, labor reporting had become a standard element of all the other newspapers in New York. Brunswick (who succeeded Levy as labor reporter at the *News* for a few months in 1888) provided a summary of that first generation of labor reporters in New York. His 1901 *Editor & Publisher* piece listed these labor reporters at work in the city's major newspapers in 1886: Thomas W. Jackson at the *Herald,* James Mulhane at the *Journal,* C. A. Mahoney at the *Sun,* William G. F. Price at the *Tribune,* Alexander B. F. Mamreov at the *Times,* James Ryan at the *Star,* John T. McKechnie at the *World,* William E. Dougherty at the *Telegram,* and Harry Levy at the *News.* Brunswick also noted the presence of labor reporters at the *Brooklyn Standard-Union* and at the German-language *Staats-Zeitung.*

At the turn of the century, labor remained an equal among the *Daily News'* fully developed civic beats. For example, on January 12, 1902, the *New York Sunday News* (as the Sunday editions of the *Daily News* were called) had a full broadsheet page evenly split among reports from the police, fire, education, and labor beats. Under the general headline of "Matters of Import in the Realm of Labor," the *Daily News* carried a wide range of reports (still without bylines) on new membership data from the American Federation of Labor (AFL); comparative statistics on labor membership in the United States and in European nations; a recommendation by the Civic Foundation (the social reform organization founded by Jane Addams and others in Chicago in 1894) to have cities write labor provisions such as minimum wages and maximum hours into street car franchise agreements in order to avoid strikes; the views of a visiting British trade union delegate to the AFL on the character of the US worker ("The whole secret of the superiority in America is the fact that workmen enforce recognition and respect," the British delegate wrote); and election results from the most recent meeting of the generously named "Metal Polishers, Buffers, Platers, Brass Molders and Brass Workers' Union."[7] The *Daily News* buttressed its regular Sunday labor column (sometimes called "News of the Labor World") with ongoing reports about labor matters throughout the week.

Yet the state of labor news at the turn of the twentieth century was already in decline, Arthur Brunswick argued. In his 1901 article he noted that "in 1886 nearly every daily paper in New York city had its own labor reporter. Now one man 'covers' it for three of them and the others only publish labor news when there is something 'special' going on." Brunswick, in an appraisal that has been echoed for more than a century since then by media critics and political economists, laid the blame for waning labor coverage on the commercial interests of the newspapers: "It would appear, therefore, that the editors are to blame for the lack of space given in the papers to labor. They are either carried away by their prejudices or lack of knowledge on the subject, or they don't want to offend the rich proprietor of the paper or the advertisers by encouraging working men's organizations and increasing their number because perfect organization necessarily means higher wages, shorter hours and better conditions generally, and consequently a positive financial loss to those who have to pay for these things."[8]

Nevertheless, the labor beat persisted, aided in part by a concurrent labor press (newspapers published by labor organizations), the Federated Press labor news service (launched in 1919), a number of labor radio stations and programs (beginning with Chicago's WCFL in 1926), and a growing labor movement both hindered and sustained by an unprecedented wave of immigration from Europe.[9] There were plenty of good stories to tell about labor and work, and the stories connected to newspaper readers' own experiences and everyday lives.

The first star labor reporter in the United States was John J. Leary, Jr., who after working at several newspapers in Boston and New York, took the labor assignment in 1918 at the *New York World*, where he stayed until the paper closed in 1931. Leary won a Pulitzer Prize in 1920, the first labor reporter to do so, for a series of articles covering the violent conflict between the United Mineworkers of America and coal mine operators in West Virginia during the national coal strike in the winter of 1919.

One of Leary's protégés was Louis Stark, who began working for the *New York Times* in 1917 and took on the labor beat full-time by 1924.[10] The *Times* added another labor reporter, Joseph Shaplen, in 1929 and a third, A. H. Raskin, in 1934. Before Stark left the beat in 1951 to become a *Times* editorial writer, he had become the second labor writer to win a Pulitzer Prize (1942).

Stark helped to expand labor writing to something beyond coverage of labor conflict. Stark's obituary in the *Times* (May 18, 1954) explained his contribution: "He was not the first labor reporter in the business, but was one of the first to go beyond the conventional concept of the labor story in dealing with strikes and lockouts." Similarly, Raskin, in accepting a Sidney Hillman Foundation Award in 1951 for his writing, argued for more expansive labor coverage. The *Times*, in a December 16, 1951, story on the awards ceremony, paraphrased him: "Mr. Raskin, in accepting his prize, said that the selection of labor reporters for the awards personified the change that had taken place in labor journalism. He pointed out that labor reporters used to consider their jobs the reporting of strikes. Today, he added, the labor reporter covers all phases of labor and industrial relations."[11]

From the mid-1940s through the 1960s, the *New York Times* had extensive labor coverage, with at least four labor writers on staff at any given time.[12] The labor writer position had cachet in that era. The *New York Times* promoted upcoming labor series in the newspaper and gave its senior labor writers programs on the company's radio station, WQXR.[13]

The events of the mid-1930s—including the passage of the National Industrial Recovery Act, the Wagner Act (the National Labor Relations Act), the formation of the Newspaper Guild, and the genesis of the CIO (Congress of Industrial Organizations)—spurred most US newspapers to assign reporters to a labor beat. At a two-day conference on labor reporting held by the Nieman Foundation at Harvard University in 1951, labor reporter H. W. Ward of the Associated Press estimated that "there are 23 [labor reporters] between here and St. Louis." Summarizing the discussions on a panel, Ward made the case for even more labor reporters: "There ought to be at least 200 labor reporters—at least part-time—because in every industrial town there is something in labor-management news and if the newspapers cannot see it to their advantage to cater to their readers, the wage earners, it is just too bad."[14]

But after the 1960s, the beat seemed to have lost its shine across the United States. The *New York Times* is emblematic of the coverage trend. After retirements and reassignments, the *New York Times* was down to two labor reporters from the 1970s to the mid-1980s, and by the late 1980s employed only a single reporter to cover labor, as most other newspapers had dropped the beat entirely (see table 2.1).

The Labor/Workplace Beat Today

I've been tracking the contemporary labor/workplace beat since 2004. At the end of that year, just less than half—twelve of the nation's top twenty-five newspapers (in terms of circulation numbers)—employed at least one full-time reporter on a labor/workplace assignment.[15] By the beginning of 2007, only five of the top twenty-five newspapers in the United States had full-time labor/workplace reporters: *New York Times, Wall Street Journal, Chicago Tribune, Boston Globe,* and *Cleveland Plain Dealer.* Thus, the labor beat, already weakened for decades, was one of the first places to cut as revenues declined in the middle of the first decade of the 2000s. With the economic shock of the Great Recession in late 2007 and 2008, the cuts continued.[16] Gone with early retirements and buyouts were such outstanding labor reporters as Stephen Franklin, a Pulitzer Prize finalist at the *Chicago Tribune,* and Nancy Cleland, a Pulitzer Prize winner at the *Los Angeles Times* (both owned by the terribly over-leveraged and mismanaged Tribune Company). By 2014, only two of the top twenty-five newspapers had full-time labor reporters: the *New York Times* (with Steven Greenhouse) and the *Wall Street Journal* (with Kris Maher).

In 2018 the labor beat had rebounded slightly. In the top twenty-five daily newspaper markets, the *New York Times* (Noam Scheiber), the *Washington Post* (Danielle Paquette), the *Chicago Tribune* (Alexia Elejalde-Ruiz), the *Philadelphia Inquirer* (Jane M. Von Bergen), and the *Boston Globe* (Katie Johnston) had full-time workplace reporters on staff, while the *Wall Street Journal* (Eric Morath) had an economy reporter who covered labor policy issues. Even in these cases, one labor/workplace reporter was not enough to cover local, regional, and national labor and workplace stories.

Table 2.1. *New York Times* labor reporter history

	1870	1880	1890	1900	1910	1920	1930	1940	1950	1960	1970	1980	1990	2000	2010
Alexander Benjamin Finkelstein Mamreov (1851–1900)	1876—			1900											
John H. McLean (?–1923)				1900	1910s										
Guy W. Seem (1894–1932)						1922–1923									
Evans Clark (1888–1970)						1925–1928									
Louis Stark (1888–1954)						1924			1951						
Joseph Shaplen (1894–1946)						1929		1946							
A. H. Raskin (1911–1993)							1934			1961					
Joseph A. Loftus (1907–1990)								1944		1969					
Stanley Levey (1914–1971)								1947		1963					
Damon Stetson (1915–2010)										1963		1984			
John D. Pomfret										1962–1968					
Murray Seeger (1929–2011)										1964–1965					
David R. Jones										1965–1968					
William Serrin (1939–2018)											1979	1986			
Kenneth B. Noble												1985–1988			
Peter T. Kilborn												1989	1996		
Steven Greenhouse													1995		2014
Noam Scheiber															2015

Source: Compiled from *New York Times* newspaper archives and obituaries. Design by Dana Potter.

In the rest of the top twenty-five—for example, *USA Today*, the *Los Angeles Times*, the *Dallas Morning News*, the *Orange County Register*, the *Minneapolis Star Tribune*, the *Arizona Republic*—either labor/workplace news is not covered at all or it's handled by a reporter in a broadly defined business beat or a related beat that might occasionally intersect with worker issues. Lydia DePillis, an excellent economy reporter for CNN who used to cover labor as a business reporter at the *Washington Post*, said that "work issues get spread across a lot of different beats, which means nobody develops expertise in the legal structures and institutional and economic history that are important to put those stories in context." That the majority of the top newspapers don't cover the labor/workplace beat on a full-time basis is significant, considering that one can safely assume that the bulk of their readers and other potential audience members *are people who work.* (In fact, about 163 million adult US civilians are in the labor force.[17]) We can also assume that few, if any, of the rest of the approximately 1,300 daily newspapers in the United States have a full-time labor/workplace reporter.[18]

It's not any better in the broadcast news world, where there are no labor/workplace reporters and finding a report about labor is almost impossible. A 2013 study that sampled three years (2008, 2009, and 2011: years in which the United States struggled with the worst recession since the Great Depression, years that gave rise to the global Occupy Wall Street movement, and years in which the political right sought to destroy public-sector unions) found that only 0.3 percent of network TV news in those three years covered labor issues.[19] On radio, NPR hasn't had a full-time labor/workplace reporter since Frank Langfitt held that position from 2004 to 2010. The beat was revived at NPR's business desk in December 2004, as NPR expanded its reporting staff with the more than $200 million bequest in 2003 from Joan Kroc, the McDonald's heir. But NPR didn't fill the position after Langfitt took a new assignment in 2010, leaving Yuki Noguchi, an NPR business desk correspondent since 2008, to sometimes cover workplace issues.

Similarly, NPR affiliates do not consistently cover labor and the workplace. An exception is KNKX (formerly KPLU) in the Seattle-Tacoma region. Erin Hennessey, the station's news director, explained that her station's proactive response to labor coverage was precisely because of the loss of the labor beat in local newspapers: "For years, newspapers had a labor beat. That beat basically disappeared in the early to mid 1990s, at least in the Pacific Northwest. I'm not sure if it was advertisers pushing back on stories, or just what was happening, but they disappeared and only 'business' was left on the 'business pages.' Sometimes, a story made it out of that section on a general assignment basis, or got wrapped into the courts beat, etc. but basically it lost its beat status which meant there was less labor coverage. Seeing this trend unfold, our station saw it as important to keep 'labor' on our radar—above and beyond general assignment."[20]

Because the labor/workplace beat just barely exists in traditional news media, despite increasing class inequality in the United States, there is some effort to cover this area in newer online media. In recent years, especially since the Great Recession of 2007–2008 and Occupy Wall Street in 2011 thrust income inequality into the public sphere, *HuffPost, Bloomberg, Politico, Buzzfeed,* and nonprofits *ProPublica* and the Center for Public Integrity have added labor and workplace reporters.[21] Mike Elk, a former labor reporter at *Politico* (who won a settlement for being illegally fired in 2015 for union organizing there), still reports on labor at *Payday Report,* a labor site he founded. All have done valuable reporting, especially the Center for Public Integrity, which won a 2014 Pulitzer Prize for Investigative Reporting on how the coal industry conspired to deny medical claims of miners dying of black lung disease.[22]

One limitation, though, particularly for the for-profit websites, is that the reporting is mostly based in Washington, D.C., covers policy issues (e.g., the Department of Labor), and is less likely to venture into the rest of the country to cover labor and workplace stories. In fact, the main focus of labor reporting at *Politico* and *Bloomberg* is special professional audiences. For example, *Bloomberg BNA* employs teams of reporters and editors to cover many topics, including the *Daily Labor Report,* which has more than a dozen reporters and many more editors and correspondents, but its products are subscription-based and priced for professional clients. Similarly, *Politico* covers some labor and workplace issues, but the bulk of the four reporters' work in that policy area is for *PoliticoPro,* another expensive, subscription-based professional service.[23]

News and opinion magazines on the left, such as *Mother Jones,* the *Nation,* and *In These Times,* and niche publications such as *Labor Notes,* cover labor unions and work more consistently than any other medium. This same level of interest and curiosity about US workers rarely seeps into the mainstream news media.

A note on defining the labor/workplace beat: some of the newspapers employ a full-time workplace columnist whose assignment focuses more on lifestyle issues—such as getting along with bosses, telecommuting, or the ethics of workplace romances—rather than work issues. This is a different kind of journalism, one that responds to a business refocus on upscale audiences, which I'll address in chapter 4. When I refer to the labor/work-place beat, my meaning is reporting that covers labor unions and other forms of worker representation, and issues affecting all workers (organized and unorganized), such as wage and salary inequality, the minimum wage, wage theft, race and gender discrimination, workplace sexual harassment assault, classification of workers (e.g., as independent contractors), workplace safety, deindustrialization, outsourcing, automation, and the continued growth of the service industry. Labor/workplace reporting can also be active at the intersection of work and other issues, such as immigration, health care, pensions, and child care.

Corporate News and Labor/Workplace Reporting

Today when we talk about the news media in the United States, we are typically talking about media corporations, publicly owned, with a Wall Street stock price to manage. These corporations have their own workers, and they usually have the same objectives as other corporations: trying to keep wages low, cutting health care and other benefits, laying off workers, categorizing long-time workers as independent contractors, stopping workers from unionizing, outsourcing workers, and automating work while also increasing executive compensation and being responsive to Wall Street needs of dividends and high profits.

In the nineteenth century and first half of the twentieth century, newspapers (the main news medium) had a different economic structure, for they were typically owned by publishers who took an active role in their newspaper's voice. The editorial position of a newspaper on labor unions and its treatment of its own workers largely depended on the views of the publisher.

The earliest US newspapers were relatively expensive, were sold by subscription, and were focused on specialized political or mercantile topics.[24] Then, in the 1830s, the "penny press" emerged. Newspapers cost much less—just one or two cents—and newspaper reading became much more widespread, while newspaper content adjusted to the new readership. News historian Alfred McClung Lee described the rise of the mass audience for journalism: "With its low price, the one-cent press of the 1830's could seek mass circulation through representing mass interests; it thus facilitated social adjustments to many current problems. Growing literacy and class consciousness among workers were finding an outlet in trade unions. Organizations were promoting voting privileges for those without property-holding qualifications, the abolition of slavery, Sunday observance, and many other objectives. Many of these movements became vocal in the cheap papers. To these appeals, the 'new journalism' added sensation, human interest, humor, and the vigor of youth in crusading."[25]

Many of the leading newspaper publishers expressed an explicit editorial allegiance to the mass audience. Joseph Pulitzer, who bought the *New York World* in 1883 and within a few years made it the best-selling newspaper in the city, announced his newspaper's commitment to a broad, democratic readership in the first issue under his direction, "dedicated to the cause of the people rather than that of purse-potentates."[26]

Edward W. Scripps, who developed with his brother the idea of a newspaper chain under the control of one ownership group starting in the late 1870s, advocated for not only a mass audience but specifically for a working-class audience. As early newspaper historian William Bleyer noted in 1927, "The Scripps papers, from the beginning, were low-priced, popular evening papers designed to appeal to what Edward W. Scripps called the '95 percent,' the plain people."[27] Historian Gerald Baldasty explained that Scripps's "working class journalism" was "a shrewd and lucrative move" in the competitive newspaper markets, and his newspapers would stake out their position in midsize markets where the broad working class was not well served by existing newspapers that had a big-business orientation: "Scripps targeted his newspapers toward the working class because he believed that newspapers needed to serve the entire population if democracy were to survive. He also served the working class because it was an untapped market that could be quite profitable."[28]

The Scripps chain was founded on newspapers (many now gone) such as the *Detroit News, Cleveland Press* (closed 1980), *Cincinnati Post/Kentucky Post* (2007), *Pittsburgh Press* (1992), *Indianapolis Times* (1965), *Rocky Mountain News* (2009), *Albuquerque Tribune* (2008), *San Francisco News* (1965), *Houston Press* (1964), *Ft. Worth Press* (1975), *Memphis Press-Scimitar* (1983), and *Birmingham Post-Herald* (2005). In 2014 the E. W. Scripps Company spun off all of its newspaper properties, which were acquired in 2016 by Gannett, the largest newspaper company in the United States. Scripps is now a broadcast company, owning dozens of television and radio stations across the country.

But in E. W. Scripps's time, the focus of the country was on newspaper journalism and appealing to the "95 percent." Even as a chain, the early Scripps company spread its stock ownership democratically, with editors, business managers, and other employees holding shares. Bleyer reported that "approximately forty percent of all the stock of the Scripps-Howard

Newspapers in 1925 was in the hands of present or former executives and managers, and several hundred employees were stock-holders in holding companies that held diversified blocks of stock in various Scripps enterprises," including a Scripps telegraphic news agency for distributing news (which became United Press International) and a syndicate for supplying its newspapers and others content such as photos, cartoons, and feature stories.[29]

On Scripps's death in 1926, *Editor & Publisher* remembered him as a publisher who "had devoted his unique genius and gigantic press power of its creation to fighting the battles of 'the forgotten man,' the worker without the prestige of wealth, political or social position."[30]

Of course, in addition to their civic role in serving their readers (who mid-twentieth-century AP labor reporter H. W. Ward called "the wage earners") and their communities, newspapers were also for-profit businesses. As journalism historian Frank Luther Mott wrote in 1952,

> Publishers of newspapers and news-magazines and owners of radio stations are themselves businessmen and their natural sympathies are with business and ownership and what President Roosevelt used to call "economic royalism." . . . Attitudes and sympathies inhere within economic groups; and those of the businessman react unfavorably toward such modern phenomena as the techniques of labor organization, the increasing socialization in many fields, controls in trade and industry, and many social reforms. This does not mean that all publishers are opposed to such things; certainly not all of them are. But a large majority of them are faithful to their own guild and naturally espouse their own causes.[31]

Some publishers were stridently antiunion, especially in the first half of the twentieth century, and it was reflected in these newspapers' coverage of labor issues.[32] The Otis and Chandler families, the longtime dynasty controlling the *Los Angeles Times*, held "a passion against labor, against social reform of any kind, against any politicians even lightly tainted by labor," wrote journalist David Halberstam.[33] Labor unions so abhorred their treatment by the *Los Angeles Times* that when William Randolph Hearst launched the *Los Angeles Examiner* in 1903, twenty thousand labor union representatives from Southern California marched through the principal streets of Los Angeles "to welcome this competitor to the anti-union-labor *Los Angeles Times*."[34] Newspaper historian Alfred McClung Lee carefully phrased his account of the labor celebrations over the *Examiner*'s opening: "The celebration on the occasion of Hearst's launching of his *Los Angeles Examiner* on December 12, 1903, demonstrates *the extent to which workers thought he represented them.*"[35]

In fact, Hearst didn't always represent *all* workers. As a reflection of anti-immigrant sentiment of the time, in 1889 Hearst's *San Francisco Examiner* responded to "the 'Yellow Menace' to white labor by setting up free employment bureaus for whites and even sending out special labor trains to collect them."[36]

Nevertheless, Lee found Hearst to be among the major newspaper publishers seeking a mass, working-class audience, but again with a caveat regarding Hearst: "Pulitzer, Hearst, Scripps, and others seeking purchasers among the near-literate tried on the whole to convince the masses, especially urban laborers, that they had popular causes at heart. Scripps and Pulitzer continued to do so even after they stabilized their properties. Hearst and many others passed on to another stage as their sheets and the industry generally attained 'firmer ground.' They still sought to 'stand' for the 'best interests' of the masses, but their ways of serving those 'best interests' were no longer necessarily the popular ones."[37]

Indeed, Hearst's commitment to journalistic democratic populism was only skin-deep. As Hearst built a newspaper chain in major cities including San Francisco, Chicago, and Boston to rival Scripps, he "became the foremost union buster," locking out or firing all union members and importing workers from his chain's other newspapers.[38]

Another newspaper chain publisher, S. I. Newhouse, founder of Advance Publications, which has long included the *Portland Oregonian*, the Newark *Star-Ledger*, the New Orleans *Times-Picayune*, and the *Cleveland Plain Dealer*, "despised" unions. He pushed reporters and writers organized by the Newspaper Guild out of his newsrooms with "a concerted program of harassment and firings," and enlisted local police to beat striking reporters and printers.[39]

Not all editors and publishers were as outspoken in their relationship with labor. As media researcher Daniel Chomsky argues, "Measuring the influence of media owners over their institutions is difficult" because of denials and the absence of evidence.[40] But in his historical study of hundreds of memos sent from publisher Arthur Hays Sulzberger to the editor of the *New York Times* between 1956 and 1962, Chomsky found that the publisher routinely intervened in editorial matters and requested that the newsroom look into his special concerns. Moreover, the requests revealed the publisher's socioeconomic interests: "The owner's requests . . . consistently favored the concerns of the wealthy over those of ordinary citizens. . . . Sulzberger never suggested a single story dealing with ordinary workers. Unions entered Sulzberger's consciousness and his blue notes only as a threat to society."[41] Chomsky also found that the newsroom had a high level of responsiveness to the publisher's many requests.

Chomsky's research doesn't present evidence that Sulzberger wanted to shrink labor coverage at the *Times*. In fact, the *Times* maintained at least four labor reporters on staff during this time. But it does demonstrate that publishers have a large degree of influence over the editorial operations of a newspaper.

At the *Cleveland Plain Dealer*, Thomas Vail was publisher and editor from 1963 to 1992. In a 1990 interview, he reflected on the careful balance in dealing with the *Plain Dealer*'s unions without offending the reading community: "Cleveland, Pittsburgh, Detroit and Chicago are four of the big union towns of the world. And you have to watch out what you are doing because it's one thing to deal with the unions in your own plant, but also you have a lot of union people in Cleveland buying your newspaper."[42] In fact, Paul Bellamy, editor of the *Plain Dealer* from 1928 to 1954, actively sought to win over union members as readers. Bellamy sent a typewritten note to Anthony DiSantis, the newspaper's labor reporter, in August 1952, complimenting him on a recent article as "labor reporting at its best," adding that "if you only keep it up long enough we will line up on our side all the thinking union people in Cleveland."[43]

Somewhat ironically, during a 1962 strike at both the *Plain Dealer* and the competing *Cleveland Press*, it was the Scripps-Howard newspaper—the *Cleveland Press*—that offended the Cleveland working-class community. Vail recounted how Louis Seltzer, the longtime editor of the *Cleveland Press*—at that time Cleveland's leading newspaper—was told by Roy Howard, CEO of Scripps-Howard, to reverse his pro-union statements regarding striking workers. Seltzer was also forced to denounce any additional Newspaper Guild organizing at the *Press*. As Vail said, "Well, now remember we are talking about 1962. Cleveland was a big union town. Seltzer's statement was so extreme it fell on the Cleveland community like a bomb shell. So here was the spokesman (Seltzer) for a blue-collar newspaper giving an antiunion speech. This turned off union people all over Cleveland in a big way. Seltzer's speech which he was forced to make was a terrible blunder. When a strike was over we picked up a swing of 35,000 or 40,000 from the *Press*."[44]

By 1962, the corporate leaders of Scripps-Howard had long ago moved away from E. W. Scripps's commitment to labor and the "95 percent."[45] In 1967 the *Plain Dealer* was purchased by Newhouse's Advance Publications, which also opposed unions. These were the two newspapers left to serve one of the "four big union towns of the world."

By the 1970s and 1980s, the shift in the target audience of most US newspapers changed how editors and publishers thought about workers, including their own. If a newspaper wrote off the working-class audience in favor of a more upscale audience, the newspaper could also be less concerned about alienating readership by cracking down on its own unions, as the *New York Times* and *Washington Post* did when breaking their typesetter unions in the early 1970s.[46]

The experiences of labor and workplace writers in the 1970s, 1980s, and 1990s illustrate the ambivalent commitment of many newspapers to the labor/workplace beat. Even as newspapers shifted their focus to upscale audiences, some maintained regular labor/workplace reporting for pragmatic reasons. For example, Stephen Franklin, who reported on labor and the workplace at the *Chicago Tribune* until it downsized and eliminated his position in 2008, explained that "there are under a million people in Illinois who belong to labor unions"—too large an audience for his newspaper to ignore.[47] However, the *Tribune's* commitment to labor is clearly not ideological: Franklin noted that on multiple occasions the *Tribune* used its editorial pages to attack his labor reports.

William Serrin, the labor/workplace reporter for the *New York Times* from 1979 to 1986, also got mixed messages about the focus of his assignment. Serrin told me that he had dinner with *Times* National Editor David R. Jones in 1979 to discuss his new position: "He and I redefined it [the beat] as *work*. You cover work, you cover everything. I got to get out in America and talk to working class people. I went all over America." Serrin also joked that "I could write about anything as long as I got 'work' in the third paragraph."[48] Yet there were also constraints on Serrin, reported *New York* magazine columnist Edwin Diamond: "Serrin began to sense that his editors thought he was 'pro-worker' and 'too opinionated'—specifically, that his stories were somehow failing to meet the *Times'* unspoken centrist standards. A top executive admonished Serrin for 'quoting too many labor people.'"[49] Diamond added that Serrin's editors "wanted 'trend stories' about the workplace and not stories about the AFL-CIO and working-class people."[50]

Those kind of heavy editorial limits on labor/workplace reporting ultimately undermine public understanding of labor and the working class. Philip Dine, a former labor journalist for more than two decades at the *St. Louis Post-Dispatch,* argued that "the marginal way labor is often covered would be tantamount to covering education by focusing on school shootings or teacher arrests, which nobody would think of doing."[51]

It is a common argument that the decline of labor and workplace reporting is the "yuppification" of the newsroom: reporters are now college-educated professionals who are generally removed from interactions with the working class.[52] There is some truth to that, especially as colleges increasingly function as "finishing schools for the affluent," and because editors tend to hire people like themselves, sustaining the lack of diversity in the nation's newsrooms.[53] Upscale journalism tends to hire upscale reporters and editors (i.e., people from "top" colleges, with the best internships, and with the familiar culture and connections of higher socioeconomic classes), which helps to make the upscale media even more insular. However, my response is not to blame reporters; although they have some degree of independence, they are reporting what they are hired and assigned to cover, and writing in the style and narrative framing they absorb as they are socialized into the newsroom.[54] As we shall see below, the most powerful force weighing on the labor / workplace beat is the overall business and editorial focus of the newspaper, which sets the tone of the newsroom.

The Move to Drop Working-Class Readers

The seeds of the decline of the labor beat were sown in the 1960s. It wasn't that union membership had precipitously fallen. Union membership was about 33 percent of the US workforce in 1955, 31 percent in 1960, and 30 percent in 1970.[55] But the newspaper industry had already begun to change. The elimination of competing city newspapers through mergers or closings had been happening since the 1920s. But the 1960s—with the advent of television as a competing news medium and newspapers battling their typesetter unions to quicken the pace of computer automation—hastened the demise of several newspapers. In 1961, sixty-one cities had two or more competing daily newspapers. That number declined to forty-five by the beginning of 1968 and to thirty by 1981.[56] In the nation's leading newspaper market, New York City, the 1967 demise of the short-lived *New York World Journal Tribune* (in its nameplate, evidence of the trail of mergers of the *World-Telegram and Sun*, the *Journal-American*, and the *Herald Tribune*) left New York a three-newspaper town. Home to fifteen daily newspapers in 1900, New York entered the last third of the twentieth century with just three major dailies: the *Times*, the *Post*, and the *Daily News*.[57] By that time, only 3 percent of US cities had competing newspapers; the rest were all single-newspaper local monopolies.[58]

The newspaper industry's further newspaper acquisitions and consolidations fueled the growth of chains, many of them becoming public corporations listed on stock exchanges in the 1960s.[59] The Times Mirror Co. and Thomson Newspapers became publicly traded in 1965, Gannett in 1967, the New York Times in 1968, and the Knight and Ridder groups in 1969 (the latter two merged in 1974).[60] With an eye on maintaining high levels of revenue (many in the 20–40 percent profit return range), the mantra for newspapers in the 1970s and onward was to be more market driven: consumer oriented rather than citizen oriented.[61] According to newspaper researcher and former journalist Doug Underwood, "The push toward conglomeration accelerated as dailies fell into chain hands in large numbers from the mid-1970s to the mid-1980s."[62] In fact, in 1960 there were 109 newspaper groups (or chains) controlling 560 papers (30 percent of dailies) and 46 percent of total daily circulation. By 1990, there were 135 newspaper groups controlling 1,228 daily newspapers (75.5 percent of dailies) and 81 percent of total daily circulation.[63]

As Michael Emery, Edwin Emery, and Nancy Roberts noted, the move of the companies from being independently owned to being publicly traded changed their focus: "Previously a media corporation had two publics: its advertisers and its readers/listeners/viewers. The corporations that became publicly owned also required a third public: investors whose interest was in the fluctuations of the corporation's stock."[64] Media economists Gilbert Cranberg, Randall Bezanson, and John Soloski similarly argue that large chain newspapers "are subject to the unceasing demands of the investment marketplace, populated by individuals, corporations, institutional investors, and other passive investors, large and small, whose interest is profits and margins and yields and share value; whose interest, in short, is business, not news."[65] An independent study of 183 US dailies linked upscale consumer market orientation to corporate size.[66] That is, the larger the corporate parent of a newspaper (measured in terms of the chain's total circulation), the more likely it is to adopt a market-based strategy designed to appeal to upwardly mobile consumers.

Even with more local monopolies for newspapers in US cities, by the 1960s there was newer competition from television, which had switched from 15- to 30-minute newscasts at the national network and local level. In an annual poll that asked respondents "Where do you get most of your news about what's going on in the world today?" the answer "television" beat "newspapers" for the first time in 1964. This response understandably concerned the newspaper industry.[67] The Newspaper Advertising Bureau, the research arm of the US newspaper industry, found that in 1961 about 80 percent of US adults read a newspaper daily, but subsequent surveys discovered that circulation growth was slowing later in the decade. As circulation numbers dropped somewhat, revenue from circulation (newspaper subscriptions and single-copy purchases) began to fall, too, although advertising revenue stayed healthy.[68]

The newspaper industry, which had generally focused on mass audiences, agonized over the reasons of and the remedies for slowing circulation. In the magazine industry, the United States witnessed the closing of three general-interest magazines that were in the top ten in the country in paid circulation. The *Saturday Evening Post* stopped production in 1969, *Look* in 1971, and *Life* in 1972. Each was popular, with a readership of more than six million per issue. Yet the magazines were expensive to produce and distribute with rising paper and postage costs, and television had garnered an increasing share of the national advertising market. The demise of these general-interest magazines "ushered in a new era of specialization" in the magazine industry, and some in the newspaper industry suggested they should do the same.[69]

Major newspapers, which had long focused on urban markets, were also struggling with the migration of more-affluent city residents to suburbs. Leo Bogart, head of the newspaper industry's Newspaper Advertising Bureau for more than twenty years, had verified the extent of the problem:

> The real reasons why readership had declined appeared to be rooted in the changes in society itself or in the changed media environment. Our studies seemed to confirm many of the observations and analyses I had offered the Bureau Board for years before the Readership Project began: the weakening of urban culture; the lost sense of identification with the central city; the growth of the underclass; changed family structure, with more mobile one- and two-person households; and the time pressures that followed entry of women into the workforce. Television was occupying more hours of the day, and news was an increasingly important component of television.[70]

The demise of urban centers was especially damaging to newspapers, for it affected not only citizens and readers but also major retail advertisers: "With the flight of middle classes, black and white, downtowns became deserted at the end of the workday, with hotels and theaters closed, storefronts boarded up, parking lots and weed-filled fields replacing abandoned buildings."[71] At a high-level meeting with publishers and editors in 1967, Bogart suggested (as he had three years earlier) that they would need to address urban decay. In a follow-up note, he wrote that "this decay also threatens the readership and the very function of metropolitan dailies as the editorial voices of the communities that are real to people who inhabit them."[72]

The publishers and editors were unmoved. In fact, they had already been shifting their focus toward upscale suburban readers, following their business out of the city. They had also been following the wishes of some advertisers and (as publicly traded corporations) security analysts, who suggested they would be most profitable if they "concentrated on the upper half of the market, and ignored the less desirable customers."[73]

This is not the first time that newspapers had deemed part of their community "less desirable customers." Although the stated mission of most US newspapers in the twentieth century was that they served the public, that public typically didn't include African Americans and other racial minorities. For example, when Ben Bradlee (later the celebrated editor of the *Washington Post* from 1968 to 1991) first started at the *Post* in 1948, he learned that "incidents were routinely not covered because they involved blacks." The *New Orleans Times-Picayune* in the same era gave its photographers instructions to shoot photos of only whites, with any blacks in the background to be cropped or airbrushed out.[74]

The reason for a black newspaper in the first place identifies the lack of attention of the nation's "white" metropolitan newspapers to black interests. In 1932 *Time* magazine bluntly explained the obstacles to the black press: "Of many efforts to establish and maintain a Negro daily none has succeeded. Discerning Negro editors recognize several reasons, 1) In large cities big department stores do not want Negro trade, would not advertise in a Negro daily. 2) White dailies widely cover the Negro field. 3) Most neighborhood stores are slow to advertise anywhere, would choose a Negro paper last."[75] By 1955, just twenty-one black reporters in the entire country were employed by white-owned daily newspapers; at the same time, there were more than 100 weeklies edited by and for black Americans.[76]

The new corporate imperatives in the 1960s and 1970s for chain-owned newspapers moved the newspapers off their central democratic function for the communities they served. According to Thomas C. Leonard of the University of California, Berkeley School of Journalism, "What changed in the 1970s was frank talk that the reading public could be separated into groups on the basis of lifestyle as well as demographic data and some readers, then, written off. This strategy meant putting aside the considerable body of research that showed that people with strained budgets were careful and loyal readers of the daily paper and in some ways better informed than the affluent."

Newspaper Readership Slides in the 1970s

By the late 1960s, major city newspapers (still very white in their operations) again shunned readers, this time based on their socioeconomic class (and/or their residency in poorer neighborhoods).[77] Race still played a factor, too. The *Washington Post* cut back distribution to black neighborhoods "in order to upgrade the quality of its demographic audience profile for demographic purposes."[78] Gannett, the largest newspaper chain, cut subscriptions to people in rural areas in the 1970s, as did the *Atlanta Journal* and the *Atlanta Constitution,* the Cowles newspapers in Minneapolis, and the *Chicago Tribune.* The *Los Angeles Times* dropped its San Diego edition and gave up on its "working-class sections of city," as did the *Nashville Tennessean.* Experts called this "rationed circulation."[79]

Philip Meyer, a former journalist and later researcher for Knight Ridder newspapers, and professor emeritus of journalism at University of North Carolina at Chapel Hill, explained the business rationale for chain owners making cuts to previously locally or regionally owned newspapers. When Gannett bought the *Des Moines Register* in 1985, "The paper covered the entire state of Iowa and had a tidy 10 percent operating margin. Gannett's finance people looked at the operation, saw no economic value in its statewide influence, and cut circulation back to the area served by advertisers in the Des Moines market. That saved money on the main variable costs, newsprint and ink. Two of the five state news bureaus were eliminated. The operating margin went quickly to 25 percent."[80]

Given that the newspaper industry intentionally dropped working-class readers and deemphasized working-class content (since they weren't writing for that group anymore), it is both surprising and ironic that the industry was perplexed that circulation rates were still declining. The industry instead doubled down on targeting its new upscale market segments, according to Doug Underwood, author of *When the MBAs Ruled the Newsroom:* "Although neither marketing or target marketing were new concepts in the newspaper business, the late 1970s and early 1980s saw a virtual stampede by the industry to get more marketing smart."[81] Most major newspapers hired marketing executives and strategized with a new class of roving newspaper consultants. Nevertheless, circulation numbers continued to slide: "In the most disastrous decade for newspapers, the 1970s, daily circulation in the 20 largest cities dropped by 21 percent while population fell only 6 percent."[82]

If a newspaper intentionally drops working-class subscribers in urban and rural areas and doesn't provide news coverage to those areas anymore, it follows that those people will likely stop reading that newspaper. As newspaper marketing professor Conrad Fink explained, "Trying to sell in an area ignored by the newsroom is futile; people want to buy a paper with news from their area."[83] Or, as Thomas Leonard put it, "Readers will not stay loyal to a publication . . . that does not look out for *their* interests and give them intelligent direction."[84]

These statements hold true in a review of data from the Newspaper Association of America about readership from 1967 to 1997, which reveals a sharp decline, particularly among the "downscale" readers the industry gave up on in the 1970s (see table 2.2). Education is a common proxy for social class. In 1967 readership rates among those who attended high school (but did not graduate) were not far from those who graduated from high school, attended college, or graduated from college: just an 11.3 percent difference across the educational spectrum. By 1977, the percentage difference in readership across levels of education grew to 19.2 percent, and to 22.9 percent by 1997. The growing disparity in newspaper readership was clearly caused by a much greater decline in readership levels in those whose education level did not reach graduation from college. Ironically, if newspapers wanted to build their circulation, their largest populations of readers (and potential readers) were in the categories with lower educational attainment: the same readers many newspapers had intentionally dismissed.

Yet the newspaper industry seemed blind to its own missteps. It did not take long for even critics of the newspaper industry to rationalize the notion

Table 2.2. US adults: average weekly newspaper readership education level, 1967–1997

Year	Attend HS		HS graduate		Attend college		College graduate	
	#	%	#	%	#	%	#	%
1967	21,459	74.1	32,286	80.0	12,581	84.5	10,815	85.4
1977	15,041	62.6	41,006	71.1	17,194	74.4	16,641	81.8
1987	12,432	55.5	44,821	65.6	22,565	70.1	23,639	77.7
1997	8,921	44.3	37,827	58.6	23,647	60.5	13,639	67.2

Note: Numbers in thousands.

Source: Newspaper Association of America, October 2004, http://www.naa.org/~/media/NAACorp/Public% 20Files/TrendsAndNumbers/Readership/Education_Daily_National_Top50_67-97.ashx.

that going upscale was the only option. For example, David Shaw, the Pulitzer Prize–winning media critic at the *Los Angeles Times*, offered this as the common wisdom as early as 1977: "Families low in income and educational and occupational achievement have always been less likely to read newspapers than the better-educated, better-off citizenry . . . this is especially true in the large cities that have become increasingly populated by low-income blacks, Chicanos, and whites."[85] However, historically that has not been true, and even independent newspaper researchers in the 1980s and 1990s argued that "blue-collar, working-class, middle-class folks are excellent newspaper readers."[86]

Ironically, industry marketers of the 1980s who used brief phone interviews to cull out unwanted subscribers created categories that "would have written off most American people" during the Great Depression and redlined "the boyhood homes of Ronald Reagan and Bill Clinton."[87] In their effort to go upscale, something more sinister was at hand in the newspaper business. "Newspaper publishers had never dared to pick winners and losers among the reading public," Leonard wrote. "Now this changed. A handbook of the 1980s on newspaper management cited the alarm over 'unprofitable circulation in areas having little corporate, editorial, or advertising value to the newspaper.' Though it's hard to know how a citizen falls below a standard of 'editorial value,' this would seem to be a complete list of all the reasons a reader may be unwanted."[88]

For the newspaper industry, working-class people were no longer newsworthy and had been even less so since the 1970s. Unless they actually addressed their working-class readers—urban and rural, women and men, white and people of color—as fully deserving citizens with real interests and concerns, they had little chance of regaining them as readers. Unfortunately, this upscale-niche marketing ideology has been increasingly ingrained in journalists since the early 1970s. In their study *The American Journalist in the Digital Age*, Indiana University researchers found that whereas 39 percent of journalists surveyed said it was "extremely important" to focus on news that is of interest to the "widest possible audience" in 1971, that response dropped to 20.2 percent of journalists in 1992 and 12.1 percent in 2013.[89]

The Consequences of a Working Class Deemed No Longer Newsworthy

There are two main consequences of US newspapers writing off the working class in the last third of the twentieth century. First, by focusing on only "quality" demographics and cutting out both working-class readers and news coverage of labor and working-class issues, news organizations ultimately damaged their own value. Philip Meyer explained the intrinsic value that newspapers had in their communities that many corporate owners had let erode over several decades: "A newspaper that depends on customer habit to keep the dollars flowing while it raises prices and gives back progressively less in return has made a decision to liquidate. It is a slow liquidation and is not immediately visible because the asset being converted into cash is intangible—what the bean counters call 'good will.' Good will is the organization's standing in the community. More specifically, it is the habit members of the community have of giving it money." Recovering and sustaining that value takes time and investment. Goodwill, Meyer argued, "is built slowly over the years. It is the result of a healthy relationship between the newspaper and the community."[90]

The other consequence is related to that goodwill. If journalism does not take the responsibility to serve citizens from all socioeconomic classes, the result is civic dysfunction. Sociologists David Croteau and William Hoynes identified already recognizable outcomes: "The news media often do not address the concerns of average citizens, focusing instead on 'insider' politics and economic information for the investor class. . . . Because, as we have seen, news media are often only interested in reaching only the particular desirable demographic groups that advertisers covet, many news media outlets do little to engage broader groups of citizens or educate them about the significance of civic affairs. The result is likely to be further alienation and disengagement from public life."[91]

When US newspapers deemed the working class no longer newsworthy, they helped create the situation they would eventually chronicle for an upscale audience: the increasing economic and political division of the United States. Working-class people (urban and rural, white and people of color) were left without a journalistic voice in public life, while middle-class people (and the more affluent) were treated to journalism that overstated their activities, overrepresented their numbers in the community, and over-catered to their interests.

The tradition and rights of a free press remain crucial to US democracy. But when newspapers piously editorialize about their important role in providing citizens the information they need to sustain it, when by their own accord they have excluded a good portion of that citizenry from their target audience, the peals for freedom ring a bit more hollow.

Chapter 3

The News Media's Shift to
Upscale Audiences

The newspaper industry's frequent use of terms such as *upscale, influential, affluent,* and *elite* to describe their readers typically avoids the sociological language of class, which could undercut the myth of a class-free United States.[1] But the news industry's own language of distinction still makes clear that its readers are extra-special and the most highly esteemed: economically, socially, and culturally. This focus on such audiences means that news organizations have written working-class readers out of their business plan.

Ideally, journalism's first loyalty should always be to its citizens, argue Bill Kovach and Tom Rosenstiel.[2] But when it comes to selling space to advertisers, not all citizens are equal. It wasn't always this way. Prior to the 1970s, when the labor beat was well established in the United States, newspapers were interested in gaining as many readers as possible and selling those readers to advertisers. As newspaper historian Herbert A. Kenny observed of this era, "Paper sales meant circulation, circulation meant advertising, and advertising meant profits."[3] In fact, *circulation* was the key word for newspapers selling advertisements in the first two-thirds of the twentieth century. Then came a dramatic shift, where mass circulation was replaced with a new key word: *readership.* In this new vision of how a newspaper should serve its community, the newspapers and their corporate owners wanted only the *right kind* of readers, those who were "well-to-do," "affluent moderns," "influentials," and people with plenty of "effective buying power" and "giant-size household incomes." Nearly every newspaper began publicizing its readers as if they were the children of Garrison Keillor's fictional Lake Wobegon: all above average.

The Telling Newspaper Advertisements in *Editor & Publisher*

The upscale consumer shift in the newspapers was well documented for industry insiders who read the leading newspaper trade journal of the twentieth century, *Editor & Publisher*. The publication, with its roots dating back to 1884, was "the bible of the newspaper industry" during the twentieth century.[4] (The fate of *E&P* correlates with the newspaper industry. In 2004, *E&P* became a monthly publication and was briefly shut down at the end of 2009 when its then-owner, Nielsen Business Media, couldn't find a buyer. Within a few months, Duncan McIntosh Company bought the journal and resurrected the print and online versions.) For nearly all of the twentieth century, until the Internet became a popular communication medium in the mid-1990s, *Editor & Publisher* was how newspapers across North America (often through a national advertising representative company they hired) communicated with their potential advertisers, particularly national advertisers. Why should a company buy a display advertisement in the *Cleveland Plain Dealer, Providence Journal, Fort Worth Star-Telegram, New York Times,* or *Portland Oregonian*? Long before newspapers could post their media kits online (which is how newspapers have reached advertisers since the mid-1990s), their advertisements in *Editor & Publisher* were the chief method for selling their audience to national advertisers.

Thus, *Editor & Publisher* advertisements are a primary source for examining how US newspapers envisioned, shaped, and presented their reading audience during the twentieth century to the other newspaper audience: advertisers.[5] In the twentieth century, newspapers were even more central than today to the discussion of democracy and commerce in the public marketplace. The *E&P* newspaper trade journal advertisements indicate who the worthy citizens (or, as a 1940 advertisement for the *Cincinnati Enquirer* put it, the "solid, substantial citizens") are in the public sphere at any given time.

The Mass Audience

In the first two-thirds of the twentieth century, the predominant appeal in newspaper ads in *Editor & Publisher* was illustrating the spending power of mass audiences. For example, an advertisement placed for the *Detroit Free Press* on January 6, 1945, emphasized the mass audience in Detroit that the *Free Press* could deliver. The ad features a raised highway paved with issues of the *Free Press,* leading directly to the nighttime skyline of "thriving, bustling" Detroit, one of the nation's largest cities at the time. The ad's boxed headline calls out "The Detroit Free Press is the High Road to the Rich Prosperous Detroit Market," where the city's only morning newspaper reaches over 380,000 families daily in a "huge market of nearly 3 million!" The *Free Press* wasn't trying to sell a segment of the market; it wanted advertisers to use the *Free Press* as "the DIRECT route to 'arriving' in Detroit."

Of course, even a "mass" audience wasn't all-inclusive in the 1930s and 1940s in the United States. In an era before the civil rights movement, the "worthwhile" mass audiences for newspapers were always characterized as white audiences and, in certain places in the Midwest, as "native born," too, unlike popular immigration destinations of the early twentieth century such as New York, Chicago, and San Francisco. The three leading newspapers in the Cincinnati-Columbus-Indianapolis triangle all played up their nativist element as a positive for their market's appeal to advertisers. For example, the *Cincinnati Enquirer* in a July 21, 1934, *Editor & Publisher* ad argued that it had a huge "mass-class" audience of readers, almost of them "native-born Americans": "It's not necessary to tell you about the financial position of Cincinnati, about the cleanness of its government! That has been widely publicized in newspapers and magazines throughout the United States. Nor do we have to tell you that Cincinnati has by far the largest percentage of native-born Americans of any large city! Talk about solid, substantial citizens! Talk about solid, substantial *circulation!* . . . Talk about a worth-while market."[6]

Similarly, the *Columbus Dispatch* in January 27, 1940, promoted Columbus as "one of the nation's best advertising test markets," in part because "It's [*sic*] population is 94.7 native born." The *Indianapolis News* (April 27, 1940) dispensed with the "native-born" euphemism and got straight to the point about race, boasting that its market had great buying power with "504,000 families, 93% white."

The Detroit Free Press paves the way into the heart of this thriving, bustling market . . . on a *smooth*, straight road. Yes, The Free Press carries your advertising message *straight* to a market of over 380,000 families daily . . . with NO CROSS ROADS to slow it down . . . NO CROSS CURRENTS OF TRAFFIC to distract attention. Your advertising in The Free Press has the road all to itself . . . for The Free Press is the ONLY *morning* paper in this entire, huge market of nearly 3 million! The Free Press is the DIRECT route to "arriving" in Detroit. *Use it!*

The Detroit Free Press

JOHN S. KNIGHT, PUBLISHER

Story, Brooks & Finley, Inc., National Representatives

A DYNAMIC NEWSPAPER SERVING DYNAMIC DETROIT

EDITOR & PUBLISHER for January 6, 1945   5

Figure 3.1. *Detroit Free Press* advertisement, *Editor & Publisher*, January 6, 1945

In these and the nation's other cities, the main appeal to advertisers was that the city's local economy was strong and that the newspaper was the way to reach this booming market. Sometimes, the success of a signature industry was the best way to make the case. For example, the *Baltimore Sun* advertisement in the July 13, 1940, issue of *Editor & Publisher* highlighted one of Baltimore's main industries (shipbuilding), listed the city's leading industrial

Figure 3.2. *Cincinnati Enquirer* advertisement, *Editor & Publisher*, July 21, 1934

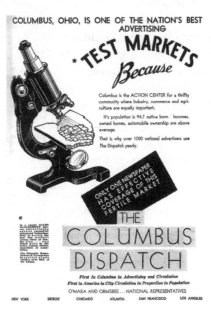

Figure 3.3. *Columbus Dispatch* advertisement, *Editor & Publisher*, January 27, 1940

Figure 3.4. *Indianapolis News* advertisement, *Editor & Publisher,* April 27, 1940

employers (including $66,850,000 for future shipbuilding contracts), and added that they are "paying good wages, making it advantageous for you to develop this market through your advertising in The Sunpapers."

A *Pittsburgh Sun-Telegraph* ad from January 6, 1940, instructed advertisers to "Hitch Your Budget to a Boom." The indicator, according to the ad, was that "Pittsburgh industrial electric power sales are up 45%." The equation was simple, the ad said: "More electric power means more *buying* power; for more electricity, used by industry, means more production, more employment, more wages, more money to spend for your products." The ad concluded that "your share is waiting. Your advertising can get it—get all of it—if you cover all the market. Remember, your retail outlets consider Pittsburgh a TWO-paper buy—and include the *Sun-Telegraph* as a must medium." As the second evening and Sunday paper, trailing the *Pittsburgh Press* in circulation, the *Sun-Telegraph*'s strategy was to recommend buying ads in both papers to encompass the Pittsburgh mass market, an approach that newspapers in other multi-newspaper markets often used.

At the *Chicago Tribune,* which bought the front-page ad of the April 6, 1940, *Editor & Publisher,* nine words in all-capital letters—"OVER ONE MILLION CIRCULATION EVERY DAY OF THE WEEK"—communicated everything

Figure 3.5. *Baltimore Sun* advertisement, *Editor & Publisher,* July 13, 1940

Figure 3.6. *Pittsburgh Sun-Telegraph* advertisement, *Editor & Publisher,* January 6, 1940

Figure 3.7. *Chicago Tribune* advertisement, *Editor & Publisher,* April 6, 1940

it wanted advertisers to know about the city's leading newspaper. If you wanted to reach an enormous audience in Chicago—then America's Second City—the *Tribune* had the massive numbers. Thus, the main message of US newspapers in the 1940s was that they had lots of readers who were making good wages in the nation's booming industries and could buy potential advertisers' products.

There were a few newspapers in highly competitive markets that targeted more exclusive, higher-income audiences at that time. The *New York Times* was a pioneer of this strategy and had been focusing on more professional audiences since 1896, when Adolph Ochs purchased the newspaper. Ochs's strategy was to avoid a head-on battle with the much more popular, mass-oriented newspapers—Joseph Pulitzer's *New York World* and William Randolph Hearst's *New York Journal*—and carve out a niche in which his smaller newspaper could grow. As news media historian Michael Schudson explained, Ochs positioned the *Times* to be the newspaper of government and business professionals and the well-educated: in short, the upwardly mobile middle class of New York at that time.[7] Yet two years into Ochs's ownership, the *Times* circulation stood at 25,000, far smaller than the *World* and *Journal,* each of which published more than a half million copies daily. Ochs decided to drop the price of the *Times* from three cents to one cent, matching the price of the two larger newspapers. Ochs wanted it both ways: his "quality" audience but also a larger audience. In an editorial announcing the price change, Ochs stepped carefully: "In appealing to a larger audience, THE TIMES by no means proposes to offend the taste or forfeit the confidence of the audience it now has. . . . THE TIMES has determined to extend its appeal beyond those readers with whom the quality is indispensable and price a matter of no consequence to the presumably much larger number to whom both price and quality are of consequence."[8]

Ochs's calculation was correct. Within a year the circulation tripled, and by 1903 it surpassed 200,000.[9] In a 1908 editorial the *Times* explained its reasoning in positioning itself against the "yellow journalism" of the *World* and *Journal:* "In the City of New York . . . a newspaper could secure a large circulation only by giving itself over to sensationalism and pictures, to startling headlines and yellowness. In other words, popularity was incompatible with self-respect, dignity, and clean living. The management of THE TIMES was not of that opinion." At one point, before it settled on its famous motto, "All the News That's Fit to Print," the *Times* employed another saying to communicate its brand: "It Does Not Soil the Breakfast Cloth."[10]

The *Times* continued to use a niche approach decades later, as it trailed the *New York Daily News* in circulation size. But instead of a sanctimonious appeal presuming its innate decency, by 1940 the *Times* went after advertisers with an appeal more pointedly based on class. For example, in an August 17, 1940, *Editor & Publisher* ad, the *New York Times* introduced a full-page ad series that would run at least six times over three months. The ad asks readers to "Meet the John Smiths and the Tom Browns," two fictitious white families, one (the Smiths) representing the mass market (presumably the audience of other newspapers), the other (the Browns) representing the *Times*' upscale market audience. The rest of the ad describes the families' socioeconomic differences without ever mentioning the term "class": "John Smith, married, lives in New York City with his wife and two children. He earns $32 a week or $1664 a year. Tom Brown, married, also has two children and lives in New York on his salary of $85 a week or $4420 a year."

The ad then compares, in chart form, the two families' typical spending on consumable goods and services, and continues: "The Browns, having more money, spend more money on everything than the Smiths, even on everyday items such as food, tobacco or the corner movie. They buy more and buy more often and thus are better and more profitable customers. That's why we call families like the Browns the *Profit Half* of New York. They are logically the first families advertisers want to reach in New York—and

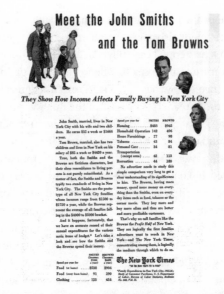

Figure 3.8. *New York Times* advertisement, *Editor & Publisher,* August 17, 1940

The New York Times, concentrating among them, is logically the medium through which to do so."

Other ads in the Browns and Smiths "Profit Half" series addressed the Browns' superior spending on home furnishings, personal care products, groceries, clothing, and entertainment (with photos contrasting the dowdy Smiths with the suave Browns in evening gown and tuxedo).[11]

The *Times* wasn't the only newspaper in New York that used an upscale niche strategy as it trailed the leading *New York Daily News* in 1940. The *New York Herald Tribune* ran an ad on August 3, 1940, with a bird's-eye view of the New York Stock Exchange building on Wall Street, claiming that it was "The Newspaper Most Read at the Heart of Business America"—that is, the one most read by members of the New York Stock Exchange.

The *New York Sun* (January 20, 1940) claimed that it "attracts a readership of young, active, progressive families . . . the worthwhile buying families throughout New York's good home areas in cities and suburbs." In another ad (June 22, 1940), with a giant sun image whose center read "Star of the Campus" and with eleven rays featuring college names, the *Sun* stated "This year the senior classes of 11 great Eastern colleges and universities again voted The Sun their *favorite* New York evening newspaper."

The elite education appeal was echoed in an ad for the *New York Times* in the same June 22, 1940, *Editor & Publisher* edition. The ad reminded

Mrs. Brown spends

3½ times as much as Mrs. Smith on her home

Mrs. Brown's budget permits her to spend $98 a year on home furnishings and equipment. Mrs. Smith can spare only $27 for these items.

If you were a refrigerator manufacturer, which family would you want your salesmen and advertising campaign to reach first—the Browns or the Smiths?

Put this way, the question may seem a little silly and the answer obvious, but every day manufacturers not only of refrigerators but of breakfast foods, automobiles and overshoes, too, have to weigh the "profit importance" of the Browns and the Smiths. Knowing how they spend their money solves many advertising problems.

"Brown" and "Smith," you see, are just a convenient way of designating two principal buying groups in New York City. The Browns represent all New York families whose income falls between $4000 and $5000; the Smiths, the group between $1500 and $1750. Studied side by side their budgets (now available in a new report*) illustrate a basic market truth: as income improves, families become better and more profitable customers for everything, even everyday staples and necessities.

The Browns each have $71 more a year to furnish and equip their homes. They can buy more and buy more often. That's why we call the Browns and other families like them the Profit Half of New York. They are logically the first families advertisers want to reach in New York—and The New York Times, concentrating among them, is logically the medium to reach them.

The New York Times

"All the News That's Fit to Print"

*Family Expenditures in New York City, 1935–36: Study of Consumer Purchases, U. S. Department of Labor, Bureau of Labor Statistics, Bulletin No. 643, Vol. II.

Figure 3.9. *New York Times* advertisement, *Editor & Publisher,* September 7, 1940

advertisers that "this year, as in years past, The Times is the favorite New York newspaper on the campuses of leading men's and women's colleges and preparatory schools throughout the North and East. Preference for The Times is expressed not only in student polls, but in student circulation as well."

Meanwhile, the *New York World-Telegram* ran a 1940 series of ads featuring its in-house research on identifying the New York market's most upscale family neighborhoods. Using fictional names for typical families revealed by their research (an approach mimicked by the *Times* later that year for its "Browns and Smiths" ad series), one ad (April 20, 1940) asked *Editor & Publisher* readers to "Consider the Lourances of Larchmont," suburban Westchester County readers of the *World-Telegram:* "They're representative of the town. They own their home, have two nice youngsters, employ a full-time maid. This year they'll vacation in Bermuda—three weeks at least, we're told. Their '38 Olds will serve through Summer, then it'll be traded in. Mr. Lourance is a corporation treasurer; he earns 'over $10,000' and carries $25,000 life insurance. Mrs. Lourance, too, is a college graduate. She's the family purchasing agent; shops in New York once a week—has charge accounts at five department and specialty stores. The World-Telegram is bought to take home each evening. . . ."

Figure 3.10. *New York Times* advertisement, *Editor & Publisher,* October 5, 1940

Figure 3.11. *New York Times* advertisement, *Editor & Publisher,* September 21, 1940

Figure 3.12. *New York Times* advertisement, *Editor & Publisher,* August 24, 1940

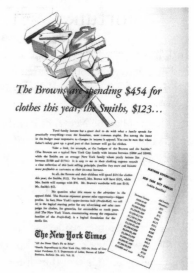

Figure 3.13. *New York Times* advertisement, *Editor & Publisher,* August 31, 1940

Figure 3.14. *New York Herald-Tribune* advertisement, *Editor & Publisher*, August 3, 1940

Figure 3.15. *New York Sun* advertisement, *Editor & Publisher*, June 22, 1940

Figure 3.16. *New York Times* advertisement, *Editor & Publisher*, June 22, 1940

Figure 3.17. *New York World-Telegram* advertisement, *Editor & Publisher*, April 20, 1940

Figure 3.18. *New York World-Telegram* advertisement, *Editor & Publisher,* April 13, 1940

Another *World-Telegram* advertisement profiles two elite Manhattan families, the Whitbys of West End Avenue and the Taylors of Tudor City, which the newspaper says it also reaches: "They could afford homes in the suburbs or estates in the country—but they choose to pay premium rentals in towers of stone and steel. They want to be 'near the office,' yet part of the taxi-riding, theatre-going, supper-clubbing night life that is the glamour of New York. And they want to be 'just around the corner' from their friends whose pursuits are the same. *For these are Manhattanites of the higher rental areas—the world-envied group which works hard at play because it can really afford to!*"[12]

The *Los Angeles Times* took a more exclusive approach as well. In a September 21, 1940, ad in *Editor & Publisher,* the newspaper used cartoon images of a smiling *Los Angeles Times* newspaper clad in a tuxedo, selling women's wear, men's clothing, and home furnishings. The ad stated: "National advertisers looking for an aggressive representative in the rich Southern California market have plenty of retail signposts to guide them. They'll find, also, that there is more to Times circulation (largest morning circulation on the coast) than volume." The subtle point was that the *Los Angeles Times* wasn't the biggest circulation newspaper of the everyman (that was the *Los Angeles Evening Herald-Express,* which the *Los Angeles Times* would surpass in circulation a few years later), but it was the newspaper for people who patronized the finer retail outlets in the market. This better class of people was implied in the ad's claim that there is "more to Times circulation . . . than volume." A similar ad placed by the *Los Angeles Times* earlier that year (May 18, 1940) made the class issue clear. In this ad, another cartoon version of the *Los Angeles Times*, this time clad in fedora hat, says "NO THANKS, I'm a family man!" to the three rougher-looking cartoon newspaper characters standing outside of a building labeled "Pool Hall." The ad illustrates the value of a family newspaper—the family man has input on the many purchasing decisions in the household—and contrasts the higher "quality" (and class standing) of the *Los Angeles Times* compared to the more common newspapers of the pool hall crowd.

For newspapers like the *New York Times*, the *New York Herald Tribune*, the *New York Sun*, the *New York World-Telegram*, and the *Los Angeles Times*, appealing to a more exclusive segment of the audience was a logical business strategy. In 1940 none of them were the largest newspaper in their market.

Figure 3.19. *Los Angeles Times* advertisement, *Editor & Publisher*, September 21, 1940

Figure 3.20. *Los Angeles Times* advertisement, *Editor & Publisher,* May 18, 1940

By 1955, the US newspaper market had begun to consolidate significantly. Consolidation fit with the business plan of most newspapers: amass the biggest circulation figures to "own" the major advertising medium in the market. Newspapers that weren't the market leaders often still took the approach that advertisers should buy into their newspaper to reach a greater proportion of the mass market or their newspaper could offer a more upscale audience niche to the advertiser.

The *Los Angeles Times* (September 17, 1955), market leader and the nation's third-largest newspaper by 1955, didn't need a niche approach when it could loudly proclaim it was "first in the nation in total advertising." Similarly, the *St. Louis Globe-Democrat* (March 19, 1955) informed potential advertisers of its record numbers: "Did you know that: Your product's advertisement in the morning Globe-Democrat reaches more people in metropolitan St. Louis than at any time in our 103 years of publication?"

Gross market size, defined by economic activity, remained significant in *Editor & Publisher* ads in 1955. A January 15, 1955, ad by the *Philadelphia*

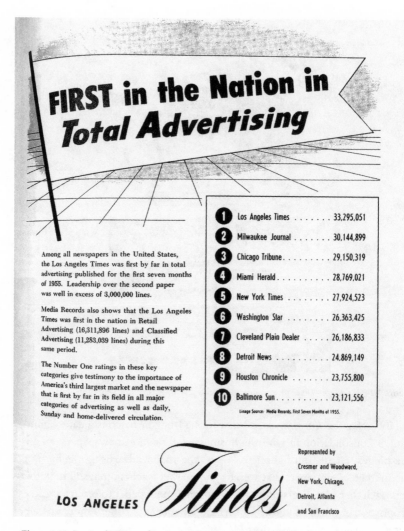

Figure 3.21. *Los Angeles Times* advertisement, *Editor & Publisher*, September 17, 1955

Inquirer noted its $8 billion market size. The *Inquirer*, the morning newspaper that was second to the market-leading evening newspaper, the *Philadelphia Bulletin*, also angled for a competitive advantage. In the advertisement, a man in a business suit at a breakfast table is reading the *Inquirer* and reaching for a cup of cream, while the headline asks "Looking for the cream . . . of an $8,000,000,000 market?" The ad continues: "THE INQUIRER takes your advertising to the most potent pocket-books in Delaware Valley, U.S.A. In

Figure 3.22. *St. Louis Globe-Democrat* advertisement, *Editor & Publisher*, March 19, 1955

Figure 3.23. *Philadelphia Inquirer* advertisement, *Editor & Publisher*, January 15, 1955

addition to intensive coverage of the city, THE INQUIRER reaches out to give advertisers thorough penetration of the rich suburbs and nearby towns that account for HALF THE SALES in the Greater Philadelphia area."

Although the *Inquirer* angles for the upscale niche in this ad, it also doesn't forsake its mass audience. It continues: "That's why you find so many new advertisers in THE INQUIRER . . . so many old ones with expanded schedules." Clearly, class is a sensitive issue. Richer demographics may appeal to new advertisers, but going "upscale" risks alienating advertisers in the city as well as core readers. By the 1970s, as more and more newspapers targeted "quality" demographics, this became less of an issue as the core of "mass" readers was increasingly shunned.

Quality Demographics, 1970s

By 1970, television already had taken the place of the newspaper as the primary news source for Americans. For newspapers, this led to even more consolidation and, increasingly, ownership by publicly traded corporate newspaper chains seeking an upscale readership and dropping their attention to working-class readers.

For some newspapers, such as the *Los Angeles Herald-Examiner*, the afternoon competitor to the morning *Los Angeles Times*, the shift from its mostly working-class readership to becoming "the rich man's newspaper" was swift.[13] In an April 11, 1970, full-page *Editor & Publisher* ad—with a stereotypical "rich man" image of a suited, cufflinked, and pinky-ringed white executive in a leather chair peering out from the stock exchange pages—the newspaper seemed rather overjoyed to target a new audience: "Suddenly, we find ourselves in the money. For about two years we've suspected a circulation shift toward richer readers. Now it's official. The latest Sindlinger report says this: over half of our households make $10,000 to $50,000. This calls for a fresh look at the whole Los Angeles market. Because now the Herald-Examiner has the power to deliver a huge number of well-to-do readers. It's just one more way we help advertisers get more money for their money."

The tagline was "Los Angeles Herald-Examiner, where the money is." On July 4, 1970, a follow-up full-page ad was even more pointed. It featured the same tagline, a one-sentence mention of the same Sindlinger report conclusion, and a big photo image of copies of the *Herald-Examiner* folded like a stack of money, fastened with a paper wrapper bearing a dollar sign.

Are we in danger of becoming the rich man's paper?

Suddenly we find ourselves in the money.

For about two years we've suspected a circulation shift toward richer readers.

Now it's official.

The latest Sindlinger report says this: over half our households make $10,000 to $50,000.

This calls for a fresh look at the whole Los Angeles market.

Because now the Herald-Examiner has the power to deliver a huge number of well-to-do readers.

It's just one more way we help advertisers get more money for their money.

Los Angeles Herald-Examiner, where the money is.

Figure 3.24. *Los Angeles Herald-Examiner* advertisement, *Editor & Publisher,* April 11, 1970

Figure 3.25. *Los Angeles Herald-Examiner* advertisement, *Editor & Publisher,* July 4, 1970

The *Herald-Examiner*'s claim that "for about two years we've suspected a circulation shift toward richer readers" is disingenuous, though. In 1967, after contract talks broke down, the Los Angeles Newspaper Guild union called a strike against the Hearst-owned *Herald-Examiner*. The strike would last ten years, as Hearst brought in replacement workers and Pinkerton guards, who often served as paramilitary forces for corporations in times of strikes. Important to the *Herald-Examiner*'s claims of an upscale audience is the fact that after the strike began, the newspaper's circulation "dropped from 750,000 in 1967 to less than 400,000 in 1968 and continued to drop annually from that point on."[14] So, yes, the *Herald-Examiner* had richer readers after its public campaign against its own unions and after working-class readers bolted from the newspaper. What was once a large newspaper with a broad readership became a much smaller one as William Randolph Hearst, Jr., made a very consequential decision to oppose his own workers and forsake LA's working-class readers. Within two decades after it claiming it had "the power to deliver a huge number of well-to-do readers," the *Herald-Examiner* newspaper failed; it folded in 1989.

Figure 3.26. Baltimore Sunpapers advertisement, *Editor & Publisher,* August 8, 1970

Figure 3.27. *Baltimore News American* advertisement, *Editor & Publisher,* November 7, 1970

At other newspapers, the new case for upscale audiences was made with greater precision. In an August 8, 1970, ad, Sunpapers (which included the *Baltimore Sun* in the morning and the *Evening Sun* as an editorially independent afternoon paper) argued that it was the only newspaper company ad buy needed to cover the city, with 70 percent of the area's newspaper advertising. However, the company argued for not only the newspaper's exclusivity but also its effectiveness at reaching higher-income households. The image of a high-powered rifle (in retrospect, a rather unfortunate metaphor) makes clear that the audience of the US newspaper is now literally a "target" for marketers. Sunpapers rolled out the data to support its targeting efficiency: "Baltimore is a major market where you can throw away the shotgun approach and use a high-powered rifle. 86% of the metro area households are in 38% of the metro land area. This is Sunpapers Primary Market Area." The ad then lists the number of households with net cash incomes of over $6,000, over $8,000, and over $10,000. (The wealthiest group accounts for 30 percent of all metro homes and 58 percent of all metro income dollars, the ad says.)

The *Sun's* main competitor, and the circulation leader in 1970, was the *Baltimore News American*. Like the *Sun*, the *News American* suggests that it delivers the best access to the Baltimore market. But unlike newspapers in previous decades, the *News American* doesn't argue that its highest circulation figures trump its competitors. Instead, the message in its November 7, 1970, ad is access to upscale readers: "Baltimore now gives you the highest gain in Effective Buying Income per household," and the *News American* "gives you the highest delivery into those households." Thus, both competing Baltimore newspapers publishers are touting access to the same upscale audience.

In Cleveland, another industrial mass market with a large working class and labor union population, the shift to upscale was even more clear. The *Plain Dealer* was, as its advertisements noted, "Ohio's largest daily and largest Sunday newspaper." But quality demographics had become more important, as evident in a campaign that the *Plain Dealer* ran in *Editor & Publisher* in 1970.

The first ad in the campaign (February 21, 1970) featured a photo of a young, white, affluent woman. She has platinum-blonde hair, is wearing a minidress, and is taking gifts and packages from the drop gate of a late-model station wagon. As the ad states, "Lines on maps don't make markets. People do. Mobile people with money. . . . In Cleveland's home county, Cuyahoga, nearly 90% of The Plain Dealer's daily circulation is in the county's top three economic quarters—people who account for more than 90% of Cuyahoga's retail purchases." The ad, in so few words, made clear that the *Plain Dealer*

Figure 3.28. *Cleveland Plain Dealer* advertisement, *Editor & Publisher,* February 21, 1970

was not targeting the entire Cleveland market (everyone within the lines on the map). It was writing off the bottom quartile of Cleveland-area residents. The ad would have more accurately said "Lines on maps don't make markets. Demographics do."

Another ad from the same campaign (March 28, 1970) featured a time-lapse photo of another affluent, young, white woman looking to each side and then straight on at the reader, with her lips parted as if she has something to say. The ad's headline stated "Our market: a perpetual emotion machine," with the copy below adding "Her many buying moods move her money to where the action is—downtown, suburban centers, corner stores. Mobile and affluent, she shops the 16-county Total Cleveland Market. The market dominated by The Plain Dealer's circulation." The woman in the ad seems vexing to marketers—she is moody and unpredictable (the stereotyping demands the inference), but the *Plain Dealer* can channel that energy into high-level shopping activity. Whew!

Our market: a perpetual emotion machine

Her many buying moods move her money to where the action is — downtown, suburban centers, corner stores. Mobile and affluent, she shops the 16-county Total Cleveland Market.

The market dominated by The Plain Dealer's circulation.*

In Cleveland's home county of Cuyahoga, 90% of The Plain Dealer's daily circulation is in the top three eco-nomic quarters — the people who account for over 90% of the county's retail spending.

And in the 15 surrounding counties, more than 70% of PD circulation is in homes valued over $25,000 — all within 40 minutes of Cuyahoga shopping.

Build the Cleveland Market — all of it — into your media plan. Start with Ohio's largest daily and largest Sunday newspaper, The Plain Dealer. Because . . .

*Daily: The Plain Dealer, 401,060 — The Cleveland Press, 377,730. Sunday: The Plain Dealer, 537,677.

The Plain Dealer is THE STARTER.

To start Plain Dealer action tomorrow, contact our National Representatives today and learn what we can do for you in the nation's 6th largest state: Cresmer, Woodward, O'Mara & Ormsbee, Inc. Eastern Resort and Travel Representatives: The Corfield Company, New York.   Newspaper 1

Figure 3.29. *Cleveland Plain Dealer* advertisement, *Editor & Publisher,* March 28, 1970

Figure 3.30. *Cleveland Plain Dealer* advertisement, *Editor & Publisher,* May 9, 1970

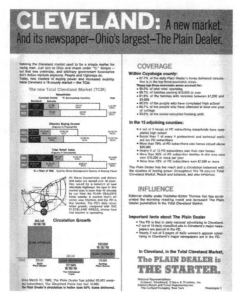

Figure 3.31. *Cleveland Plain Dealer* advertisement, *Editor & Publisher,* December 12, 1970

The move toward "modern" was also apparent in an ad from May 9, 1970, that featured a line drawing of a young, fashionable woman on a black-and-pink striped chair. The design's flattened image, bold color, and wavy stripes style echoed George Dunning's 1968 animated Beatles fantasy film *Yellow Submarine*. The text of the ad also made a break with the *Plain Dealer's* former mass readership goals: "Our readers are the first people— affluent moderns who are the first with new things for better living. And who find where to buy them first in The Plain Dealer."

A fourth ad (December 12, 1970) took the more traditional approach— no design, but data-driven arguments with much more demographic precision than in the past. Bar charts comparing 1960 and 1969 illustrate that the growth in households, effective buying income, and total retail sales had all shifted noticeably from Cleveland to the Cuyahoga County suburbs and to the fifteen surrounding counties of the Northeast Ohio market. In terms of coverage, the *Plain Dealer* also unveiled new demographic markers beyond household income: how many readers completed high school, attended at least one year of college, were a professional or technical worker, had homes valued at $25,000 or more, and lived in owner-occupied housing. The first paragraph of the full-page ad described a new way for advertisers to think about their audience: "Defining the Cleveland market used to be a simple matter for media men. Just turn to Ohio and check under 'C.' Simple— but that was yesterday, and arbitrary government boundaries don't define markets anymore. People and highways do. Today, new clusters of buying power and increased mobility make Cleveland a 16-county market—the TCM [Total Cleveland Market]." Again, here is an explicit argument for how the *Plain Dealer* isn't interested in "arbitrary government boundaries," which include all people, but the new clusters of upscale people in Cleveland and its suburbs who are linked together by freeways.

On the other side of the country, we see the same approach from the *Seattle Post-Intelligencer* (June 6, 1970), where the readers "represent able-to-buy households." The illustration shows a white nuclear family of five with all the hallmarks of prosperity: a new ranch house, a shiny convertible sedan, and a hulking camper trailer in tow. The message is simple: *Post-Intelligencer* families are far richer and far better educated than the average western US household: "These are the kind of people who will respond to your advertising message."

Another way that newspapers appealed to "quality" demographics by 1970 was to make an appeal for the newspaper's relevance. The reasoning is that upscale advertisers would want to place ads in newspapers that are so

Post-Intelligencer Readers Represent Able-to-Buy Households

67% of Post-Intelligencer families have annual incomes of over $10,000

. . . and that 67% is a way-above-average figure. (The Western U.S. household average is 32%.) A high 41% of these readers are employed in professional, technical, managerial or other decision-making positions. (The Western average is 27%.) The average Post-Intelligencer reader is bet- ter educated, too. A greater share, 53%, have attended or graduated from college, compared with 32% for Western U.S. households. These are the kind of people who will respond to your advertising message . . . and they live in one of the richest parts of the nation. Reach them through The P-I.

Sources: P-I readership survey conducted by Gerhardt Research Service, Seattle; P-I Reader Forum, October 1969–January 1970; Analysis of Sunset Magazine's Western Market Almanac, 1967–68.

The Seattle Post-Intelligencer

IF YOU'RE NOT IN THE P-I, YOU'RE NOT IN THE NORTHWEST!

The Post-Intelligencer is represented by Key Market Advertising Representatives, Inc.

Figure 3.32. *Seattle Post-Intelligencer* advertisement, *Editor & Publisher,* June 6, 1970

meaningful and important to the community that the "right" kind of people will want to read them. It was a pitch with a certain amount of irony: as the newspapers were writing off their working-class readers, they were simultaneously making the case for their relevance to their readers. Rarely before had social significance of editorial content been something trumpeted in *Editor & Publisher* ads.

In previous decades, the Rochester (New York) *Times-Union* and *Democrat and Chronicle* (sister afternoon and morning newspapers) would promote the city's well-paid employees to advertisers in *Editor & Publisher.* In April 13, 1940, their ad trumpeted "$1,621,256 Kodak Dividend Paid to 17,745" and featured seven smiling workers who were ready to spend their dividend checks. In a November 26, 1955, ad the banner was "Kodak Announced New Record High 1955 Wage Dividend" for 34,500 employees in the area.

By April 4, 1970, it wasn't about the local workers anymore. Instead, it was about local consumers. The Gannett-owned *Democrat and Chronicle*'s

ad in *Editor & Publisher* featured its new "HELP! For the Consumer" column, which "helps make readers smarter shoppers." The newspaper's ad
explained "We created a once-a-week page to rescue our readers from the
inflation pinch. It's helped find the date codes on perishable foods, warned
against fraudulent wig-selling practices, described the pleasures and pitfalls
of credit cards, and reported poor handling practices in Rochester restaurants." The *Democrat and Chronicle* argued for its relevance to the community: "Great newspapers must react with relevant features when readers
need them. We are. And we do." Yet at the same time, Gannett had become
a growing, publicly traded corporation (since 1967) with a new emphasis on
market-oriented journalism. A feature that focused on readers as consumers,
and not as citizens, fit that new strategy.

Similarly, a *Chicago Tribune* ad on the cover of *Editor & Publisher* on
June 20, 1970, featured (as did several of its ads that year) the editorial

Figure 3.33. *Rochester Democrat and Chronicle* advertisement, *Editor & Publisher*, April 4, 1970

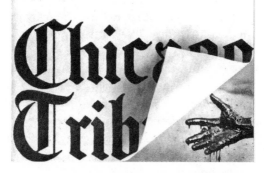

"Too thick to drink,
too thin to plow."
In 1967 the Tribune was first to focus nation-wide attention on the appalling polluting of Lake Michigan and the other Great Lakes. In recent years we have intensified this reporting. Our aim: to halt this pollution . . . before our Lakes become too thick to drink, too thin to plow.
Our aim was good.
Recently, President Nixon asked Congress for legislation and money to outlaw dumping of polluted dredgings in our Lakes. "This bill," said Mr. Nixon, "represents a major step forward in cleaning up our Great Lakes."
The Tribune helps make good things happen.

Figure 3.34. *Chicago Tribune* advertisement, *Editor & Publisher,* June 20, 1970

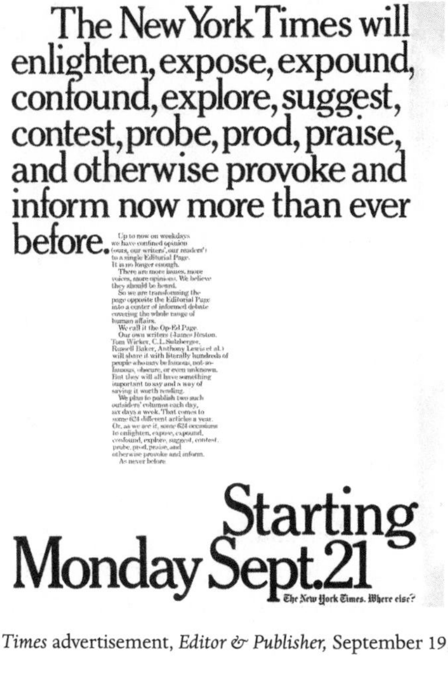

The New York Times will enlighten, expose, expound, confound, explore, suggest, contest, probe, prod, praise, and otherwise provoke and inform now more than ever before.
Up to now on weekdays we have confined opinion (ours, our writers', our readers') to a single Editorial Page. It is no longer enough.
There are more issues, more voices, more opinions. We believe they should be heard.
So we are transforming the page opposite the Editorial Page into a center of informed debate covering the whole range of human affairs.
We call it the Op-Ed Page.
Our own writers (James Reston, Tom Wicker, C.L. Sulzberger, Russell Baker, Anthony Lewis et al.) will share it with literally hundreds of people who may be famous, not-so-famous, obscure, or even unknown. But they will all have something important to say and a way of saying it worth reading.
We plan to publish two such outsiders' columns each day, six days a week. That comes to some 624 different articles a year. Or, as we see it, some 624 occasions to enlighten, expose, expound, confound, explore, suggest, contest, probe, prod, praise, and otherwise provoke and inform.
As never before
Starting Monday Sept.21
The New York Times. Where else?

Figure 3.35. *New York Times* advertisement, *Editor & Publisher,* September 19, 1970

impact of the newspaper's reporting. The ad, which included an image of a hand dripping with oily sludge, briefly outlined the *Tribune*'s achievement in bringing public notice to water pollution: "In 1967 the Tribune was first to focus nation-wide attention on the appalling polluting of Lake Michigan and the other Great Lakes. In recent years we have intensified this reporting. Our aim: to halt this pollution . . . before our Lakes become too thick to drink, too thin to plow. Our aim was good. Recently, President Nixon asked Congress for legislation and money to outlaw dumping of polluted dredgings in our Lakes. 'This bill,' said Mr. Nixon, 'represents a major step forward in cleaning up our Great Lakes.' The Tribune helps make good things happen."

Likewise, the *New York Times* advertised its centrality to progressive politics of the day. In a September 19, 1970, advertisement, the *Times* introduced its op-ed page, an innovation to feature its own writers and guest writers who "all have something important to say and a way of saying it worth reading." The invention of the op-ed page was indeed historic, became the model for US editorial sections, and became one of the most widely read elements of the *Times* and its "quality" audience. By the first decade of the 2000s, the *Times* marketing materials would be calling this same kind of desired quality audience "influentials"—a term coined by market researchers Ed Keller and Jon Berry.[15] These people are defined as the 10 percent in a community or market who are highly engaged and regularly influence the other 90 percent—including what they purchase—through word of mouth.

To paraphrase a 1970 *Cleveland Plain Dealer* ad, defining a newspaper market used to be a simple matter for media men. But by 1970, a new audience—an upscale consumer niche audience—was either "hailed" directly or inferred through images, brief stories, sophisticated content, or other socially relevant elements associated with upwardly mobile (and always white) readers.

Two other signature 1970 *Editor & Publisher* campaigns, from the *New York Times* and the *Washington Post*, typify this even more targeted approach—not the "Profit Half" of the *Times* circa 1940 but the even more exclusive proto-influentials: the well-educated, well-traveled, high-consuming managerial and professional class in New York, and the Washington, D.C., power brokers ("the people who need to know," says the *Post*).

The *Times* series, which included eight different advertisements, cleverly riffs on the newspaper's Gothic nameplate style to promote its upscale readership (completely white, and with clear gender roles, as depicted in 1970). The black-and-white photos—photojournalistic images of the wealthy

The New York Spenders
They enjoy a family income
79 per cent greater than the national median.
They're the people who read
The New York Times.

Figure 3.36. *New York Times* advertisement, *Editor & Publisher,* March 21, 1970

The New York Smarties

Two-thirds of them have attended college.
More than 500,000 hold post-graduate degrees.
They're the people who read The New York Times.

Figure 3.37. *New York Times* advertisement, *Editor & Publisher*, April 11, 1970

caught enjoying the pleasures of their everyday elite lives in New York—dominate each full-page ad. The "headlines" below the photos serve as the caption, and just a little additional text makes the argument.

The ad "The New York Spenders" features a stylish white woman wearing an expensive scarf while in an antique shop: "They enjoy a family income 79 percent greater than the national median. They're the people who read The New York Times." Another ad, "The New York Smarties," shows three middle-aged white men playing squash: "Two-thirds of them have attended college. More than 500,000 hold post-graduate degrees. They're the people who read The New York Times." Others in the series include "The New York Travelers" (a white family of husband, wife, boy, and girl are greeted as they appear to be walking on a ramp to enter a cruise ship), "The New York Chargers" (three well-dressed white women—one with a young boy in her lap—in a candid moment during lunch in a café distinguished by white table-cloths and decorative palms in the background), and "The New York Managers" (three white men in English saddled horses trotting on a forest path).

A 1970 campaign by the *Washington Post* portrays the *Post* as the medium for upscale, influential readers in the nation's capital. The first full-page ad plays off the floor-length maxi-dress fad in 1970, tagging the Post as "Maxi Medium," with readership income being the "maxi" focus. The ad's tagline states: "The higher the income, the greater the Post's coverage." The theme of elite readership continues in the ad titled "Majority leader in the Senate," which dubs the *Post* "the newspaper official Washington follows closest of all." The theme is echoed in other ads that boast "Commands attention at the Pentagon" and "Blue-chip buy at the SEC." Even before the term "influentials" was coined, the *New York Times* and *Washington Post* were unabashedly selling those readers to advertisers.

Maxi Medium

The Washington Post. Reaches 60% of all adults daily...77% of over $15,000 families. Leading medium by far...in the major market with the highest income per household. And the higher the income, the greater the Post's coverage.

Source: Washington ARI

The Washington Post
First in circulation ... First in advertising ... First in awards

Figure 3.38. *Washington Post* advertisement, *Editor & Publisher*, December 5, 1970

Figure 3.39. *Washington Post* advertisement, *Editor & Publisher,* January 3, 1970

What has changed from 1940 to the twenty-first century is that the newspaper business consolidated further and almost all of the big afternoon papers went out of business. Yet no matter that almost every newspaper market in the United States is a monopoly, nearly every newspaper in the nation—the *New York Times* and *Washington Post* included—entered the twenty-first century still targeting its "upscale" audience rather than the demographics of the entire community. For example, in its advertising literature the *New York Times* 2007 media kit boasted of the "high-quality demographic profile" of its readership and even highlighted "white collar occupations" to signify that its readers were "twice as likely to be in professional/managerial occupations" compared to the US adult population. The *Washington Post* media kit of 2007 announced it "delivers a high-income target audience" that is "No. 1 in $100,000+ income households."[16]

Even at the more conservative competing newspapers in those two markets, the emphasis in their marketing materials was toward an upscale audience. The *New York Post*'s 2006 media kit touted its "smart, savvy, and affluent readership," adding "Post readers are young, educated, and enjoy spending money," with a household income that is "12% over the market average!" Similarly, the *Washington Times* 2006 materials touted its website, with bar charts illustrating how its readers greatly exceeded the national average in household income, education, and managerial job positions. Moreover, their readers had an exceptionally high index for "purchased/transacted stock mutual funds (last 6 months)."

The same appeals emanated from the *Oregonian* in 2006 ("Readership higher among upper incomes"), the *Cleveland Plain Dealer* in 2008 ("Affluent readers in key demographic groups"), and the *Chicago Tribune* in 2007 ("We have the highest reach of any newspaper in the Chicagoland area among key demographic targets," which meant high household income, high home value, college graduate and above, and professionals/managers/executives).

The targeting of upscale audiences isn't an East Coast/West Coast phenomenon. The business plan could be found in every part of the country in 2017. In Phoenix the *Arizona Republic*'s marketing site proclaimed "We love Big Bucks. Good thing we reach nearly 50% of Phoenix readers who make $75K+."[17] In Boise the *Idaho Statesman* told potential advertisers that its readers "are more educated, have higher incomes and are more likely to own homes than the market average."[18] In Indianapolis (site of the embattled Carrier furnace assembly plant), the *Star*'s media kit said "We deliver a premium audience," adding "66% of our audience has a college or advanced degree."[19] In Greensboro, North Carolina, the *News & Record* stated that "our readers are your best prospects—upper income, highly educated, homeowners."[20] In Alaska the *Anchorage Daily News* promotes its "educated consumers with high household incomes who take action on the ads they see in the paper."[21]

Even in newspapers that do not make explicit statements about their readership being better than average, the data presented implicitly tell the same kind of story about having "quality" customers. For example, the *Tulsa World* lists its online readership's demographic profiles on several dimensions. The category of "occupation" is telling: only four types are listed: "Professional/Managerial, 40%; White Collar, 57%; Sales and Office, 18%; Retired, 9%."[22] Discounting the fact that "white collar" is not an occupation, it nevertheless evident which Tulsa citizens the *World* is not inviting to its pages.[23]

The *Editor & Publisher* advertisements and more contemporary newspaper appeals to advertisers empirically illustrate a trend identified by critical media scholars. By the late 1970s, journalism scholar Ben Bagdikian documented that many daily newspapers had already shifted to a strategy of fewer but wealthier subscribers, often cutting circulation to low-income subscribers in urban and rural areas in favor of richer suburban readers. As he observed, "Newspapers and magazines in the main do not want merely readers; they want affluent readers."[24] Sociologist Herbert Gans observed the same trend under way in the late 1970s: "Local newspapers are already stratified by class, at least in some larger cities."[25] By the 1990s, the shift in newspapers' focus from a mass audience (inclusive of all potential readers and citizens) to "quality" demographics (inclusive of only affluent consumers) was virtually complete. As media scholar Robert McChesney noted, "A telling indication of this turn came in Detroit, where the city's last full-time labor reporting position at the *Detroit Free Press* was eliminated in 1998, while the newspaper added fifteen new editorial positions in the suburbs."[26]

A Business Model for Making Workers Visible

The trend toward upscale readership that so many US chain-owned metropolitan newspapers joined in the late 1960s and 1970s didn't make its way to family-owned small-town dailies and weeklies. Instead of going for only the affluent residents in the market (which also would be an impractically tiny segment), most smaller newspapers still focused on the entire community and in editorial matters as well.

An interesting example of this is the *Storm Lake Times*, a twice-weekly newspaper with a circulation of about 3,000 published in Storm Lake, the seat of Buena Vista County, population 20,000, in Northwest Iowa. The *Times'* staff of ten includes its editor, Art Cullen, winner of the Pulitzer Prize in Editorial Writing in 2017 for a series of editorials taking powerful agribusinesses to task for secretly financing a case to defend against a lawsuit that sought to regulate runoff pollution of rivers and streams.[27] Cullen's brother established the *Storm Lake Times* in 1990, competing with the existing town paper, the *Pilot-Tribune*. As another Iowa newspaper reported, "For a time Storm Lake was the smallest city in the country with competing daily newspapers."[28] The *Storm Lake Times* now has a circulation higher than that of the *Pilot-Tribune*.

Storm Lake and Buena Vista County have been through difficult times, losing a high-wage, unionized meatpacking employer in 1981, part of a restructuring of the industry that gave rise to new meatpacking companies that "drove down wages and benefits, increased productivity, neutralized unions, experienced high employee turnover, and relied increasingly on immigrant and refugee labor."[29] Today, Storm Lake has one of the most diverse populations in Iowa, with nonwhites about 20 percent of the population and more than 24 percent of the population Hispanic or Latino.[30] Dozens of languages are spoken in the local public schools. Cullen regularly supports Storm Lake's recent wave of immigrants, which helps to make the county one of the state's rare locations with positive population growth.[31]

The conversational, honest style of Cullen's editorials is also reflected in the business side, where the newspaper's circulation includes a broad socioeconomic range of readers. Those same readers (not just the upscale ones) are proudly sold to potential advertisers on the *Times'* website:

$476 MILLION!

That's the buying power of the readers you reach through The Storm Lake Times.

OUR READERS ARE YOUR CUSTOMERS. They are bankers, lawyers, doctors, farmers, merchants, teachers, laborers and others with money to spend.

In today's competitive marketplace, it's more important than ever to direct your marketing efforts carefully at the sector that spends money.

Go where your message will stand out. The Storm Lake Times is that medium.

Thousands of households invite us into their homes twice each week by paying for a subscription to The Times. That's guaranteed readership!

That's a market you can't afford to miss.

What's different about the *Storm Lake Times* business plan is that it does not shun its working-class readers, even when competing with another newspaper in the same small market. That inclusive approach to the community shows in its news pages as well. Douglas Burns, a friend of Cullen's and co-owner of the *Daily Times Herald* in Carroll, Iowa (fifty-six miles southeast of Storm Lake), smartly identified the connection between the business model of a newspaper and the newspaper's editorial freedom: "As more and more newspapers are consumed by corporations and the shareholder shackles that come with Wall Street ties, it's harder and harder to find fearless newspaper owners willing to tell truth to power—damn the torpedoes from readers and advertisers."[32]

Chapter 4

The Changing News Narrative
about Workers

On a rainy March 11, 1941, the headline of the *New York Times'* front-page lead story shouted "WALKOUT HALTS 1,305 BUSES, NO SETTLEMENT IS IN SIGHT; THRONGS JAM SUBWAYS, CABS." So began the story of the strike of 3,500 Transport Workers Union employees, which stopped buses operated by two companies that supplied 95 percent of surface mass transit to Manhattan and affected 900,000 daily riders. And what of the riders? The long story, which ran the full length of the front-page right column and then jumped inside to take up more than half of another broadsheet page, said only this: "Warned well in advance of the likelihood of a strike, the 900,000 riders normally using the bus lines resorted to the subway and elevated routes, or traveled by taxicab." No riders were quoted; none were identified in photos. The rest of the story discussed the disputed contract issues between the transport workers and the company, and the response of New York Mayor Fiorello LaGuardia. Three photos inside, where the story continued, showed warehoused buses, the chairman of the bus company with telephone and tobacco pipe in hands, and a long shot showing taxi cabs filling a city street as far as the eye could see. The caption to the photo took a positive angle on the strike and read "Fifth Avenue: Where opportunity knocked for hackmen." To summarize: the story of a bus strike in New York in March 1941 features no consumer complaints as nearly a million riders instead take subways and taxis. Good news for taxi drivers.

On another rainy day forty-two years later, March 8, 1983, in the same top-right corner of the front page, the headline of the *New York Times'* lead story read "RAIL STRIKE CLOGS TRAFFIC ON ROADS IN NEW YORK AREA." The reason for the story was a strike of 622 conductors and United Transportation Union workers from the Metro-North suburban commuter lines against the Metropolitan Transit Authority. Whereas the 1941 story showed no photos of displaced riders, the 1983 story featured a large rectangular photo at the top center of the front page, with three middle-aged executives from Westchester (one of New York's wealthiest suburbs to the north) on a subway car leaving a station in the Bronx (one of New York's poorest neighborhoods). It is a wonderful fish-out-of-water photo: three well-groomed businessmen dressed in almost identical trenchcoats, with briefcases on their laps, on their way to jobs in Manhattan, riding in a dirty, graffiti-caked subway car. The man to the left is writing something, the man to the right is reading a newspaper, and the man in the middle—looking a bit more rumpled with a loosened necktie—is in the midst of a gaping yawn, expressing the misery of having to wake up much earlier for a patchwork commute to the office.

The image of the photo communicates the main point of the text: although only 90,000 commuters were affected by the strike (a mere 10 percent of the number affected by the 1941 bus strike), the story's primary focus is on the displaced commuters, the "shoulder-to-shoulder crowds," and the "rain, fog, delays, long queues, unfamiliar routes and a bit of grumbling" they experienced. Moreover, the displaced commuters have a voice in this story. "'I'm lost,' said Don Gilbert of New Canaan, Conn., bound for work at the Chemical Bank at Park Avenue and 47th Street. 'I've never done this before. If I didn't follow the crowd, I wouldn't know where to go.'" Another commuter quoted, referring to the strikers, got the final word of the story: "'The idea of such a small minority having such an impact on such a huge majority is just not right,' said a 25-year-old man from Dobbs Ferry, N.Y." To summarize: a suburban commuter rail strike in New York in March 1983 affected only one-tenth as many passengers as were affected by the 1941 strike, but in the 1983 strike the story's emphasis is on the discomfort of the displaced commuters and the unfairness of the strike to them.

The two stories, similar in events and in the placement they received in the newspaper, yet so different in the narrative focus, illustrate a discursive transformation in labor news in the second half of the twentieth century. Over this course of time, US newspapers shifted their target market from a mass audience of the working and middle class to a niche, "upscale" audience. This chapter critically analyzes news reports of transit (e.g., rail, bus, and airline) strikes and how the framing of those strikes dramatically switched from a pre-1970s orientation of worker struggles to a post-1970s orientation of high consumer inconvenience. To track how newspapers have shifted their target audience from mass to upscale audiences in the narrative framing of transit strikes, I analyze two major newspapers, the *New York Times* and the *Washington Post*.[1]

The purpose of the chapter is to demonstrate how the target market of the newspaper business clearly affects the language of news. In other words, to paraphrase British linguist Roger Fowler, the US newspaper industry's refocusing of its target audience changed the social, economic, and historical conditions that govern the semiotic structure of news discourse.[2]

Of course, presently there are still working-class and "downscale" readers of newspapers, but they don't seem to count when it comes to the business side. As I'll argue below, since the 1970s they've been increasingly written out of the editorial side of the newspaper as well.

The Transformation of Transit Strike Narratives

Transit strikes immediately impact transit customers to varying degrees, compared to an industrial strike, which may have little or no direct or immediate effect on consumers' lives. Thus, the roadway, rail, or airline passengers—the consumers—are available as potential actors in these stories, along with others, including union members on strike (and those members who might not be participating in the strike), their families, the management, and government officials. Journalistic accounts of transit strikes might characterize passengers as fellow citizen workers—compatriots with the strikers—rather than consumers inconvenienced by the strikes.[3] It all depends on how the story is told. As journalism critic James W. Carey wrote, "News is not information but drama. It does not describe the world but portrays an arena of dramatic forces and action; it exists solely in historical time, and invites our participation on the basis of our assuming, often vicariously, social roles within it."[4]

These dramas, existing in historical time, are crafted into news narratives that have a particular structure, or frame. These frames organize verbal and visual discourse, and determine "who are virtuous, who are threats to the good life, and which courses of action are effective solutions."[5] This act of framing news discourse is consistent with the influences on news language that Fowler identified: "News is not a natural phenomenon emerging straight from 'reality,' but a *product*. It is produced by an industry, shaped by the bureaucratic and economic structure of that industry, by the relations between the media and other industries, and most importantly, by relations with government and other political organizations. From a broader perspective, it reflects, and in return shapes, the prevailing values of a society in a particular historical context."[6] As we shall see below, the particular historical context for the transit strike narrative is the newspaper industry's shift from a mass-audience orientation to a market-driven orientation of a newspaper industry that had become more consolidated and publicly traded.

Before the 1970s

There were a number of strikes in the United States in 1940, but more in heavy industry than transport. Nevertheless, a bus strike occurred in New York that year which lasted more than five weeks during the summer, as forty employees sought a raise in their minimum hourly wage from 58 cents to 70 cents. The headline in the *New York Times* on July 18 for the first story about the strike read "EAST SIDE BUS LINE TIED UP BY STRIKE." The lead paragraph of the story laid out the basic information: "Eighteen buses operated by the Triangle Bus Corporation, serving 10,000 persons on the East Side, were idle yesterday as a result of a strike of forty employees, including thirty-five drivers, called early yesterday morning by the Transport Workers Union, C. I. O. affiliate. The strike was called to enforce wage demands."[7]

The narrative quickly introduces the word "demands" to represent the union's bargaining perspective. As the Glasgow University Media Group noted in its three foundational reports from the 1970s and 1980s, workers' positions are typically framed in the negative language of "demands," whereas management's positions are more positively framed as "offers."[8] Although the stories for this specific strike didn't use the word "offer" (it seemed that the bus company ultimately didn't have anything to propose), it frequently used variations of "demand" in reference to the workers. This vocabulary of management "offers" and union "demands" is consistent throughout news reports analysed from 1940 to 2000.

But despite the negative vocabulary of "demands," more significant to the six articles the *New York Times* published on the 1940 bus strike— particularly in contrast to contemporary transit strike accounts—is what they *didn't* say. Other than the mention in three of the stories that the idle buses normally provided transportation for 10,000 passengers, there was no reference to the inconveniences of the displaced East Side bus riders. Instead, the narratives invited the reader to consider the struggles of the workers as they strategically wrangled with the bus company and the mayor of New York. The individual stories could be quite compelling and captured details of the strikers' experiences not typically covered today. For example, on the third day of the strike, a few of the company's executives attempted to operate some of the buses themselves. The situation arising as striking workers attempted to thwart them reads like a scene from a farcical comedy:

> At Houston and Pitt Streets, [company president] Mr. Hagler's bus was boarded by nine strikers as "passengers." Each of them handed Mr. Hagler a $1 note. His inability to provide change caused a delay of more than half an hour, during which Mr. Hagler sought in vain to prevail upon the strikers to leave the bus. The intervention of a policeman likewise failed to produce results, the strikers contending that they had the right to ride as passengers.
>
> Meanwhile they had hung signs out of the bus windows announcing the strike and appealing for public support. A large crowd gathered and finally the strikers and Mr. Hagler were all taken to the police station near Stanton and Houston Streets, where the lieutenant on duty found it difficult to decide on what charge they should be booked, so he released them.[9]

All of the striking workers were ultimately rehired at the end of the strike, as New York's mayor requested another bus company take over the service and grant the workers an increase in wages and benefits.

Many transit strikes from the 1950s displaced even more passengers, but stories in the *Washington Post* and *New York Times* rarely made the customers major actors in the strike narratives. A strike of about five hundred flight engineers at United Air Lines between October and December 1955 generated ten stories in the *New York Times* and one in the *Washington Post*, but none of the stories had a word about affected passengers. The strike did not shut down the airline but did cause cancellations of several flights during the two months. The engineers were mostly nonpilots and were required to work as the third person in the cockpit on larger aircraft. The stories instead focused on the conflict between the flight engineers union and the Air Lines Pilot Association, which didn't support the strike and kept pilots on the job.

A huge, 52-day city transit strike in the steamy heat of Washington, D.C., began July 1, 1955, idling about 750 buses and 375 trams as 3,000 transit union members walked off their jobs over a wage dispute with the privately held Capital Transit Company. The system carried 400,000 passengers taking about 900,000 rides on an average weekday. The buses and streetcars were the primary mass transit system in the nation's capital until the Metro subway system opened in 1976. The *Washington Post*, which kept the story on page 1 for the duration of the 1955 strike, ran a total of 92 articles from the transit union strike vote on June 25 until the last postmortem of the strike on August 23.

As with other transit strikes of the era, the majority of the stories focused on the details of the negotiations (called "parleys" in the language of the day), the work of the city commissioners to resolve the dispute, the involvement of Congress and the president, and the haughtiness of Capital Transit's absentee owner, Louis E. Wolfson. Yet because of this story's magnitude for the US capital, the *Post* did include stories about the displaced passengers. But the framing in both stories and accompanying photo images was unlike anything in a contemporary transit strike news story. These weren't annoyed, irritated consumers personally offended by the inconvenience (despite having lived through a big transit strike just four years earlier) but instead were citizens who stoically, even cheerfully, weathered through a labor dispute that involved some of their fellow Washingtonians.

For example, the July 2, 1955, issue of the *Post*, covering the previous day's first full day of life with the transit strike, led with a photo looking down Pennsylvania Avenue toward the capital, the street jammed with large sedans (including those parked in the center on unused trolley tracks). The three-line banner headline above read, "TRANSIT STRIKE PARLEYS DEADLOCKED; WOLFSON REFUSES TO RETURN NEXT WEEK; CAPITAL'S WORST TRAFFIC CRUSH SOLVED."[10] Thus began the coverage, somewhat pessimistic about a speedy resolution but optimistic about metro-area residents commuting efficiently. In fact, the *Post* almost seemed to be celebrating the disruptions of the strike as pleasures for the citizenry (clearly from a male, heteronormative perspective, though). Page 2 of the July 2 issue showed a photo of three smiling women leaning against a convertible as they propositioned the male driver. In the words of the *Post*'s caption, "Government girls, holding signs naming their destinations, try their luck at getting a ride home yesterday. The girls, from left, are Mary Fitzgerald, Stella Deinzer and Ruth Speakman, all of the State Department. If the signs didn't work, they walked."[11] Under the banner headline "Washington Takes Its Transit Strike in Stride!" page 10 of the same issue showed photos of parked, empty buses, traffic jamming Connecticut Avenue, and a full-figure shot of a smiling woman in sunglasses, wearing a dress and a short-sleeve jacket with white high heels and matching handbag. The caption identified her as "Florence Gallo," who "walked three miles to her job in the Commerce Department and eight hours later walked three miles back to her home again."[12]

The theme of orderliness, stoicism, and even small pleasures in the face of disruption continued with the strike coverage. The July 6 front page featured a wide-angle photo (covering three-quarters of the page's width) of government workers peacefully walking home on crowded sidewalks. Inside the same issue, photos showed a busy street (the caption read "the early rush-hour traffic was surprisingly orderly"), a man holding an electric fan waiting for a ride, and a woman asking a passing driver for a ride ("a common scene during the transit strike").[13] The next day, on page 2, next to an article titled "Rush Hour Traffic Finds Only a Few Rough Spots," the *Post* carried a photo of another smiling person, a woman in a black dress and a string of pearls (identified as "Mrs. Etta Jenkins of 4000 Livingston Road SE") in front of a car-pool sign-up board at a drugstore.[14] Perhaps the most gratuitous photo of a female commuter was on July 8. The page 2 image was a full body shot of a smiling, platinum blonde woman, barefoot in a wet clinging dress, holding up a hose spouting water and waving to the photographer. The caption had a title, "Cooling Off," and read "Not bothering to change her clothes, Judith Launt, 20, of Silver Spring, cools off with a garden hose after a trip home made doubly tiring by the transit strike."[15]

In fact, the only story of resolutely angry people during this hot-summer strike came in a report about the workers themselves, titled "STRIKERS ARE GRIM, BITTER AT WOLFSON," the Capital Transit Board chairman. The workers interviewed all said they had been reluctant to strike because of the financial hardship, and hoped for arbitration. They were uniformly angry at Wolfson, with one stating "if Mr. Wolfson and his clique would have given his employes a little of the money they paid in dividends, there wouldn't have been a strike."[16]

The workers were right about Wolfson, and the *Washington Post* concurred on his legacy of greed more than a half-century later in Wolfson's 2008 obituary: "He was considered one of the city's chief villains while he was principal shareholder of Capital Transit from 1949 to 1956. He did little to diminish that image when he admitted to *Time* magazine of 'milking' the company of its past surplus as he paid huge dividends to shareholders, many of them his associates. Meanwhile, profits dragged, fare prices shot up and a strike shut down operations for much of the summer of 1955. Congress, responding to public uprisings against Mr. Wolfson's stewardship, revoked his franchise."[17] There would be similar villainy against workers in the coming decades, but the narratives about transit strikes and other labor stories began to evolve in the 1970s, increasingly identifying more with upscale consumers and less with the workers involved.

The 1970s and Beyond

The theme of citizen responsibility during strikes fades and then disappears completely in the 1970s. The year 1970 in particular is transitional, with worker-oriented narratives shifting toward more consumer-oriented stories.

The *New York Times* coverage of an air traffic controllers strike in 1970 set up the new narrative of negative consumer impact. The story began on March 25, 1970, when several hundred of the nation's 9,000 PATCO (the Professional Air Traffic Controllers Organization)[18] workers conducted a "sick-out" action (calling in sick to work without really being ill) against the US Federal Aviation Administration to unofficially protest inadequate pay, general work conditions, and the job reassignments of some controllers. The *Times'* first article covering the sick-out, on March 26, 1970, mildly suggested some consumer difficulties as it calculated that "100,000 air travellers were inconvenienced." But the story later morphed into a more tragic tale, as it tapped into the timeworn melodramatic story of young boys' crushed dreams:

> Airlines tried to reach passengers to tell them about delays and canceled flights. But not everybody got the word.
>
> Fifteen-year-old Joseph Campbell of Brentwood, L. I., had planned to see the National Collegiate Wrestling Tournaments starting today in Chicago.
>
> He arrived at La Guardia Airport and learned that his flight had been canceled.
>
> "I sold candy, hats, buttons and wrestling programs for about a month just to get enough money to go," he said, as an airline clerk tried to find him an available seat.
>
> Neil Moss, 14, of the Bronx, arrived at La Guardia for his first airplane ride and was told that his jet to Toronto had been grounded.
>
> "I waited all my life to ride an airplane, and now I find that I might not get a chance," he said.[19]

The *Times* handled these two anecdotes as tragedies foisted upon innocent children, although it is plausible that both boys were rebooked onto other flights that day. *Times* readers would never know the outcome.

The *Times*' coverage of the PATCO strike on March 27, 1970, continued the new upscale-consumer–oriented framing of the transit strike narrative: on the eve of Easter weekend, bad weather and the sick-out brought "near-chaos," "harried airline employees," and "disgusted" and "angry" passengers, many of whom "milled around, simply waiting with blank expressions on their faces."[20] The story's headline—"TRAFFIC DISPUTES AND WIDE STORMS SNARL AIRPORTS"—attributed the delays to two causes. In fact, the story noted that "the effect of the widespread snow and rain over the Northeast and Midwest—where most of the fight delays occurred—made it difficult to measure the full impact of the absence of the controllers from their control towers and radar stations." Nevertheless, the story added that "overall, the F.A.A. estimated only 10 per cent of the nation's total air commerce was substantially affected by the absenteeism on Wednesday." Still, the two photos that accompanied the story made little attempt to depict snow problems as the main factor and instead visually suggested the air traffic controllers as the primary cause. The top photo had a high-angle view of a jam-packed terminal in Chicago, with the caption "CHICAGO: Travelers jamming O'Hare Airport yesterday. Snow added to delays caused by traffic control absences." The bottom photo showed a sparsely populated air control room, with the caption "NEW YORK: Control room of MacArthur Airport in East Islip, L.I. About half of the normal staff was at work yesterday."[21]

The travelers quoted in the March 27 story supported the same consumer-oriented story frame. " 'I think this is disgusting,' one passenger, Dr. Norman Mitnick of Wayne, N.J. exclaimed, as he waited at Kennedy International Airport with his wife and two children," the *Times* wrote. " 'The air traffic controllers picked a poor time to get sick,' said another angry passenger, Mrs. Ilene Halpern, of Woodmere, L.I."[22]

By the next day, March 28, the *Times* reported that "thousands of passengers waited with surprisingly good humor at New York's three airports" despite the now "crippling effects" of the three-day-old sick-out.[23] Thus, the expectation of what constituted normal behavior in the face of a transit strike had changed; the responsible citizen was now the disgusted, angry consumer. "Good humor" by consumers in the face of a labor disruption was now an unexpected surprise.

The transit consumer, to be pitied in despair and indulged in anger, became a significant actor in transit strike narratives after 1970. A formulaic photo of the impatient, exhausted, or sleeping commuter in a train station, bus terminal, or airport emerged as the iconic image of the consumer narrative frame. In 1970 this iconic image and the consumer narrative frame was just arriving on the US news scene. By the 1980s, it was the commonsense news narrative for transit strikes.[24] The iconic photo could be found in newspaper coverage of numerous strikes, including the 1985 Pan Am strike in the *Post*, the 1985 United Airlines strike in the *Post* and the *Times*, the 1985 New York City bus strike in the *Times*, and, of course, the 1983 rail strike covered by the *New York Times*, mentioned at the beginning of this chapter.[25] The corresponding narratives of the angry consumers were there as well. For example, the *Washington Post*'s May 18, 1985, coverage of the United Airlines pilot strike included statements from several travelers, including these two couples:

> Peter Stein, a Chicago physician, and Diane Camp, 26, a nurse, were trying to get to Philadelphia where they planned to talk over wedding ideas with her parents. But their United flight, scheduled to depart at 8 P.M., had been canceled at 9 A.M. this morning and they were searching for seats on another flight.
>
> "We had enough to do without this happening," they said as they waited to learn whether they could get aboard any rival airline's flight.
>
> A Chicago couple was headed to New York for a surprise party marking a relative's 25th wedding anniversary. Somehow, they had missed the news that United had been struck last night after management and the pilots could not agree on a new contract.
>
> "Just as we got here, we saw the pilots," said the woman who asked not to be identified. "We didn't know and now we're very disappointed and trying to find out whether we can make the surprise party at all."[26]

The mainstream news media refocused their target audience in the late 1960s and early 1970s and began to make stoking middle-class grievances against the working class a fundamental element of their coverage. In stories of labor actions that in any way negatively affected middle-class life (which extended from transit delays and cancellations to the wider presumed inflationary impact of bargained wage increases and the "red tape" of union-negotiated workplace rules), it became normal to present middle-class consumers as the disgruntled victims of working-class demands.[27] It is not that many of the news audience members were not also part of the same broadly defined US "working class." It is that the mainstream news media began to address their audience as either aspirational or true upwardly mobile consumers, somehow different from unionized workers.

The Break in Narrative Solidarity

The consumer-oriented frame communicated a new sense of privilege for the transit passengers, giving them the implicit permission to express their irritation, annoyance, anger, and disgust at a labor dispute. Consequently, this consumer-oriented perspective served management's interests more than labor's because what the consumer wants is for workers to stop complaining and end the strike immediately, no matter the damage to their bargaining position.

The consumer-oriented approach to news harms the working class and labor in two broader ways. First, targeting upscale news consumers contributes to class inequality as the working class is excised from news discourse and evidence of systemic socioeconomic inequality disappears. As Pulitzer Prize–winning journalist and later journalism scholar Ben Bagdikian explained, "People who are not affluent seldom see stories about their day-to-day pains and pleasures and have little reason to buy a daily paper. As a result, the daily newspaper has become the medium for the middle and upper classes."[28] Ironically, growing class inequality hastens an even greater shift in marketing to upscale consumers as advertisers increasingly prefer consumers with more disposable money.[29]

Second, consumer-oriented discourse is "an expression of a profoundly fragmenting individualism," with significant political consequences, according to historian Gary Cross.[30] Instead of news stories that refer to labor's long collective movement for economic and social justice, newspapers began to focus on individuals organized into collectives only for occasions of "spontaneous interest."[31] The rise of individualistic consumerism as a news frame in the 1970s fit nicely with the aims of the larger project of political conservatism in the late 1970s and 1980s, led by Ronald Reagan in the United States, Brian Mulroney in Canada, and Margaret Thatcher in the United Kingdom. They successfully used "consumer interest" as the selling point for deregulation of transport and other industries, corporate tax cuts, and attacks on labor unions.[32]

Thus, newspapers' target market can affect the discourse of labor news stories, and the discourse of labor news stories can affect views on class politics. Over time, the consumer-oriented narrative frame has helped to drive a wedge into the narrative solidarity that existed between striking transit workers and passengers in newspaper stories of the pre-1970s era. If news invites its audience to assume social roles in relation to its stories, as media theorist James Carey said, then the post-1970s consumer-oriented frame invited its audience to interpret transit strikes from only their own individualistic point of view as upscale consumers, not as fellow citizens.³³

The Shift to News of Workplace "Lifestyles"

As newspapers moved their focus to upscale audiences, they often supplanted the labor beat with a lifestyle-oriented workplace feature column. Whereas the labor beat traditionally located its stories in collective worker action within a class-based economic system, the new workplace column found its stories in striving individuals within an economic system featuring "pink-collar" or "white-collar" employees (not workers) often identified in business-speak as "associates," "team members," or "office staff," laboring in cubicles and trying to climb the corporate ladder. These were people who were more likely to write résumés and cover letters to get their jobs than to fill out job applications. The workplace feature column was (and is) about the lives of young professionals and their concerns about office gossip, job interview strategy, expense accounts, and office party etiquette.

One of the first workplace reporters in the nation was Carol Kleiman, columnist at the *Chicago Tribune* from 1967 to 2006. Kleiman ultimately handled three columns ("Women at Work," "Jobs," and "Letters") for the *Tribune* during her career, wrote several books, and was once called "the undisputed godmother of workplace reporting" by Barbara Presley Noble, the *New York Times* "At Work" columnist in the early 1990s.³⁴ Kleiman's own story reflects the focus and development of the workplace beat. In her final column for the *Tribune* on January 31, 2006, Kleiman wrote the following:

> Four decades ago, when I was a part-time copy editor and freelance writer for the *Chicago Tribune*, a suburban wife of an executive and mother of three children, the features editor of the *Tribune* called me. He had noticed something unusual: Women were going to work! He said as he rode on his commuter train he actually saw women going into downtown Chicago, not to shop but to work. Would I cover this revolution, would I write the

column, Working Woman, that he had dreamed up, the first of its kind in the U.S.? And to convince me, he sagely pointed out that I was living it.

"Absolutely," I said, though I assured him women, particularly African-American women, had always worked in the paid labor market. And almost all women worked hard at home for free, taking care of their husbands and family. He looked at me suspiciously. He knew I was an active participant in the civil rights movement, both down South in Alabama and "up South" in Chicago. "OK," he said, "you have the job. But keep your politics out of it." I promised I would try but told him that male columnists express their opinions, why shouldn't I? But I never promised to keep my emotions out of my column. And I never have.[35]

Kleiman's focus was honorable, and she brought her perspective as a civil rights activist and feminist to the job. Her voice also brought new readers to the *Tribune*: "I covered what was happening and also tried to empower people—women, minorities, the disabled, the elderly—who had very little positive exposure in the media. I made sure my columns and photos included a diverse population."[36]

Eventually, business editors at the *Tribune* noticed her work and her ability to attract women readers, and brought her column to the business section. The beat's move from features to business reflected the improving status of women in the (office) workplace.

Yet for all of the good intentions of a workplace column (and writing about women's struggles in the workplace is certainly important, in 1967 and still today), the solutions are almost always individualistic instead of collective. For example, in Kleiman's 2002 book *Winning the Job Game: The New Rules for Finding and Keeping the Job You Want* (based on many of the same themes in her work as a columnist at the *Tribune*), she wrote: "This book is written for both job seekers as well as those who are currently employed. I will help you learn how to find out what's going on in your profession and industry—and how to use that knowledge to your advantage. I'll also help you build your confidence. You will know what to expect in order to play the interview game, make a good impression, and land the job. And then I'll help you move up the career ladder and be the one who still has a job, no matter what happens to the economy."[37]

Although Kleiman included mentions of what labor unions can do for workers in her columns and books, she also was cognizant that a workplace column alone was not sufficient for providing complete coverage of work for a newspaper. "Every paper should have labor reporters. Unions have given us all the good things we have, such as overtime, pensions, health insurance, paid vacation, sick leave, though I do expect the current anti-labor adminis-tration to try to continue to cut back on these necessities," she said in 2006.[38]

Nevertheless, the trend in newspapers was away from covering labor unions and issues (including comprehensive coverage on how those "good things" that unions had won were under constant attack) and toward the more upscale workplace beat that avoided any issues of collective bargain-ing or collective engagement. The focus of the new workplace beat was predominantly "job coaching": advising readers how to get a job, keep a job, and climb the corporate ladder. In 2006 Penelope Trunk, *Boston Globe* and "Brazen Careerist" columnist, described her column's approach for the *Globe:* "It's targeted, it has to be advice and trends for people in their early 20s to their early 30s."[39] Mackenzie Dawson of the *New York Post* similarly said "our idea is basically approaching workplace issues as almost as a lifestyle topic."[40] Workplace reporting is fine but limited: the assumption, of course, is that all readers hold or desire such white-collar or pink-collar jobs, that they aspire to climb a careerist corporate ladder, and that the solution for any job dissatisfaction is to figure out how to either ingratiate oneself to the boss or look for another job.

At Kleiman's own former newspaper, the *Chicago Tribune,* labor beat reporter Stephen Franklin resigned in 2008 in a wave of downsizing.[41] He was one of the last experienced labor beat reporters in the country, in a city known for the strength of its labor membership. (Kleiman retired from the newspa-per after the Tribune Company, victim of its enormous debt from the ill-timed $8.3 billion merger with the Times-Mirror Company in 2000, announced its first round of cuts in 2005.) By 2013, Franklin still had not yet been replaced, but after several more rounds of cuts, the *Chicago Tribune* maintained a work-place columnist.[42] The headlines of Rex Huppke's "I Just Work Here" pieces provide a clear outline to the focus of the column—glib, and a long way from the well-intentioned social justice thrust of Kleiman's best work. Instead, they read like episode titles from the television comedy *The Office:*

- A field guide to spotting office jerks (February 11, 2013)
- How to connect with your employees (February 4, 2013)
- Psst: Be more flexible. Pass it on (January 28, 2013)
- Do emotions have a place in the office? (January 14, 2013)
- New year, new boss—same old fear (January 7, 2013)
- More doughnuts, and other 2013 office resolutions (December 31, 2012)
- Panic at the office party (December 17, 2012)[43]

Huppke's last column was on May 26, 2017, after which he became the *Tribune*'s humor columnist. Two of Huppke's final columns took a strong stance on issues of workplace inequities. The titles tell the story: "Bosses Must Become Vacation Evangelists" and "It's Time for CEOs to Address Stagnant Worker Pay." Indeed, Americans work far too many weeks each year without a break, for not enough money. But the titles also reveal where the locus of workplace power unquestionably resides for the workplace columnist: with the boss.[44]

The Rise of Personal Finance Journalism

A related news media narrative that also began its ascendancy in the 1970s was personal finance. The focus was again on individualism: people had to take care of themselves. Time Inc.'s launch of the magazine *Money* in 1972 helped to kick off a "boom in the literature of personal finance."[45] The magazine was Time Inc.'s first magazine launch since *Sports Illustrated* in 1954, and it was created "for the general reader," said the Time Inc. executive guiding the magazine's development.[46] In 1978 the *New York Times* started "Business Day," the first stand-alone business section for the *Times*. When *USA Today* launched in 1982, it followed the trend and created "Money" as one of its four regular sections.

The burgeoning personal finance news genre followed several initiatives by the federal government in the 1970s that encouraged the rise of the subject. First, in 1972 the Securities and Exchange Commission (SEC) authorized money market funds, enabling small investors to buy into pooled investments that could beat the high rates of inflation in the 1970s.[47] Congress then passed the Employee Retirement Income Security Act (ERISA) in 1974, which enabled people to established tax-beneficial IRAs (individual retirement accounts) to invest for their own retirement. IRAs were initially permitted only for cases in which employers did not provide pension benefits, but they were opened to all investors in 1981. In 1975 Charles Schwab & Company became one of the first discount brokerage services after the Securities & Exchange Commission deregulated the commissions that brokerage firms could charge for stock trades.[48]

The rise of a new petit-investor class perfectly fit the desired upscale audience for a US news media that was tossing the working class overboard. The news media made extensive moves to "meet the growing interest in business and money," according to media critic and former business journalist Dean Starkman: "Great metropolitan dailies ramped up staffing on their business-news desks, once newsroom backwaters."[49] *Columbia Journalism Review* charted the growth in the business staff sizes of several US newspapers from the early 1980s to 2000. For example, the *Washington Post* grew from 18 to 81 business desk reporters in that time; the *Los Angeles Times* expanded from 20–25 to 90; the *Dallas Morning News* from 8 to 54; the *Tampa Tribune* from 2 to 14; the *Cleveland Plain Dealer* from 9 to 24–25; the *Milwaukee Journal Sentinel* from 7 to 19; and the *Rocky Mountain News* from 6 to 14. Business magazine titles grew from 358 in 1988 to 694 in 1999. In 1996 alone, a record 22 personal finance magazines were introduced. CNBC launched in 1989, as did the Bloomberg financial wire service. The time that network TV news devoted each week to the NYSE and NASDAQ stock exchanges almost doubled, from 152 minutes in 1988 to 296 in 1999.[50] The total number of published English-language business stories jumped from fewer than 100,000 in 1984 to more than 400,000 in 2010.[51]

As the personal finance industry and media grew, there was a "pivotal moment" in its evolution, Starkman notes. The fateful event was in August 1995, when the New York Stock Exchange permitted a journalist—Maria Bartiromo of CNBC—for the first time to do a live daily report from the exchange floor. Bartiromo brought "a new air of glamour, vitality, urgency, modernity, and sex appeal" to the stuffy institution of the NYSE, consequently boosting CNBC's ratings and making Bartiromo "the attractive face of the people's capitalism."[52]

A new mythology of "market democracy"—aided by the "democratic" opportunities for everyone (with capital) to make stock trades—achieved full bloom by the 1990s, and the media of personal finance celebrated the "populist entrepreneur." Thomas Frank wrote that "economic democracy was finally at hand, the observers proclaimed, but not by the actions of any of its usual historical protagonists—government or labor unions. Yes, the people were coming at last to claim what rightfully belonged to them, to smash the barriers of social class and halt the scoffing of the arrogant plutocrats, but they were doing it entirely through mutual funds, or investment clubs, or online chat-rooms, or day-trading."[53] In fact, the investors were part of a financial services industry that became a leading economic force, eclipsing manufacturing. As historian Judith Stein noted, "The industry's share of corporate profits rose from 10 percent in the early 1980s to 40 percent in 2007."[54]

However, in this proclaimed age of "market democracy" and "people's capitalism," something went awry: wealth in the United States was becoming *more* unequal. In 1969 the top 1 percent of households held 35.6 percent of net assets (wealth), the top 20 percent households held 82.5 percent, and the remaining 80 percent held 17.5 percent. By 2013, the top 1 percent enjoyed 36.7 percent of the wealth, the top 20 percent had 88.9 percent, and the remaining 80 percent had 11.1 percent. Moreover, the bottom 40 percent of US households held –0.9 percent of the wealth, meaning that as a group they had negative wealth and were in debt.[55]

As it turned out, a huge swath of Americans didn't have large stashes of money to play in the financial markets. The share of income for the top 20 percent of US households had increased from 48.9 percent to 61.8 percent from 1969 to 2013, while the other 80 percent saw their share of income drop from 51 percent to 38.3 percent over the same period.[56] The richest Americans have been highly engaged in personal investments. In the very wealthiest top 1 percent of households, 84 percent hold corporate stock, financial securities, mutual funds, and personal trusts. In the top 20 percent of wealthy households, 60 percent hold such investments. But only 14.2 percent of the middle 60 percent of households (sandwiched between the richest 20 percent and poorest 20 percent) hold these kinds of financial investments.[57] For most Americans in the middle, their home is their chief investment asset, and it often carries long-term debt.

During the time of the rise of personal finance journalism, there was, of course, the decline of labor and work reporting. Diana B. Henriques, a financial writer at the *New York Times* and a business reporter since 1982, was a front-seat witness to the expansion of business journalism and wrote about it retrospectively in 2000 for *Columbia Journalism Review*: "Most new business writers back in 1980 instinctively and perhaps wrong-headedly approached local business news from the perspective of workers involved—after all, we were workers ourselves, with a healthy mistrust of what passed for management in the newspaper business. As the 1980s rocketed along, our 'readers' became 'consumers.' As the 1990s unfolded, those 'consumers' morphed into 'investors.'"[58]

There was a sense of regret in Henriques's account for what had been lost in the transformation of journalism:

> A sad thing happened along the way: as our intended audience has gotten narrower, so have we. . . . The men and women who scrambled to explain the economic turmoil of 1970s—the gas lines and the shuttered factories and the apparent erosion of American competence—were not writing for consumers or investors. They were writing for citizens, for people who

cared deeply about how this nation turned out. They assumed an audience whose concerns stretched far beyond the performance of their 401(k) and the leasing arrangements on their Jeep Grand Cherokee. I don't know about you, but I'd rather be writing for those people again.[59]

However, business news carries on in the same fashion. Its voice is substantially oversized for the small slice of US society actually doing investing. It largely operates in a bubble, unaware that its audience is rarified and also not attuned to the financial realities of most Americans. For example, Bob Pisani, CNBC's "On-Air Stocks" editor, lamented the lack of new investors in 2017, a decade after the Great Recession: "The investment class in the United States is small, and it's not getting bigger." He further noted that "the bottom 80 percent of households owns only about 7 percent of stock." Yet he was completely confounded that despite record highs in the market, "There is no stock euphoria or a rush to buy stocks by people who are not already investing. . . . What would it take to get more households to own stock?" Money, perhaps.

The move away from stories about labor and work to stories about workplace lifestyles and personal finance was an intentional one for the newspaper industry as it reconfigured its market objectives. But the transformation in the editorial outlook left unanswered an enormous question: what would happen to the working class—union members or not—that they abandoned in their marketing and editorial strategy? With the demise of the mass audience, who would speak to the working class?

The Abandonment of the Working Class: Conservative Media Fill a Big Gap

The working class is the majority in the United States, now and during the past fifty years. It consists of people of all genders, sexualities, races, ethnicities, faiths, and urban-rural classifications. When the mainstream news media in the late 1960s and early 1970s chose to pursue readers based chiefly on their upscale socioeconomic status, they forfeited their working-class audience, millions of Americans whose stories were going untold.

At approximately the same time, political conservatives had envisioned a project of building a conservative media. Early conservative media strategist Richard Viguerie—who labeled as "liberal" any news medium that is not wholly conservative in politics and purpose—got the idea for conservatives to have their own "printing press," that is, for conservatives to create their own conservative media. Although conservative books and journals (such as William F. Buckley's *National Review* magazine, launched in 1955) existed as the first media of the modern conservative movement, Viguerie developed the first truly mass medium of the movement—direct mail—in the 1960s.[60] "Neither the Republicans nor the Democrats, *being* the establishment, understood [direct mail's] true potential or had the will to use it. The conservatives did. They had no choice but to adopt a populist bent, since establishment venues were closed to them," Viguerie wrote with David Franke in *America's Right Turn: How Conservatives Used New and Alternative Media to Take Power.*[61] Viguerie and Franke emphasized "how important it is to be first" with new media and using the new channels to reach audiences that "establishment" media were not accessing.[62] In fact, the history of conservative media is based on its ability to exploit relatively new media forms—direct mail, cable news, talk radio, and the Internet—to reach audiences that mainstream media discounted. Given their regional, religious, and nativist political interests, the conservative media aimed for a potentially like-minded segment of the working class that had been abandoned by the mainstream media: the mostly white, male, suburban/rural, Christian working class. (No corresponding major media news organizations targeted the broader, more diverse working class.)

After Viguerie's work with direct mail, the right-wing media complex got its start with Rupert Murdoch's purchase of the *New York Post* in 1976. As *Wall Street Journal* journalist and author Sarah Ellison noted, "Murdoch was unafraid to use his media outlets, particularly his tabloid newspapers, as instruments of influence."[63] As he had done in Britain and Australia before, Murdoch used the *Post* to boost his favored political candidates.

Although the *Post* was part of a traditional news medium, the next element of the conservative media established a beachhead in the new format of nationwide cable television. Televangelist Pat Robertson founded CBN, the Christian Broadcasting Network, as a basic cable channel in 1977, just a year after Ted Turner founded WTBS as the nation's first basic cable channel. The cable network and its "news" program, *The 700 Club,* moved from religious content to a full embrace of conservative politics.[64] CBN founder Robertson became a 1988 Republican presidential candidate himself and continued to wield political power with his program and the Christian Coalition (founded 1989), which supports conservative politicians. The Christian Coalition was modeled on other conservative religious media groups that formed to actively participate in politics, including Focus on the Family (established in 1977) and the Family Research Council (1983). Viguerie argued that adding social conservatives (Christian evangelicals and their collection of issues) to national defense conservatives and economic conservatives created a three-pronged "winning political movement" for conservatives that helped deliver Ronald Reagan to the presidency in the 1980s.[65]

Right-wing media became more powerful with nationwide conservative talk radio. Again, conservatives got in at the beginning of a new medium, this one created by a regulatory change. From 1949 to 1987, the Federal Communications Commission enforced what was called the Fairness Doctrine. This allowed "a station to editorialize, provided it made air time available for 'balanced presentation of all responsible viewpoints on particular issues.'"[66] As media historians Robert Hilliard and Michael Keith explain, the demise of the Fairness Doctrine changed the tenor of talk radio: "Ostensibly this put no limits on any ideas, philosophies, or other political matter a station might wish to advocate. In reality, it swung the tide of radio and television political advocacy to the right."[67]

In 1988 ABC Radio brought a talented talk radio host from Sacramento to New York, making Rush Limbaugh the first conservative talk host to go national. As Limbaugh, still one of talk radio's biggest stars, says of himself, "My success has spawned dozens of imitators. It has touched off a frantic scramble to cash in."[68] Limbaugh is correct: from its debut, conservatives have dominated commercial talk radio.[69] The late author David Foster Wallace described Limbaugh as "a host of extraordinary, once-in-a-generation talent and charisma—bright, loquacious, witty, complexly authoritative."[70] Limbaugh is an effective conservative messenger as well. His persistent political attacks on President Bill Clinton and support of conservative causes led to Republicans gaining control of the House of Representatives in 1994. Republicans acknowledged their debt to Limbaugh and named him an "honorary member of their class."[71]

The emergence of the Internet as a mass medium in the 1990s enabled a whole additional group of conservative activists. The first notable one was Matt Drudge, who began the *Drudge Report* in 1994, which evolved into one of the first political blogs. He gained national notice a few years later, particularly with the leak of a journalist's story about Bill Clinton's affair with a White House intern. One of Drudge's assistants was Andrew Breitbart, who in 2007 began his own conservative internet media sites. Breitbart received a major $10 million infusion in 2011 from billionaire Robert Mercer, who donates heavily to conservative causes. Steve Bannon, a founding member of Breitbart's board, succeeded Breitbart after his death in 2012 as executive chair. At Breitbart, Bannon was an early booster of Donald Trump's candidacy and joined his presidential campaign in August 2016 as chief executive. According to Jane Mayer in the *New Yorker,* Bannon was already an unofficial player in the Trump campaign: "A year before Bannon joined Trump's campaign staff, he described himself in the e-mail as Trump's de-facto 'campaign manager,' because of the positive coverage that Breitbart was giving Trump."[72] After Trump's election, Bannon served as chief strategist and senior counselor to President Trump until he was pushed out by chief of staff John F. Kelly in August 2017.

The biggest institution in conservative media is Fox News, the cable network founded in 1996 by Rupert Murdoch and Roger Ailes, a former Republican media operative who got his start with Richard Nixon's campaign. Fox News answered a long-awaited dream of conservatives. Nixon aide Patrick Buchanan (later White House communications director for Ronald Reagan) alluded to the idea of conservative cable television in 1973 as an answer to the "liberal bias" of the mainstream media: "Dr. Milton Friedman, distinguished economist and disciple of Adam Smith, believes the long-range answer lies in more and competing channels of communication, to be achieved partly through the rapid expansion of cable television. But that is a long-range solution."[73]

Although CBN gave conservatives an early place in cable television, Fox News fully realized the vision. As NPR media correspondent David Folkenflik aptly explained, "Above all, Ailes wanted Fox News to referee Republican Party politics."[74] Ailes did this by rewarding former GOP politicians by putting them on the Fox payroll as commentators or show hosts. He ran Fox News until he was forced to resign in a sexual harassment scandal in 2016. Announcing Ailes's resignation, Rupert Murdoch said that "Roger shared my vision of a great and independent television organization and executed it brilliantly over 20 great years. Fox News has given voice to those who were ignored by the traditional networks and has been one of the great commercial success stories of modern media."[75] Murdoch's comment about Fox News giving voice "to those who were ignored by the traditional networks" comes full circle on how conservative media were able to fill the fateful gap in traditional news media for their chosen segment of the estranged working class.

In the hands of Donald Trump, the social media micro-blogging service Twitter became another new conservative media outlet. The Twitter platform gives Trump direct access to 57 million followers (fans, news media, critics, and monitors of the US president around the world).[76] Twitter wasn't exactly new when Trump first engaged in it; it was released in 2006, and

Citizen Trump established his @realDonaldTrump account in 2009. But with Twitter, Trump blew up the typical format for political communication for presidential candidates and presidents.

Donald Trump's mobile phone with the Twitter app is his own printing press. It is his primary method of communicating ideas, drumming up support for policies, and trolling perceived enemies and the mainstream press. Twitter enables Trump to constantly be part of the media conversation without having to take pesky accountability questions from the press. As the *Columbia Journalism Review* put it, "It allows him to state untruths with impunity, knowing that his tweets will be widely redistributed by his followers and the media, and to dodge follow-up questions or criticism."[77] On Twitter, Trump also regularly stokes the media and cultural divide, praising and retweeting messages from sources such as Sean Hannity or *Fox & Friends*, while trolling the mainstream press (which included the "failing @nytimes, @NBCNews, @ABC, @CBS, @CNN" in a February 17, 2017, tweet).

In December 1972, as journalists were methodically investigating President Richard Nixon's growing Watergate scandal, a paranoid Nixon privately told his national security advisors to "never forget that the press is the enemy, the press is the enemy."[78] With that sentiment, the dream of Nixon's staff to build a parallel conservative press ecosystem was made easier by the gap created by the traditional news media's upscale turn in the late 1960s and 1970s. Like Nixon, Donald Trump doesn't like an independent-minded traditional news media. But Trump can publicly proclaim the news media to be both "the enemy of the American people" and "the opposition party" nearly a half century later, and he has the advantage of his own Twitter printing press and a many-tentacled conservative media system to maintain his version of reality.[79]

Stoking White, Working-Class Grievances

Trump's rhetorical approach on Twitter has long been used successfully by the conservative media: attract white, working-class audiences by drawing attention to the fact that the mainstream media has alienated them. The conservative media campaign becomes one with the conservative political campaign. Rush Limbaugh articulated this idea in 1992, early on in his national talk radio career: "The Media is now considered just another part of the arrogant, condescending, elite, and out-of-touch political structure which has ignored the people and their concerns and interests."[80] Thus, Limbaugh cultivated the notion that the mainstream media were part of the political structure that alienated white, working-class Americans and held himself up as their chief advocate and ally.

Limbaugh was the "first great promulgator of the Mainstream Media's Liberal Bias idea," David Foster Wallace argued. "This turned out to be a brilliantly effective rhetorical move, since the MMLB concept functioned simultaneously as a standard around which Rush's audience could rally, as an articulation of the need for right-wing (i.e., unbiased) media, and as a mechanism by which any criticism or refutation of conservative ideas could be dismissed (either as biased or as the product of indoctrination by biased media)."[81] In effect, Limbaugh was filling the gap that was left when the mainstream media dropped the working-class audience. It was a relatively easy turn to make mainstream media the bogeyman; it had, after all, turned its back on the working class in favor of more-upscale citizens. Media historian Susan Douglas concurred that Limbaugh tapped into "a sense among many Americans, and especially many men, that they were not being addressed or listened to by the mainstream media."[82]

Fox News incited the same grievances. Bill O'Reilly, one of Fox News' biggest stars (and who later followed Roger Ailes out of Fox after serial allegations of sexual harassment and assault), described one of the typical complaints: "The no-spin truth is that the elite media think the degeneration of American popular culture is beneath them and not very important."[83] The "culture wars" element (the grievance about the erosion of various elements of traditional US popular culture) became crucial to Fox, Limbaugh, and others in the conservative media complex in relating to the white, working-class audience. This masked the conservative media's inability to deliver an honest critique of the economic problems of the working class because of their political position and wealthy Republican sponsors and owners. (Using culture wars to mask an honest economic appraisal also works for billionaire political leaders.) The cultural battles are a stand-in for a class critique that is never waged.[84] Therefore, instead of discussing the merits of things such as an increase in the minimum wage, publicly funded health care, or full support for postsecondary education for working-class people, the conservative media focus on abortion, the "war" on Christmas, not taking a knee during the national anthem at football games, and the evils of immigration (from Hispanic, nonwhite, or Muslim populations)—all cultural wedge issues embraced by the Republican Party. As Andrew Breitbart, founder of the eponymous conservative website, said, "I want to change the cultural narrative."[85]

Meanwhile, in the politically centrist world of the mainstream media, the pursuit of upscale audiences remains the main objective. As Indianapolis hemorrhaged thousands of working-class jobs in recent years, marketing materials at the *Indianapolis Star* matter-of-factly stated "it's about reaching the right people, motivating them & inspiring them to act. Indy Star attracts a premium audience because it delivers a premium content experience that is both relevant and engaging."[86]

Chapter 5

Workers and Political Voice

Discourse about workers has clearly changed over the last century, and the news played a major role in normalizing that discourse. The US government's responses to the biggest national crisis of the twentieth century and the biggest national crisis of the early twenty-first century illustrate the enormous shift in discourse about the role of the nation's workers.

After the attack on Pearl Harbor on December 7, 1941, a rallying cry went out to all US industries, workers, and consumers to sacrifice for the common good. President Roosevelt requested that workers and businesses increase wartime production in basic industries to 24 hours per day, 7 days per week, and maintain peaceful relations. Sidney Hillman, former union leader and associate director of Roosevelt's Office of Production Management in 1941, put workers at the center of the nation's efforts: "Our victory depends on greater and yet greater production from the workshops of democracy. Today our soldiers, sailors, airmen and industrial workers share the front line of battle. Our fighting forces rely upon your skill and your energy for the implements of war."[1] Consumers also sacrificed, as fuel, food, clothing, rubber, nylon, and metal were limited with rationing, and families were urged to be thrifty and grow vegetables in "victory gardens."

Sixty years later, the economy of the United States had changed, becoming less industrial and much more service oriented. US citizens also had been steeped in decades of consumer-oriented news narratives. After the terrorist attacks of September 11, 2001, President Bush, who likened the attacks to Pearl Harbor, briefly praised those airline workers who resumed their regular duties.[2] Then he requested that all Americans do this: "Get on board. Do your business around the country. Fly and enjoy America's great destination spots. Get down to Disney World in Florida. Take your families and enjoy life, the way we want it to be enjoyed."[3] Commerce Secretary Donald Evans concurred, saying that "consumers must have confidence during the holiday shopping season. . . . Every dream you had before Sept. 11 is still there."[4]

If the appeal to only consumers wasn't indicative enough of a refocusing of life in the United States, Bush soon created the Department of Homeland Security and insisted that its 170,000 new workers not be unionized, ironically denying frontline national security employees a measure of job security.[5]

One of the long-standing fundamental goals of journalism, as noted by Bill Kovach and Tom Rosenstiel, is to "monitor power and offer voice to the voiceless."[6] By the end of the twentieth century, most of US journalism seemed to have lost its way with this objective, especially when it involved exposing the uncomfortable issue of socioeconomic class.

Instead of giving voice to the working class (increasingly forsaken by both Republicans and Democrats), journalism largely followed the political trade winds, chronicling—and even advocating—the consolidation of corporate economic and political power, and sidelining the working class and labor.[7] The story of what was happening to the working class and labor in corporate America was mirrored inside the business of news corporations, which were consolidating, moving against their own unionized workers, and refocusing their priority audience from citizens to consumers.

In this chapter I'll look at two indicators that chart the disappearance of the working class from public discourse. First, I will analyze postwar, twentieth-century presidential rhetoric, in which the working class becomes invisible starting in the 1970s. On this count, the working class drops out of the news via journalism's passive coverage of the presidency and national politics. Second, I'll review data on the larger trend of the symbolic annihilation of socioeconomic class and corresponding rise in representations of consumers, Wall Street, investors, and entrepreneurs by searching key terms in the texts of millions of books published in the United States from 1900 to 2008, using Google's Ngram tool.

Class and Political Voice: How Presidential Campaigns Hail "The People"

French theorist Louis Althusser described communication as a process of interpellation, or hailing. By addressing or hailing someone, we create a relationship between the communicator and the subject: the person who is hailed. A man calling an unfamiliar man "sir," "mister," "bro," "hey you," or "stupid" creates a relationship between the communicator and the subject with each term. (The subject's response to the manner in which he is addressed accepts or rejects the implicit terms of the relationship, too.) The news does this as well, most often hailing the audience as consumers rather than citizens.[8]

Presidential campaigns do the same thing. They select the words that they use to address citizens and in doing so establish their "terms" for our relationship with them. So begins the "voice" of citizens as they either respond as identified by the campaign or respond in a way opposed to the campaign's hailing (a difficult path, if they want their opposing voice to be heard). Finally, a third scenario is that the campaign doesn't even bother to hail some citizens: it's talking to some other kind of person. In that case, the citizens, unfortunately, do what most US citizens do (including a majority of Iowans at caucus time): they don't participate at all. In short, when the campaigns hail citizens, some say "That's me," some disagree and say "That's not me," and some decide that the campaign is ignoring them and say "You're not even talking to me" and drop out of the political conversation.

My focus will be how presidential campaigns hail US citizens in terms of socioeconomic class. Which terms, concepts, and ideologies relating to socioeconomic class are in the political mainstream at various points in modern US history, and which are not? How people are hailed has significant impact on the voice of citizens as socioeconomic beings. If "it" really is "the economy, stupid," as in the popular catchphrase of the 1992 Bill Clinton campaign, exactly where do workers and the concept of socioeconomic class fit into the economy? Are citizens hailed as the participating *subjects* of the economy or hailed merely as its passive *objects,* taking what the economy (or campaign) gives to them?

My argument is that beginning around the early 1970s, there was a wholesale shift in political rhetoric about people and their social economic status.[9] The public went from being valued as citizen workers whose productivity created the US economy to consumers in an economy led by Wall Street and business entrepreneurs ("job creators," in the current parlance). In that shift, Americans have become less often identified as participants in the institution of "labor" or people of the working class or the middle class, and more likely to be hailed with the class-free appellation of "working families" or just "families."

Meanwhile, corporations—more dominant than ever in the US political system—are less likely to be explicitly identified in political discourse since the 1970s. In the discourse, people do not work for corporations (which might suggest the implicit power of a top-down hierarchy) but in more-democratic-sounding *workplaces*, and the political benefits for corporations are framed in more personable terms such as *aid for small businesses* or as *job creators*. As the presumptive Republican presidential candidate Mitt Romney was happy to remind listeners at the Iowa State Fair in 2011, "Corporations are people, my friend. . . . Everything corporations earn ultimately goes to people. Where do you think it goes?"[10]

Trends in Presidential Party Nomination Acceptance Speeches from 1956 to 2016

To put the socioeconomic hailing of presidential campaigns into context, I'll reach back to the middle 1950s, the time when organized-labor membership in the United States attained a peak of nearly 35 percent of the workforce. It's been a mostly downward trajectory ever since. Membership dropped to 20.1 percent of the nation's wage and salary workers by 1983. In 2017 the rate had fizzled down to 10.7 percent overall, with a 34.4 percent union membership rate for public-sector workers and a 6.5 percent rate for private-sector workers.[11]

Since the 1950s, the hailing voice of presidential campaign rhetoric has shifted from respectful mentions of labor and US workers as equal subjects in the US economy to workers being cast as the objects of an economy run by corporate masters (who are often identified more benignly as entrepreneurs or CEOs). Along the way, presidents jettisoned terms like "working class" and thereafter only occasionally referenced a "middle class." The "working family" gained favor with politicians as a term that avoids invoking socioeconomic class. At some points in the last half century, workers disappeared completely from the lips of presidential candidates, except where workers were strategically hailed as cover for policies that ultimately benefited corporate profits.

Presidential party nomination speeches are where candidates, for the first time, get to introduce their message to the entire US public, not just to their party. For the candidate who eventually wins the presidency in that year, a key in the speech is how the nominees hails the US public, either providing voice to the citizens of the vast working class or treating them like consumers.

In 1956, as labor unions were at their greatest strength, President Dwight D. Eisenhower gave his acceptance speech for his nomination by the Republican National Convention for a second presidential term. In the speech, Eisenhower made it clear that workers and their organizations were on equal footing with business management: "Science and technology, labor-saving methods, management, labor organization, education, medicine—and not least, politics and government—all these have brought within our grasp a world in which backbreaking toil and longer hours will not be necessary." His speech also included a section discussing labor relations in which he explicitly stated his principle: "Free collective bargaining without government interference is the cornerstone of the American philosophy of labor-management relations."[12]

Four years later, Democratic nominee John F. Kennedy spoke of a New Frontier, but he hailed the working class and forged a link with those who had been forsaken by the new economy: "For the families forced from the farm will know how to vote without our telling them. The unemployed miners and textile workers will know how to vote. The old people without medical care—the families without a decent home—the parents of children without adequate food or schools—they all know that it's time for a change."[13]

In 1964, as he was seeking his first full term as president, Lyndon B. Johnson accepted his party's nomination "in the midst of the largest and the longest period of peacetime prosperity in our history." However, Johnson argued that "prosperity for most has not brought prosperity to all. And those who have received the bounty of this land—who sit tonight secure in affluence and safe in power—must not now turn from the needs of their neighbors." In his move toward the Great Society, he urged his listeners to "extend the hand of compassion" for "medical care for older citizens . . . fair and stable prices and decent incomes for our farmers . . . a decent home in a decent neighborhood . . . an education for every child to the limit of his ability . . . a job for every man who wants to work" and "victory in our war against poverty."[14] Johnson's fight against socioeconomic inequality was sincere (e.g., the Civil Rights Act of 1964), although his statement of "a job for every man who wants work" was unfortunately literal. Johnson and most of his political contemporaries envisioned a workforce of male breadwinners, with women workers as contingency labor.[15]

Nevertheless, Johnson's speech hailed a broad range of people, with business and labor on equal footing, and he attempted to maintain and expand his party's coalition: "The needs of all can never be met by parties of the few. The needs of all cannot be met by a business party or a labor party, not by a war party or a peace party, not by a southern party or a northern party. Our deeds will meet our needs only if we are served by a party which serves all our people."

Richard Nixon, who lost the election to Kennedy in 1960, returned as the nominee in 1968. In accepting his nomination, Nixon set a tone for law and order, and made specific reference to a voice that answers the nation's ills: "It is another voice. It is the quiet voice in the tumult and the shouting. It is the voice of the great majority of Americans, the forgotten Americans—the non-shouters; the non-demonstrators."

Thus, Nixon introduced an appeal that did not address citizens as much in terms of their economic position but more in terms of their cultural position as traditional patriotic Americans: "They are not racists or sick; they are not guilty of the crime that plagues the land. They are black and they are white—they're native born and foreign born—they're young and they're old. They work in America's factories. They run America's businesses. They serve in government. They provide most of the soldiers who died to keep us free. They give drive to the spirit of America. They give lift to the American Dream. They give steel to the backbone of America. They are good people, they are decent people; they work, and they save, and they pay their taxes, and they care."[16] This message became part of Nixon's efforts to peel white, male workers away from their labor unions and the Democratic Party. Nixon's theme begins a cultural complaint that builds to a never-ending list of grievances by the era of Donald Trump.

Nixon's political strategy became the familiar Republican approach that has endured through today: leverage culture, race, and gender as wedge issues.[17] As Democrats opened up civic life in the mid-1960s, embracing civil rights and later the antiwar and women's movement, the party's traditional coalition among northern liberals, labor unions, and southern Democrats frayed, unraveling in clear view along generational and other fault lines at the 1968 Democratic convention in Chicago.

Nixon—for whom winning elections trumped ideology, ethics, and everything else (see Watergate)—schemed that he could bypass his party's traditional opponents, the union leaders, and go straight to the rank-and-file workers and woo them to his side. Jefferson Cowie, in his superb book *Stayin' Alive: The 1970s and the Last Days of the Working Class*, explained that Nixon's approach was to "dispel the notion that his party and his presidency were anti-worker, cleverly manipulate the race issue, and peg the label of 'elitism' on the liberals" to build a new "Silent Majority" that united many blue-collar union workers with management against common enemies: hippie college draft dodgers, uppity blacks and women, the press, and unpatriotic liberal snobs. The strategy was not to aid working-class white men in any economic sense (that would have gone too far) but to appeal to them psychologically.[18]

Four years later, in his 1972 nomination speech, Nixon had no references to workers or laborers but to *wage earners*. The focus was less about the working class and their position in US society and more about hardening their position against taxes. Nixon's new approach marked a significant transition in how workers were hailed by a presidential campaign. That is, prosperity was less about what workers did for the nation than about workers protecting their income from the government.

"Listen to these facts: Americans today pay one-third of all of their income in taxes," Nixon said. "If [our opponent's] programs were adopted, Americans would pay over one-half of what they earn in taxes. This means that if their programs are adopted, American wage earners would be working more for the Government than they would for themselves. . . . Once we cross this line, we cannot turn back because the incentive which makes the American economic system the most productive in the world would be destroyed. . . . Let us always be true to the principle that has made America the world's most prosperous nation—that here in America a person should get what he works for and work for what he gets."[19] Nixon's message turns away from solidarity among all Americans and encourages citizens to think of themselves as individuals, battling a government that would take away their hard-earned money.

Jimmy Carter's Democratic nomination acceptance speech in New York City in 1976 gave a traditional nod to a sense of equality among institutions and Americans from various walks of life: "Business, labor, agriculture, education, science, and government should not struggle in isolation from one another but should be able to strive toward mutual goals and shared opportunities."[20] However, Carter, a southern Democrat, offered little hope to the working class in terms of "mutual goals and shared opportunities." He was unable to pass labor reforms in 1978 with a Democratic majority in Congress, and was more concerned with fighting inflation, reducing the deficit, deregulating the transportation industries, and launching austere monetary policies with the appointment of conservative Paul Volcker to chair the Federal Reserve Board in 1979. The sum of these policies "brought approval from Wall Street and denunciation from AFL-CIO headquarters."[21] Prominent Democratic Congressman Augustus Hawkins described Carter's policies in 1977 as "slightly more conservative than Richard Nixon's."[22]

Ronald Reagan's 1980 Republican nomination acceptance speech advanced on the rhetorical path that Nixon had set. In this case, workers are not a central subject of the economy, but merely a trickle-down beneficiary, via tax cuts for businesses that presumably cause businesses to create jobs. Moreover, Reagan moved into new rhetorical territory, shifting from the economic centrality of workers toward the centrality of the family, which corresponded with his embrace of cultural conservativism: "Work and family are at the center of our lives; the foundation of our dignity as a free people. When we deprive people of what they have earned, or take away their jobs, we destroy their dignity and undermine their families. We cannot support our families unless there are jobs; and we cannot have jobs unless people have both money to invest and the faith to invest it."[23]

Reagan's philosophy quickly became clear. He destroyed a major union—firing more than 11,000 striking air traffic controllers of the PATCO union in 1981—and made the Department of Labor and the National Labor Relations Board essentially anti-worker, pro-business governmental organizations. Reagan significantly weakened the power of the working class and refocused the economic battle lines. Instead of a coexistence among government, labor, and management—a three-pillared tenet of the modern US economy—Reagan reframed labor and government as the enemies of consumers, relieving big business of the only two economic institutions that served as a check on its power and ethics.[24] Corporate profits soared, even more with the additional boost of lower taxes for the wealthy, while workers' wages stagnated.

In 1984 Reagan's second nomination acceptance speech furthered the shift in who is hailed. For the first time in a presidential party nomination acceptance speech, we hear the hybrid term "working families." The rhetorical move reinforces the cultural conservative thrust of the Republican Party and fully supplants the working class with the working family. Hailing "workers" addresses citizens at a class level; hailing "working families" addresses citizens only as a consumption unit. Reagan celebrated their additional "purchasing power" gained through reduced tax and inflation rates:

Together, we began the task of controlling the size and activities of the government by reducing the growth of its spending while passing a tax program to provide incentives to increase productivity for both workers and industry. Today, a working family earning $25,000 has about $2,900 more in purchasing power than if tax and inflation rates were still at the 1980 level.

They call their policy the new realism, but their new realism is just the old liberalism. They will place higher and higher taxes on small businesses, on family farms, and on other working families so that government may once again grow at the people's expense.

Our tax policies are and will remain prowork, progrowth, and profamily.[25]

Notably, Reagan called his tax policies "prowork" but not "proworker."

In his 1988 nomination acceptance speech, George H. W. Bush, Reagan's vice president, delivered his famous line likening America to "a thousand points of light." That line was eclipsed by an even more famous line in the speech (one that eventually led to just one term as president): "Read my lips: no new taxes."

In Bush's speech, labor unions are treated like just another US organization. Bush puts unions in a list that includes "the Knights of Columbus, the Grange, Hadassah, the Disabled American Veterans, the Order of Ahepa": all organizations, along with the "union hall," that are given a mention as sample points of light.

Bush's speech follows Reagan's trickle-down dictum: low taxes (on business and the wealthy) "create" jobs. It's clear in the rhetoric: the tax cutters are ultimately the job creators. Workers cease to be central to the functioning of the economy and are instead just the objects of federal policies.

Bush made it certain who is hailed in the Republican Reagan-Bush era: "An election that is about ideas and values is also about philosophy. And I have one. At the bright center is the individual. And radiating out from him or her is the family, the essential unit of closeness and of love. For it is the family that communicates to our children—to the 21st century—our culture, our religious faith, our traditions and history."

Missing from this history was the story of workers in the US economy. Gone was the notion from both Republicans and Democrats that workers and businesses were the main economic forces. Instead, corporations (subsidized through tax cuts and corporate welfare) became the job creators, and workers are left with no voice, to take what was offered. Individuals and families (of a culturally conservative bent) were hailed, but workers were not.

Another section from Bush's speech (also ironic in retrospect) is the notion that workers—now excluded from the economy as helpless objects—need to be retrained for a future planned by technocrats. That job apparently fell to Bush's vice president, Dan Quayle. "And we're going to win with the help of Senator Dan Quayle of Indiana—a young leader who has become a forceful voice in preparing America's workers for the labor force of the future," Bush said.[26]

By 1992, the political discourse about work had changed so much that Bill Clinton's Democratic nomination acceptance speech was an awkward combination of seemingly old-fashioned acknowledgments of workers with a primary appeal that favored the emphasis on business entrepreneurialism. Workers were again merely objects of the economy, a labor force in service to business, to be retrained as needed: "What is the vision of our New Covenant? An America with millions of new jobs and dozens of new industries, moving confidently toward the 21st century. An America that says to entrepreneurs and businesspeople: We will give you more incentives and more opportunity than ever before to develop the skills of your workers and to create American jobs and American wealth in the new global economy. But you must do your part, you must be responsible. American companies must act like American companies again, exporting products, not jobs."[27]

Clinton's warnings to companies to "be responsible" were a reaction to corporate excess since the 1980s. Yet with labor and government disempowered, the warnings to business carried few measures of accountability. The power of the neoliberal ideology entrusted nearly every part of the US government and society to the needs and demands of the entrepreneurial (the trendy way to say "capitalistic" in the 1990s) overlords, whom Clinton gladly hailed: "One sentence in the Platform we built says it all. The most important family policy, urban policy, labor policy, minority policy, and foreign policy America can have is an expanding entrepreneurial economy of high-wage, high-skilled jobs."[28]

In 1996, riding a better economy, Clinton failed to mention labor unions but said that "I want to build a bridge to the 21st century that ends the permanent under class, that lifts up the poor and ends their isolation, their exile, and they're not forgotten anymore." Despite sharp resistance from Republicans in Congress in his first term, Clinton was able to cite some accomplishments for US workers in his second party nomination speech, including low unemployment and inflation rates, ten million new jobs, portable health insurance, and a tax cut.[29]

Yet perhaps the only indication that the business- and entrepreneur-driven economy had been a class war on workers was the name of Clinton's legislative proposal: "I have proposed a new G.I. Bill for American Workers—a $2,600 grant for unemployed and underemployed Americans so that they can get the training and the skills they need to go back to work at better paying jobs—good high-skilled jobs for a good future." Recalling Reagan's use of the term "working families," a bromide for workers that avoids the realities of class, Clinton's address included other tax cuts and credits for "middle-income families," "every working family," and "every middle-income working family in this country."

George W. Bush's 2000 Republican nomination speech contained a passing sentiment for workers: "Corporations are responsible . . . to treat their workers fairly, and leave the air and waters clean."[30] But it was evident in his speech that the economic responsibility for the country was in the hands of the financial elite. He hailed workers twice; in both cases, Bush deceptively invoked workers as he advocated policies that benefit the wealthy and Wall Street.

First, Bush noted that "on principle . . . every family, every farmer and small businessperson, should be free to pass on their life's work to those they love. So we will abolish the death tax." Significantly, he didn't mention that the US working class and middle class do not have estates large enough to even be affected by the estate tax (reframed as the "death tax"), so such a repeal would be a gift to the super-wealthy.

Second, he directly hailed young workers to entrust their retirement security to Wall Street, thus undermining the Social Security program and creating a windfall for loosely regulated capitalists. The deal might have sounded good to a generation primed by personal finance journalism: "For younger workers, we will give you the option—your choice—to put a part of your payroll taxes into sound, responsible investments. This will mean a higher return on your money, and, over 30 or 40 years, a nest egg to help your retirement, or pass along to your children. When this money is in your name, in your account, it's not just a program, it's your property." Congress never approved the proposal, though.

Post-9/11, in his 2004 nomination speech, Bush envisioned an economy with no mention of social class but one in which he professed belief "in the energy and innovative spirit of America's workers, entrepreneurs, farmers, and ranchers—so we unleashed that energy with the largest tax relief in a generation. Because we acted, our economy is growing again, and creating jobs, and nothing will hold us back."[31] (Meanwhile, Bush and the nation were fighting two major wars in Afghanistan and Iraq.)

In addition to the "largest tax relief" (which went chiefly to the higher-income brackets and was followed by a stagnant economy and then an enormous recession),[32] Bush claimed to create jobs with the same old trickle-down economics. Bush also proposed family-friendly measures: "In this time of change, government must take the side of working families.

In a new term, we will change outdated labor laws to offer comp-time and flex-time. Our laws should never stand in the way of a more family-friendly workplace." Yet no such family-friendly laws were signed in Bush's second term.

In 2008 Barack Obama shifted the target of a presidential speech back to the middle class (synonymous with working families) in his Democratic nomination address: "I will cut taxes—cut taxes—for 95 percent of all working families. Because in an economy like this, the last thing we should do is raise taxes on the middle class."[33]

Obama used the earlier comments of his presidential opponent John McCain in sharp contrast to his own hailing of the US middle class: "Now, I don't believe that Senator McCain doesn't care what's going on in the lives of Americans. I just think he doesn't know. Why else would he define middle class as someone making under five million dollars a year? It's not because John McCain doesn't care. It's because John McCain doesn't get it."

In his balancing act, Obama hailed both workers and entrepreneurs, the working class (although he didn't call them that) and the economic elite (who, despite the many small campaign contributions Obama garnered, contributed significantly to his campaign coffers):

> We measure the strength of our economy not by the number of billionaires we have or the profits of the Fortune 500, but by whether someone with a good idea can take a risk and start a new business, or whether the waitress who lives on tips can take a day off to look after a sick kid without losing her job—an economy that honors the dignity of work.
>
> It's a promise that says the market should reward drive and innovation and generate growth, but that businesses should live up to their responsibilities to create American jobs, look out for American workers, and play by the rules of the road.

Obama's statement regarding businesses responsibilities echoed Clinton's 1992 nomination speech, but with labor further weakened and a federal government still predisposed to neoliberalism (supported by Republicans and many Democrats), the warnings had little strength.

In his 2012 reelection convention speech, Obama again walked a very tight line, balancing business interests and worker interests. He anecdotally argued against extremes of capitalism but did not quantify growing class inequality or specify the ongoing corporate and political war against labor unions and the working class. The speech reflected the legacy of a generation's worth of political rhetoric about labor and the working class in which the discourse had so tilted in favor of unbridled individualism, deregulation of business, excessive profiteering, corporate irresponsibility, the antitax movement, and the reduction of government oversight that Obama found it necessary to reintroduce the basic concepts of citizenship and social obligation. (As Obama aimed for the moderate middle, his speech mentioned "middle class" five times but never "working class.")

> As Americans, we believe we are endowed by our Creator with certain inalienable rights—rights that no man or government can take away. We insist on personal responsibility and we celebrate individual initiative. We're not entitled to success. We have to earn it. We honor the strivers, the dreamers, the risk-takers who have always been the driving force behind our free enterprise system—the greatest engine of growth and prosperity the world has ever known.
>
> But we also believe in something called citizenship—a word at the very heart of our founding, at the very essence of our democracy; the idea that this country only works when we accept certain obligations to one another, and to future generations.[34]

Obama's 2012 speech mentioned "unions" only once and in a manner that certainly gave them no privilege: "We don't think government can solve all our problems. But we don't think that government is the source of all our problems—any more than are welfare recipients, or corporations, or unions, or immigrants, or gays, or any other group we're told to blame for our troubles."

Amazingly, the next president moved even further from rebalancing the power of big business with labor unions and government oversight. In bits and pieces, Donald Trump's 2016 Republican party nomination speech touched on many of the themes of prior presidential nominees. Borrowing from Nixon, Trump claimed without subtlety that he was the law-and-order candidate. Borrowing from Reagan (and every Republican presidential candidate since then), he honored the myths of trickle-down economics—"Reducing taxes will cause new companies and new jobs to come roaring back into our country"—and the horrors of regulations— "Then we are going to deal with the issue of regulation, one of the greatest job-killers of them all. Excessive regulation is costing our country as much as 2 trillion dollars a year, and we will end it." And even sounding a bit like

Kennedy or Johnson's nomination speeches, Trump noted that "every day I wake up determined to deliver a better life for the people all across this nation that have been ignored, neglected and abandoned."

Overall, though, Trump's speech was unlike any other in the past sixty years. The *Washington Post* called it "a compendium of doomsday stats that fall apart upon close scrutiny. Numbers are taken out of context, data is manipulated, and sometimes the facts are wrong." FactCheck.org found "plenty of instances where Trump twisted facts or made false claims."[35] The speech was also unusual for its dark assessment of crime in the United States, even as violent and property crime rates have fallen sharply since the early 1990s.[36]

Yet after decades of presidential nomination speeches from both parties that ignored or tiptoed around the condition of the working class, and decades after the mainstream news media had dropped the idea of a mass audience, Trump's speech connected directly: "I have visited the laid-off factory workers and the communities crushed by our horrible and unfair trade deals. These are the forgotten men and women of our country. People who work hard but no longer have a voice. *I am your voice.*"[37] Like Nixon, with his reference to "the voice of the great majority of Americans, the forgotten Americans" in 1968—the last time that the United States was so politically divided—Trump sought to mobilize this population for his presidency. And like Nixon, Trump's idea of "forgotten Americans" included only white, working-class voters.

From Eisenhower to Trump there has been a slow but dramatic tectonic shift in political discourse about labor unions and the working class. Presidents have lost the ability to speak of the essential role of labor unions in the US economy (in 1998, George H. W. Bush weakly identified unions as one of his thousand points of light; by 2012, Obama's only mention of unions in his Democratic nomination speech was as part of a list of groups that we shouldn't blame for our troubles); they've become true believers that tax cuts and regulation cuts are job creators; they've mostly become lost in a Mobius strip of crazy reason whereby one should not increase wages or benefits to make jobs sustainable because that would kill jobs; they decry the loss of community but kneel at the altar of individualism when it comes to solutions. Today, it would seem outlandish for a president to express anything approaching what Eisenhower, a moderate Republican, said in 1956: "Free collective bargaining without government interference is the cornerstone of the American philosophy of labor-management relations."[38]

The change in political discourse has been mutually reinforcing between political leaders and the news media. As the mainstream media moved to upscale audiences and reported on workplace lifestyles and personal finance from the 1970s onward, they left little room to consider the fate of America's working class in such an era of economic transformation. Meanwhile, the conservative media pushed a strong antiunion agenda in support of the Republican Party. And Democrats moved to the right as well, taking organized labor for granted. A mainstream news media with an editorial focus on their *entire* community would have kept stories of the working class in the public sphere. But with no watchdog, politicians were left to wander away from a real commitment to the economic well-being of America's working class.

The Loss of the Idea of Class in Public Discourse

Ironically, as the United States has become a more divided nation economically in the past fifty years, the notion that there is a working class has become less relevant in the news media. The same diminishment of relevant concepts and terms is also apparent in books that capture the larger themes of political discourse and the journalistic record, the two main agenda setters of our sociocultural atmosphere.[39]

In 2010 Google released the Google Books Ngram Viewer, which enables users to search and graph the occurrences of words or phrases in a corpus of millions of books already scanned in the Google Books project.[40] I used the Google Ngram Viewer tool to get a sense of the general use of terms relating to work and socioeconomic class as they appeared in books published in US English from 1900 to 2008.[41] Across several terms related to work and the economy, the 1970s appear to be a period of significant transition as certain terms rise and fall, reflecting the changing importance of the terms in news and political discourse.

Figure 5.1 looks at the use of the terms *citizen, consumer, worker,* and *employee.* By the mid-1970s, *consumer* had surpassed *citizen,* and *employee* and *worker* were on an upward trend. By about 2000, *employee* and *consumer* had surpassed *worker* in frequency, whereas *citizen*—the dominant of the four terms in the early twentieth century—was the least frequently used.

Figure 5.2 charts the frequency of the terms *working class, middle class,* and *Wall Street. Working class* and *middle class* hit their ascendancy in the mid-1970s. By the 1980s, the terms *working class* and *middle class* were out of favor and were surpassed by *Wall Street* (a term and place favored by the Reagan Administration and critically portrayed in Oliver Stone's 1987 movie of the same name), the capital of the flourishing financial industry.

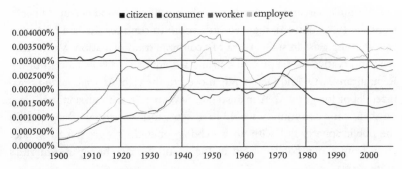

Figure 5.1. Google Ngram, tracking terms *citizen, consumer, worker,* and *employee* in the corpus of books published in US English, 1900–2008

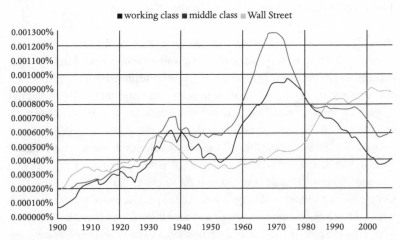

Figure 5.2. Google Ngram, tracking terms *working class, middle class,* and *Wall Street* in the corpus of books published in US English, 1900–2008

Figure 5.3 analyzes the same terms as figure 5.2, plus the term *entrepreneur.* In the 2000s, *entrepreneur* surpassed the term *working class* in books published in US English. The emphasis on Wall Street and entrepreneurs was also reflected in the news media, particularly as personal finance journalism continued its growth. By the year 2000, the unprecedented news media emphasis on Wall Street, high-flying CEOs, and millionaire entrepreneurs led a writer for the *Columbia Journalism Review* to call the genre "wealth porn." As Gary Andrew Poole wrote, "Do we over-celebrate the New Wealth, giving the reader the impression that he's the only one who isn't loaded, or that being rich is all that matters? Are we analyzing the ramifications of the new prosperity?"[42]

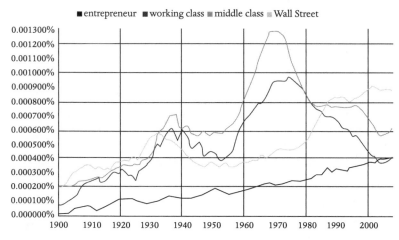

Figure 5.3. Google Ngram, tracking terms *entrepreneur, working class, middle class,* and *Wall Street* in the corpus of books published in US English, 1900–2008

Figure 5.4. Google Ngram, tracking terms *corporation* and *workplace* in the corpus of books published in US English, 1900–2008

Figure 5.4 charts the terms *corporation* and *workplace*. Although corporations were still the dominant force in the economy (firms of 100+ workers employed about 65 percent of workers in private industry, versus about 35 percent of workers for smaller businesses in 2008), discussion of

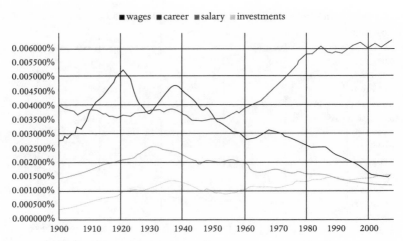

Figure 5.5. Google Ngram, tracking terms *wages, career, salary,* and *investments* in the corpus of books published in US English, 1900–2008

corporations as places of work has waned since the mid-1970s.[43] Meanwhile, the term *workplace* has gained favor since that time and surpassed the term *corporation* in the early 2000s. The workplace is the site for the lifestyles-centered column that commenced in US journalism in the 1970s and continues today.

In the 1970s the term *career* began to gain new prominence, reflecting journalism's emphasis on the lives of upscale, career-minded people, while discussions of *wages* and *salary* fell (see figure 5.5). Since the 1970s, the term *investments* has also gained favor, corresponding to the rise of *Wall Street* (see figure 5.2) and journalism's emphasis on personal finance reporting. Although the term *career* has grown in popularity since the 1970s, it is worth noting that the clear majority of US workers labor in jobs that pay hourly rates. As the US Bureau of Labor Statistics noted in 2010, "58.8 percent of all wage and salary workers" were paid at hourly rates. Six percent of those hourly paid workers—4.4 million workers—in 2010 were paid at or below the minimum wage of $7.25 an hour.[44] The stories of those people's economic lives are less likely to be told in newspapers and, it seems, in books.

The Google Ngram graphs chart meaningful economic concepts as they appeared in books published in US English from 1900 to 2008. The rise and fall of certain words reflects journalism's priorities since the 1970s and illustrates the spread of this cultural and economic shift, from the daily stories of the news media to the more lengthy and durable narratives of books. On a downward trajectory are words and terms such as *worker, work-ing class, middle class, wages, salary,* and *citizen.* On an upward trajectory are words and terms such as *employee, career, entrepreneur, investment, Wall Street,* and *consumer.* These words reflect the everyday framing of journalism and the determination of important or sellable ideas by the book industry. The graphs track the diminishment of the idea of class in public discourse and its replacement by an emphasis on upscale careers, personal finance, and our lives as consumers, not citizens. With its daily stories—news has been called "the first rough-draft of history"—journalism helped create this world.[45]

Finding Voice When You're Not Hailed

In October 2011 the Congressional Budget Office released a study, "Trends in the Distribution of Household Income between 1979 and 2007."[46] The main point of the study was that "the rapid growth in average real household market income for the 1 percent of the population with the highest income was a major factor contributing to the growing inequality in the distribution of household income between 1979 and 2007."

The average real household market income for the top 1 percent income group grew by 275 percent over that period; market income increased by about 19 percent for a household at the midpoint of the income distribution. The study noted further that the share of total market income received by the top 1 percent of the population hit 20 percent in 2007, up from about 10 percent in 1979.

Another extensive study of income inequality in the United States, analyzing the period from 1913 to 1998, confirms that income inequality began to increase sharply in the 1970s, returning to income inequality levels not seen since the 1920s and 1930s.[47]

Annual income is just one measure of economic inequality. Wealth—a household's total net assets in bank accounts, stocks and bonds, real estate, and material goods—is the other indicator of Americans' socioeconomic status. Lagging somewhat behind income increases, by the 1980s the trend was for the wealthy to grow even wealthier. The share of wealth for the richest fifth increased from 81.3 percent in 1983 to 87.2 percent in 2009. For the bottom 80 percent of society's households, their share of wealth shrank to just 12.8 percent.[48]

"The gap between rich and poor is the least reported story in the last 25 years," Michigan State economics professor Charles Ballard said in 2011.

Workers invisible in the eyes of the news media and political leaders were left with one option: find a voice for themselves. Yet rhetorical scholar Michael C. McGee reminds readers that there is usually not a single "public" or "the people" at any one time: " 'The people' exist, not in a single myth, but in the *competitive relationships* which develop between a myth and objective reality, and between a myth and antithetical conditions of the collective life."[49]

True to McGee's observation, there were at least two forms of "the people" that emerged from the Great Recession of 2007–2009. Both groups were confronted by the painful objective reality revealed by the financial crisis: that Wall Street institutions might be too big to fail but working-class Americans were not. In the long view, working-class people also began to realize that they had gotten a bad deal and an increasingly smaller portion of the expanding economy over the past several decades. The myth of the American Dream was at odds with their own experience.

Two groups emerged with their own distinct voices and philosophies. The Tea Party arrived first, launched with an on-screen rant by Rick Santelli, a commentator on CNBC reporting live from the Chicago Board of Trade on February 19, 2009, regarding a plan by President Obama to help millions of debt-bound homeowners avert foreclosure in the wake of the Great Recession. Santelli challenged Obama "to have people vote on the Internet as a referendum to see if we really want to subsidize the losers' mortgages." Cheers and applause rose from traders on the floor. He continued: "This is America. How many of you people want to pay for your neighbor's mortgage that has an extra bathroom and can't pay their bills." Boos erupted from the floor. "President Obama, are you listening?" Later, CNBC pulled out to a wide shot, revealing Santelli surrounded by white, middle-aged male traders: "These guys are pretty straightforward, and my guess is a pretty good statistical cross section of America, the silent majority."[50]

It was a moment made for the conservative media. Sarah Jaffe, in her excellent book *Necessary Trouble: Americans in Revolt*, noted that "though Fox's competitor, CNBC, had launched the idea of the Tea Party, conservative Fox hosts like [Sean] Hannity and Glenn Beck quickly jumped into the fray, publicizing Tea Party events and even hosting their own." The movement grew to about a thousand local groups by the end of 2010, Jaffe reported. Santelli's estimation of white, middle-class traders as "a pretty good statistical cross section of America" exemplified what the "silent majority" had always represented in US politics: white, working-class/middle-class people. Jaffe observed that "Tea Partiers saw themselves as regular people working with their neighbors to take their country (and the Republican Party) back."[51] Moreover, "Its members were not the most likely to have been hurt by the recession, but they were psychologically affected by the crash. When the stock market plunged, so did retirement accounts, alongside the drop in home values caused by the bursting of the housing bubble, hitting Tea Partiers and other older Americans in what had seemed like safe investments." Tea Party membership was also associated with racial stereotypes and anti-immigrant views from the beginning, and the signs and shouts at Tea Party events were clear evidence of such animus.[52]

On the left, the response to the financial crisis developed gradually. Groups conducted protests at the American Bankers Association convention in Chicago in October 2009, and later at bank shareholder meetings and a march of thousands on Wall Street in April 2010. Huge protests at the statehouse in Madison, Wisconsin, against Governor Scott Walker's attack on public-sector unions in the first half of 2011 then inspired more protests in New York and anti-austerity protests in Spain.[53] In June and July 2011, protesters on Wall Street made a "Bloombergville" encampment, named after New York City's billionaire mayor, Michael Bloomberg, whose fortune was connected to digital financial trading systems and financial news.

A few months later, the Occupy Wall Street (OWS) movement began with a question posed in *Adbusters* magazine: "Are you ready for a Tahrir moment?"[54] Inspired by the then-recent Arab uprisings, especially those at Tahrir Square in Cairo, the Twitter hashtag #OccupyWallStreet was born, and on September 17, 2011, a group of protestors gathered in Zuccotti Park in New York's financial district. This effort clearly resonated with people across the country. Soon there were at least 600 Occupy encampments in the United States spread across every state, and more than 900 Occupy-related protests worldwide.[55] With their growing occupation of Zuccotti Park (called Liberty Plaza by the occupiers) and the global reach of social media, the protesters eventually attracted the attention of the news media. Early coverage simply pitted angry protesters against dismissive Wall Street executives and politicians, many of whom questioned the movement's longevity. But as retirees, teachers, labor unions, off-duty police officers, firefighters, and other workers joined college students and the jobless in Occupy protests across the country, the coverage and narratives in the media became more complicated and nuanced. Unlike the Tea Party, OWS did not have a major media advocate. However, OWS was able to establish a broader, nonpartisan message. Jaffe, who reported from Zuccotti Park, explained how OWS brought the idea of class back into public discourse: "The expression of solidarity that 'We are the 99 percent' offered, that we were all in this together, allowed people to move beyond the easy politics of moral superiority or purity. . . . With one slogan, it appeared that Occupy had both pointed the finger squarely at the rich and gathered the other classes together in opposition."[56]

Although OWS faced criticism for having a vague agenda and no charismatic leaders, a clear focus did emerge: discontentment with overpaid CEOs, big banks, and Wall Street, all players that helped cause the 2007–2009 financial collapse but still enjoyed a government bailout.[57] OWS supporters found their voice by giving the United States the words to understand the threat to democracy in the ever-growing disparity between the wealthiest 1 percent and the other 99 percent of the population. The Tea Partiers found their voice as well, and using the conservative media as their megaphone they expressed their aim to take over the Republican Party, cut government spending, and not pay for other people's bailouts. (Later, one of their leaders also expressed he didn't want "other people's babies" either—a tweet by US Representative Steve King (R-Iowa) regarding his desire to maintain white racial supremacy in the United States.[58])

Iowa Struggles to Find a Voice

Iowa is a state with millions of acres of corn and soybean fields, but most of its 3.1 million people live in small towns and cities. The state occupies a unique place in the nation's presidential elections. Since the 1970s, Iowa has held the nation's first caucuses, an event in which presidential candidates of the political parties compete to earn delegates toward the goal of winning their party's nomination later in the year. Compared to most other states, Iowa is active in political participation, and it regularly has one of the highest voter turnout rates of any state.

As one drives from the Mississippi River on the east border to the Missouri River on the west, the landscape of Iowa changes, getting less forested, more flat, and more dry. It changes politically, too. The eastern half of Iowa is more traditionally liberal and Democratic, and that generally carries through to the central Iowa region of Des Moines and Ames. The east and central regions are home to Iowa's three major public universities (University of Iowa, Iowa State, and University of Northern Iowa) and seven of the state's ten most populous counties. Beyond Des Moines, the western half of the state is reliably Republican.

My home state of Iowa famously gave Barack Obama a convincing victory in the Democratic caucuses in 2008, the triumph that helped launch a young US senator from Illinois to become the first African American president.[59] Obama ultimately won two terms, and each time Iowans favored him by considerable margins in the general election, with Obama winning 53.9 percent of the vote in 2008 and 52 percent in 2012. Iowa was also part of a block of midwestern states (Iowa, Wisconsin, Michigan, and Ohio) that famously flipped from being reliable Democratic strongholds (especially based on two terms of support for Obama) to voting for Donald Trump in the 2016 general election.

After all of the votes had been counted in the 2016 election in Iowa, Donald Trump won with 51.1 percent of the vote. Clinton lost with 41.7 percent of the vote; third-party candidates finished with more of the vote in 2016 than they had in the previous two presidential elections (see table 5.1). Looking at a map of Iowa's 99 counties, the final results highlight just 6 county wins for Clinton. Trump won the remaining 93 Iowa counties, including the 31 counties that almost inexplicably switched to Trump after voting for Obama in the two previous elections. These "pivot counties" are all generally in the east and central regions of the state. Nationwide, there were 206 counties that voted for Obama in both 2008 and 2012, then flipped parties to vote for Trump in 2016.

Although pivot counties occurred in 34 states, Iowa had more than any other, with 31 pivot counties out of 99 counties statewide.[60] This makes Iowa a useful microcosm to analyze the nature of Trump's victory. Was Trump's victory, as the *New York Times'* Nate Cohn reported, won by "an enormous wave of support among white working-class voters"?[61] Or were there other factors in play? For the 2016 presidential election, the rhetoric of the Tea Party and Occupy Wall Street movements still hung in the atmosphere, ready for candidates to engage citizens who believed that they didn't have a voice. Both the Tea Party and Occupy Wall Street movements called for drastic change to the economic status quo. Which candidates would best embrace them in their political discourse? And what role did the news media play in the election?

Table 5.1. Iowa votes and turnout: 2016, 2012, and 2008 presidential elections

Year	Democratic candidate	Vote (%)	Republican candidate	Vote (%)	Statewide turnout (%)
2016	Clinton	653,669 (41.7)	Trump	800,983 (51.1)	72.77
2012	Obama	822,544 (52.0)	Romney	730,617 (46.2)	73.28
2008	Obama	828,940 (53.9)	McCain	682,379 (44.4)	72.60

Source: "Election Results and Statistics," Iowa Secretary of State, https://sos.iowa.gov/elections/results.

No Wave of New Working-Class Voters

Overall, the voter turnout in Iowa was 72.77 percent, down from the 73.28 percent in 2012 and slightly above the 72.6 percent in 2008.[62] Thus, it's fair to conclude that Trump's candidacy did not bring a great mass of new voters into Iowa's electorate. Even in the pivot counties, there was no strong evidence indicating that Trump brought out more voters in just those counties. In the 31 pivot counties, 17 had higher turnout compared to 2012, and 14 had lower turnout. If we look closer at the pivot counties that had increased turnout, most were less than one percentage point increase. Only 8 of the 31 pivot counties had a turnout increase of more than one percentage point. Of the 14 pivot counties that had decreased turnout, 10 had a turnout decrease of more than one percentage point. Overall—and this must bring him great angst—Trump won Iowa with fewer statewide votes than Obama had in either of his election victories (see table 5.1). So, if there was "an enormous wave of support among white working-class voters," then the wave was not caused by a mass of new people jumping in the pool. It was more like most of the same people in the same water were wading from one side to the other side of the pool, as voters shifted from Democrat to Republican in Iowa for the 2016 presidential election. Most significantly, even with Iowa's 72.77 percent turnout, 27.23 percent of potential Iowa voters—591,614 people—did not participate in the 2016 presidential election. Nationwide, people's estrangement from the political process was even worse: about 42 percent of eligible voters sat out the 2016 presidential election.[63]

Income, Education, and Urban-Rural Divides in Iowa

Although Clinton won just six counties in Iowa, they were six of the seven largest counties in the state: Polk (Des Moines), Linn (Cedar Rapids), Scott (Quad Cities), Johnson (Iowa City), Black Hawk (Waterloo and Cedar Falls), and Story (Ames).[64] As in the national election (in which Clinton won the popular vote, another matter which brings great angst to Trump), Clinton did much better than Trump in most large metropolitan areas. In the 31 pivot counties, all but one were rural (which is to say that all but one had populations of 87,000 or less and were not in the top ten of Iowa's most populous counties).[65] In Iowa, the urban-rural divide was a salient element in the campaign, similar to what political scientist Katherine Cramer discovered in her adjacent state of Wisconsin.[66] (In fact, the three Northeast Iowa counties that border Wisconsin along the Mississippi River all pivoted to Trump.)

The urban-rural divide in Iowa is also reflected in income and education. The estimated Iowa per capita income in 2016 was $28,872. In the United States it was $29,829. As in most states, income in Iowa is not spread out evenly. Per capita incomes in 77 of Iowa's 99 counties are below the state per capita income level, whereas 22 are above it. Four of the 6 urban Iowa counties that Hillary Clinton won are above the Iowa per capita income. These are also the 4 largest counties in the state, which means that Donald Trump won the other 18 counties with the above-average per capita income (all of these reliable Republican counties, including Dallas County, west of Des Moines, which has the highest per capita income in the state). And it also means that Trump won 75 of the 77 counties with below-average per capita income. Of the 31 pivot counties that Trump won, 28 had below-average per capita income. Therefore, Trump won some of the richer counties and most of the less-rich counties (the majority of Iowa's counties), but he didn't win the wealthiest major urban counties.

In terms of education, 25.7 percent of Iowans have a bachelor's degree or higher. (Iowa also has an extensive community college system; another 32.3 percent of Iowans have "some college" or a two-year associate degree.[67]) As an indicator of class, I'll use "bachelor's degree or higher" as the standard, since a four-year college degree serves as not only an economic marker but also a sociocultural one.[68] (This divide is at the fore of our political discourse, too. The Democratic Party implores workers to use higher education to get ahead, while the Republican Party often targets higher education as the province of elite snobs.) Citizens in Iowa with a college education tend to be concentrated in or near urban areas and/or in locations with colleges or universities. Only 11 of Iowa's 99 counties have high rates of citizens with a bachelor's degree, that is, greater than the state rate of 25.7 percent. Hillary Clinton won five of those counties.[69] Of the 31 pivot counties, 27 have rates lower than the state rate for higher education.

Considering the urban status, income, and college education rates of Iowa counties that pivoted to Trump in 2016, Cramer's idea of rural consciousness seems apt, with its "strong identity as a rural resident, resentment toward the cities, and a belief that rural communities are not given their fair share of resources or respect."[70] In fact, resources and development in Iowa are increasingly unequal. An analysis of Iowa at the county level understates the size and impact of Iowa's largest multicounty metropolitan areas. In the center of the state, Polk and Story counties are adjacent along the I-35 corridor, creating a larger metro area that stretches from Ames and Iowa State University in the north to Des Moines and its many suburbs, including those that stretch into a third county, Dallas County, to the west. Similarly, in the eastern part of the state, Linn and Johnson counties are adjacent on the I-380 corridor, creating a district that runs from Cedar Rapids and its suburbs in the north to Iowa City and the University of Iowa in the south. Both of these "corridors" (and they do market themselves that way) are the wealthiest, most populous, and fastest-growing regions of the state, with plenty of government-funded institutions and research, headquarters of the largest corporations, excellent hospitals, and the state's best sports, recreation, and shopping.[71]

Life can be quite different in one of Iowa's more distant counties, where population might be declining, school districts get consolidated (meaning there may not be local schools nearby for children anymore), access to doctors and quality hospitals lags, new investment is rare, the closing of a single long-time manufacturing facility can be devastating, and young adults often move to places such as Des Moines or Iowa City to find better jobs. These kinds of disparities aren't apparent in the larger cities of Iowa that national reporters might visit when they cover the caucuses or general elections. But away from the population centers, the majority of Iowa's rural counties are on a much more feeble economic trajectory.[72] Although Iowa appears to have a sound economy when looking at state-level data, the lived experience of personal income, higher education, and the long-term hope for opportunity and prosperity can vary widely across the urban-rural divide of Iowa's 99 counties.

A Poor Performance by Clinton and a Sufficient Performance by Trump

Hillary Clinton's problems in Iowa started in 2008, when Obama won the January Democratic caucus with a record turnout. Clinton finished third, just behind John Edwards. Clinton ultimately lost a close nomination race to Obama later that year. After Obama finished two terms, an even more experienced Clinton seemed to be the heir apparent for the Democratic nomination and was expected to be the first woman president of the United States. However, although Obama had led the country through the worst of the recession, an even more unequal economy emerged as labor's share of increasing revenues flowed up and away from the working class.

In 2016 Clinton almost had the same problem in Iowa again, facing a serious challenge by an insurgent candidate from the left. With the slimmest of margins, 49.9 percent to 49.6 percent, she edged out Bernie Sanders in the 2016 Iowa Democratic caucuses and fought him most of the way

to the nomination.[73] Although they were both aiming for the same Democratic Party nomination, Clinton and Sanders had very different rhetorical
approaches to the economy. In her victory speech late on the night of the
caucus, Clinton's words about the economy were vague, spare, and unre-
markable: "I know what we are capable of doing, I know we can create more
good-paying jobs and raise incomes for hard-working Americans again."[74]
The same night, Sanders spoke directly to those who felt alienated by politics
as usual: "What Iowa has begun tonight is a political revolution. A political
revolution that says when millions of people come together, including those
who've given up on the political process, they're so dismayed and so frustrated with what goes on in Washington, with young people who before had
never been involved in the political process, when young people and working
people and seniors begin to stand up and say loudly and clearly, enough is
enough, that our government, the government of our great country belongs
to all of us and not just a handful of billionaires, when that happens we will
transform this country."[75] Sanders was able to build a strong coalition with
his change-oriented message inspired by Occupy Wall Street, but Clinton's
message of incremental reforms struggled to give her resounding caucus
and primary victories in Iowa and other important states.

Donald Trump could also wear the mantle of change, although his lack
of experience was unprecedented. Iowans did not immediately take to him.
He lost the Iowa Republican caucus to Ted Cruz, finishing second, just ahead
of Marco Rubio.[76] Voter turnout for the general election was lower than
in 2012, and Trump won with 2.75 to 3.5 percent fewer votes in Iowa than
Obama received in his two elections. Yet Trump's performance was sufficient to beat a poor performance by Clinton.

If you were an Iowan who supported Obama in 2008, you were patient
enough to wait out the recovery to the Great Recession, which hit just before
Obama was elected. In 2012 you could be sufficiently optimistic that the economy was improving to throw your support to him again. By 2016, however,
you might have been concerned. By that time, the economy was reportedly
improving: the unemployment rate was down, the stock market was up, and
corporate profits were great again. Yet most of the benefits to this economy
did not show up on your doorstep. If you lived in rural Iowa, the inequality was even more apparent. So if a very unlikely presidential candidate—
one made famous by playing the role of super-successful billionaire in a
network reality television show and countless movie cameos—shows up
and says to the "forgotten men and women of our country" that "*I am your
voice,*" you might listen to him. And when he gives his explanation for the

dimming prospects of the white working class and states that the problem is politicians like his opponent, you might feel like this is the answer you've been waiting for:

> I am going to turn our bad trade agreements into great trade agreements. America has lost nearly one-third of its manufacturing jobs since 1997, following the enactment of disastrous trade deals supported by Bill and Hillary Clinton. Remember, it was Bill Clinton who signed NAFTA, one of the worst economic deals ever made by our country. Never again. I am going to bring back our jobs to Ohio, and Pennsylvania, and New York, and Michigan and to all of America—and I am not going to let companies move to other countries, firing their employees along the way, without consequence.[77]

Despite all of the obvious and ugly flaws of this candidate, Trump was the only one remaining who seemed to be completely candid about the fact that the economy wasn't helping the working class and that perhaps the trade agreements from earlier decades had not brought prosperity, at least to some parts of America. Therefore, if you were a rural, working-class voter in Iowa in 2016 (and white, which is a strong likelihood in a state where 91.4 percent of people are white), then you might be willing to take a chance with a vote for Trump.[78] An analysis by a political scientist found that "about 12 percent of Bernie Sanders supporters from the Democratic primary crossed party lines and voted for Donald Trump in the general election."[79]

Of course, Trump's economic message was not for the *entire* working class. Trump specifically targeted white, working-class men (he could already be assured of capturing typical Republican voters). To reach them, he appealed to both their economic status and cultural status, both inextricably linked. Research by Diana Mutz argues that a perceived "status threat" was a major factor for these voters. Mutz analyzed responses by a panel of subjects who were surveyed in both 2012 and 2016 that revealed changes in their thinking over time. Significantly, voters moved closer to the Republican Party on three issues: trade (agreeing more with "the United States should have fewer trade agreements"), immigration (agreeing more with "returning illegal immigrants to their native countries"), and China (agreeing more with China being "a threat to our jobs and security").[80] In practical terms, "The whole slogan of Make America Great Again really speaks to this desire . . . it's a nostalgic desire for the kind of status hierarchies that we used to have, and that meant men were more powerful, whites were more powerful," Mutz explained.[81] More directly, given all of Trump's dog-whistle appeals, winks, and nods to white male cultural status that accompanied his economic message and limited it to a subset of the working class, this also meant, as columnist Leonard Pitts, Jr., wrote, "A vote for Trump was a de facto vote for racism and misogyny."[82]

What the Media Had to Do with Iowa Voters and Political Voice

The upscale-audience focus of the mainstream news media and the existence of an explicitly partisan conservative media played out perfectly for candidate Trump. To the extent that the mainstream news media critiqued Trump as a candidate (and there was plenty to critique), it may not have reached working-class voters who weren't the audience of those news media. For example, many editorial boards of the nation's top 100 newspapers were alarmed by the idea of a Trump presidency. A number of newspapers, such as the *Tulsa World*, the *Dallas Morning News*, the *Cincinnati Enquirer*, the *Arizona Republic*, the *Omaha World-Herald*, and the *San Diego Union-Tribune*, had not endorsed a Democratic candidate for seventy years or more. Clinton received fifty-seven endorsements, Libertarian candidate Gary Johnson received four, "none of the above" received five, "not Trump" received three (including that of *USA Today*), and Trump received only two.[83] Never had the nation's newspapers been so certain about their lack of support—and even disdain—for one of the major presidential candidates. Yet given the upscale readership profile of most US newspapers, did these editorials ever reach a white, working-class audience? One of those top newspapers, the *Des Moines Register*, Iowa's largest daily, endorsed Clinton (after endorsing Romney in 2012). Thirty-five percent of the *Register*'s readers have a college education, almost 10 points higher than the state average.[84] Is this evidence that the *Register* has a low rate of readership by the white working class that Trump was courting?

On shores opposite of the mainstream news media, conservative media were a boon for Trump in Iowa and elsewhere. To the extent that mainstream news media critiqued Trump as a candidate, the conservative media could dismiss, ridicule, play the victim, argue every point, and attack the mainstream media itself (as Trump did) or just offer steady, unqualified support for Trump, blotting out any controversy. Fox News, Rush Limbaugh and his band of imitators, religious radio (Iowa has at least twenty-seven Christian stations), and conspiracy websites were just part of the conservative media complex that supported Team Trump.[85]

In Iowa and across the nation, the mainstream news media belatedly discovered the blind spot in their journalism: the working class. Meanwhile, the conservative media, after decades of assembling a white, working-class audience, finally found the perfect vessel who matched their message and political ambition. Donald Trump said he would be the voice for "forgotten men and women of our country." He didn't mean the whole working class, only the white, working-class audience with a vision of the nation framed by the conservative media and its Tea Party movement, who were primed and ready to flip for a presidential candidate just like him.

What does political voice mean for US citizens today? For journalism, enshrined in the highest ideals of the Constitution's First Amendment, political voice took a commercial turn in the late 1960s toward valuing a more exclusive, upscale audience. For the conservative media, founded on a partisan (but still commercially lucrative) vision, political voice always meant ingratiating themselves to the "real" Americans: the mostly white, male, Christian, heterosexual working-class audience. For America's entire working class—the majority of Americans—political voice is fractured: mostly ignored by the mainstream news media and actively split along class, racial, gender, ethnic, and religious lines by conservative media. These fractures represent our politics, too. We aren't citizens; instead, we are branded political factions: "Soccer Moms," "NASCAR Dads," and "Lunch-Pail Catholics."[86]

Should journalism follow wherever our current politics takes us? Or should it set its own agenda, putting its historically democratic function—loyalty to all citizens—first, betting that hailing a mass audience might ultimately find more readers and viewers than its current business plan and ultimately do better for our country?

Chapter 6

"Job Killers" in the News

When Donald Trump cited regulation as "one of the greatest job killers of them all" in his nomination speech in Cleveland in July 2016, he was already deeply committed to the same long list of things the Republican Party for years had been calling "job killers": environmental regulations (including those dealing with global warming); financial reform; National Labor Relations Board rules; public health and safety regulations by the Environmental Protection Agency, the Occupational Safety and Health Administration, and the Consumer Product Safety Commission; voluntary healthy food marketing guidelines proposed by the Federal Trade Commission; student loan reforms; tax code changes; health care reform; and minimum-wage increases.

It is always fine for liberals and conservatives to debate the direction of government policies, particularly with regard to the economy. But "job killer" became a figurative shape-shifter for conservatives; *anything* could be deemed a job killer if Republicans didn't like it, and by giving the undesired policy that label, it seemed as if they were making a principled stand on behalf of the working class.

However, in a news media that is focused on upscale audiences, allegations that something is a "job killer" for working-class Americans can easily get ignored. After all, they aren't talking about jobs for upscale Americans, right? But if there is no reporting, no verification, who will know what's true? That is the case with "job killers," a term whose durability is a great failure of journalism.

Mass communication researchers have long identified the role of the news media in shaping public opinion and influencing political debate. This is known as the media's *agenda-setting* effect, when persistent coverage puts issues on the public agenda.[1] Moreover, the news media can put interpretive spin on the issue through the way in which they *frame* the narrative.[2] Political communication consultant Frank Luntz observed that the key to framing an issue, or a candidate, in the popular mind is constant repetition. According to Luntz, "There's a simple rule: You say it again, and you say it again, and you say it again . . . and about the time that you're absolutely sick of saying it is about the time that your target audience has heard it for the first time."[3]

Political scientists find that the use of "continual engagement and repetition of themes" reinforces the public's opinions about those themes and keeps them from weakening.[4] Moreover, getting that message repeated without any competing themes further strengthens the message. As political scientists Dennis Chong and James Druckman explain, "If one side can establish the relevant terms of debate over an issue, it can successfully persuade individuals to support its position."[5]

To understand how and why the phrase "job killer" has entered the political discourse and repeated so frequently that it almost becomes conventional wisdom—thus setting the agenda of discussion and framing the debate—Peter Dreier of Occidental College and I analyzed the frequency of the "job killer" term in four mainstream news media from 1984 to 2011, how the phrase was used, by whom, and—most importantly—whether the allegations of something being a "job killer" were verified by reporters in their stories.

In the world of news, sources sometimes make false statements. Ideally, the job of journalists is to verify what the newsmakers say. Are they telling the truth or not? According to Bill Kovach and Tom Rosenstiel in *The Elements of Journalism*, verification is "the essence of journalism." It is what separates journalism from propaganda, "which selects facts or invents them to serve the real purpose: persuasion and manipulation."[6] Verifying the truth—getting the story right—is the standard by which journalism can be defined as credible, and verification should be done despite pressures to publish immediately to beat the competition or publish just because others have already done so, Kovach and Rosenstiel explain. Similarly, first on the Society of Professional Journalists (SPJ) Code of Ethics list is to "seek truth and report it," with the directive to "take responsibility for the accuracy of their work. Verify information before releasing it."[7]

However, as our findings illustrate, allegations about public policies and programs being "job killers" were unsubstantiated in 91.6 percent (349) of stories in four major national news organizations from 1984 to 2011. Moreover, stories alleging "job killer" policies and programs shot up after Obama's November 2008 election. More than half (52.75 percent, or 201 stories) of the 381 stories using the phrase "job killer" (or a variation) from 1984 to 2011 occurred in just three years: 2009–2011.[8] This study finds that over 28 years—a period from the midpoint of Ronald Reagan's presidency, through the administrations of George H. W. Bush, Bill Clinton, George W. Bush, and the first three years of Barack Obama—"job killer" changed from an occasional accusation to a politically charged bludgeon swung predominantly by Republicans and business groups and used to try to weaken support for government policies and proposals that regulate business, primarily to protect consumers, employees, public health, and the environment.

The term "job killer" has become a powerful political weapon. In 2011 the Republicans in Congress even embedded the phrase in the name of actual legislation. On January 5, 2011, in one of the first official acts of a new Republican majority in the US House of Representatives, Majority Leader Representative Eric Cantor (R-Virginia) introduced H.R. 2, titled "Repealing the Job-Killing Health Care Law Act," the first time that "job killing" (or a variant) has ever been used in the name of a congressional bill. The measure passed two weeks later on a mostly party-line vote.

A study by the Institute for Policy Integrity at New York University School of Law found that the introduction of H.R. 2 was part of a concerted effort by the new Republican majority in the House to focus attention on Democratic-sponsored legislation and policies that allegedly killed jobs and undermined economic growth: "During roughly the first twenty days the 112th US House of Representatives sat in session, congressional committees scheduled at least twenty separate hearings on the purported link between regulations and the nation's job woes, the study reported."[9]

Leading into the 2012 and 2016 presidential elections, the news media— both mainstream outlets and opinion magazines and blogs—continued to deploy the term, primarily by reporting what Republicans, business lobby groups, and conservative pundits said about Democrats and their policy proposals. (During the GOP primary seasons, Republicans occasionally leveled similar charges at other Republicans.)

To compare themselves to Democratic "job killers," Republican candidates and their supporters began using the term "job creators" with reference to businesses and business leaders. The Republican effort to use and popularize the term "job creators" is similar to their deployment of the term "job killers." In 2011, Bernie Marcus, cofounder and former CEO of Home Depot and a major GOP funder, created, along with other corporate leaders, a Dallas-based group called the Job Creators Alliance (now the Job Creators Network). The group's goal is to promote deregulation, the lowering of corporate taxes, unregulated trade, opposition to health care mandates, and carbon-based energy. Toward that end, it pledged to deploy "our spokespeople in every type of media . . . to generate constant message repetition."[10]

Our research found that the news media, by failing to seek to verify allegations made about government policies and proposals, typically acted more like a transmission belt for business, Republican, and conservative sources than an impartial seeker of truth when it came to the term "job killer." This had the effect of communicating serious falsehoods about government policies and programs, including suggestions that several government policies and programs that help the working class—including affordable health care, increasing the minimum wage, regulation of Wall Street, and more worker-friendly National Labor Relations Board rules—are instead somehow responsible for taking jobs away from workers. Years before Trump became president, Americans had years in training listening to unverified "job killer" allegations to become familiar with Orwellian turns of phrase.

The Rise of a Conservative Attack Phrase

During the twenty-eight-year period we examined, the United States experienced the deindustrialization of the national economy, the acceleration of job outsourcing to other countries, the decline of labor union membership and political influence, attempts to dismantle environmental laws, campaigns for health care reform, rollbacks of taxes on the wealthy, and an unprecedented growth in wage and wealth inequality.[11]

As our study found, the use of "job killer" surged during the Clinton administration and again—much more dramatically—during the Obama administration. This is a testament to the new focus on language to frame the debate by House Republican Leader (and later Speaker of the House)

Newt Gingrich and political consultant Frank Luntz, who was hired by the Republican National Committee to hone its communications capacity for the party's "Contract with America" political strategy.

"The change in Republican language began with Newt Gingrich in 1994," Luntz told PBS, although our findings chart the partisan deployment of "job killer" a year earlier.[12] Even before the "Contract with America," Gingrich was focused on using words that demonized opponents and their policies.[13] Gingrich was working on a communication framing strategy at least as early as 1990, when as House Republican Whip and chairman of GOPAC (a conservative political action group) he commissioned market research to formulate a list of "optimistic positive governing words" that could be used favorably for Republicans and a list of "contrasting words" to be used to undermine Democrats and their policies.[14] The findings were distributed to Republican candidates and politicians across the country in a memo titled "Language: A Key Mechanism of Control." Although the memo didn't contain the precise phrase *job killer,* the list of sixty-four "contrasting words" were of the same ilk, including *destroy, impose, liberal, mandate, welfare, taxes, bureaucracy, unionized,* and *anti-* (flag, family, child, jobs, etc.). The memo instructed Republicans to "apply these to the opponent, their record, proposals and their party."

Studying Job Killers

We looked at four leading national news organizations—the Associated Press, the *New York Times,* the *Wall Street Journal,* and the *Washington Post*—that have full, searchable text archives for the entire twenty-eight-year period of study.

The Associated Press (AP) is a news wire organization that syndicates stories to thousands of other news sources. As a result of this ripple effect, AP stories reach more readers (and broadcast viewers and listeners) in more locations than any other news organization. According to the AP, "More than half the world's population may read, hear or see news from The Associated Press." AP's national news stories are sent to the organization's 1,700 newspaper members in the United States.[15]

The *New York Times* is the nation's most prestigious and influential newspaper. It maintained one of the highest national circulations during the period. The *Wall Street Journal* is the nation's leading business newspaper and has long had the largest national newspaper circulation. The *Washington Post* emerged from the 1970s as the leading newspaper in the nation's capital and has one of the strongest political reporting staffs over the period in review, as well as a large circulation.[16]

From 1984 to 2011, there were 381 stories by the four news organizations that contained the phrase "job killer" and its variations, such as "kill jobs."[17] AP had 115 stories, the *New York Times* 55 stories, the *Wall Street Journal* 151 stories, and the *Washington Post* 60 stories.

Key Findings

Increasing Use of the "Job Killer" Phrase since the Early 1990s

The data reveal that use of the phrase "job killer" has increased dramatically in recent years. Its appearance is not random. Since 1984, the appearance of the phrase "job killer" in the mainstream media increases during election seasons and during Democratic administrations. The candidacy of Barack Obama triggered a dramatic increase in use of the term beginning in 2008. Business and Republican leaders consistently targeted Obama administration's proposals and policies as job killers (see figure 6.1). In charting the history of the use of the term "job killer" during the Reagan, Bush, Clinton, Bush, and Obama administrations, one can see that the term was barely on the radar screen until Clinton took office, virtually disappeared during the eight years of the George W. Bush presidency, and skyrocketed in use

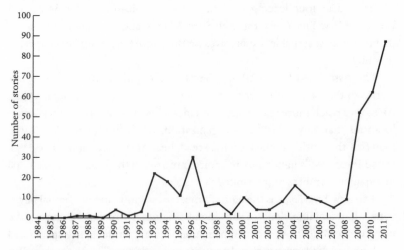

Figure 6.1. News stories in the Associated Press, *New York Times, Wall Street Journal,* and *Washington Post* that contained the phrase "job killer" and its variations, 1984–2011

once Obama was elected. The number of stories with the phrase "job killer" increased by 1,156 percent between the first three years of the George W. Bush administration and the first three years of the Obama administration.

Just 10 "job killer" stories (2.6 percent of our 28-year period of study) appear from 1984 to 1991, during Ronald Reagan's second term and George H. W. Bush's administration. (There were no uses of the term in 1984–1986.) Beginning abruptly in 1993, the trend of "job killer" stories begins in earnest, resulting in 27.8 percent (106) of stories using the "job killer" term in our study appearing during the eight years of the Clinton administration (1993–2000). During the Clinton presidency, Republican leaders in the House of Representatives, including Newt Gingrich, John Kasich, Dick Armey, Rick Lazio, and Tom DeLay, and business figures such as Charles DiBona, who was the president of the American Petroleum Institute, led the "job killer" assault on the Clinton administration.

During the following eight years of the George W. Bush administration (2001–2008), the term appeared just 64 times, 16.8 percent of the 28-year study period. In contrast, during the first three years of Obama's administration (2009–2011), sources deployed the "job killer" charge with a vengeance, accounting for 52.8 percent (201 stories) of all mentions in the four news organizations under study. Similar to our findings concerning the Clinton administration, top House Republicans such as Eric Cantor and John Boehner, Senate Republican Leader Mitch McConnell, Business Roundtable President (and former Republican Michigan Governor) John Engler, and former House Speaker Newt Gingrich (by then a business consultant and media pundit) were leading sources of "job killer" charges against Obama.

Figure 6.1 clearly links the frequency of the deployment of the "job killer" term to periods when Democrats controlled the White House. Moreover, each of the four news organizations under study showed a similar pattern.[18]

All four of the news organizations climbed to new heights in "job killer" stories beginning in 2008, with the Obama candidacy and even more so after he took office. This reflected the reality that these news organizations' key sources were deploying the term more frequently. Interestingly, while frequencies of "job killer" stories for the AP and the *New York Times* subsided somewhat during Obama's first three years, the trajectory of the *Wall Street Journal's* frequencies climbed consistently and sharply from 2008 to 2011. The difference is that the *Wall Street Journal* had a high number of stories in which the source of the "job killer" was the news organization itself; that is, the *Wall Street Journal's* editorials, columns, and reports deployed "job killer" as conventional wisdom, with no attribution. *The Wall Street Journal* generated sourceless "job killer" allegations in 45 stories (about 30 percent of its 151 total stories), the *New York Times* did so in 8 stories (14.5 percent of its 55 stories), the *Washington Post* 5 times (about 8 percent of its 60 stories), and the AP in 5 stories (about 4 percent of its 115 stories). The *Journal's* editorial allegations of "job killer" policies are consistent with other studies identifying the *Journal* as a key component of the conservative media echo chamber.[19]

"Job Killer" Deployed in Battles over Federal and State Policies

The phrase "job killer" was used most often—in 65 percent of the 381 stories examined—to criticize proposed federal policies. For example, in February 2009, House Republican Leader John Boehner alleged that President Obama's proposed federal budget was a "job killer, plain and simple," as reported in an AP story.[20] Similarly, a front-page *Washington Post* story on November 5, 2009, noted that "critics of the [Democrats'] climate-change legislation before Congress say it would be a job-killer."[21] The story failed to name who these opponents were or what evidence, if any, they provided to back up their "job killer" accusation. Both stories, in other words, focused on political scorekeeping resulting from the allegation rather than treating the charge as something to be fact-checked in the larger narrative of a proposed policy. Readers were not given any information to help them understand whether the charge of "job killer" was accurate or even whether the proponents of the policy had rebuttals to the charge made by the opponents.

In the 28-year period analyzed, rarely has "job killer" been lobbed at an individual (4 percent of the stories), an organization (1 percent), or an event (1 percent). Even international, national, and subnational issues—such as a strong Chinese yuan, credit checks on job applicants, or liquor license delays for restaurants—were infrequent targets as "job killers." Rather, more than three-quarters (78 percent) of the "job killer" charges were targeted at proposed or existing government policies at the local, state, and federal levels.

At the state level, California has been a hotbed of "job killer" allegations. Since 2003, the California Chamber of Commerce has annually released a list of "job killer" bills, along with a continuous campaign of media communications and lobbying against those bills.[22] Almost all of these bills are proposals to regulate business, increase taxes, improve worker safety, defend workers' rights, or protect consumers and the environment. The news media often simply repeat the chamber's own label of these proposed bills as "job killers" without providing any scrutiny or analysis. For example, in

an August 28, 2011, story on a bill introduced to ban the dispensing of food
in polystyrene containers in California, the Associated Press wrote that "the
California Chamber of Commerce has labeled the measure as one of its
'job-killer bills,' saying it threatens manufacturing jobs while increasing costs
for restaurants that will have to spend more on alternative containers." The
story had only the anecdotal evidence of one restaurant owner who estimated that biodegradable containers would cost more, and despite the story's own mention of "more than 50 California cities and counties" and other
places across the nation with similar bans, it failed to check the Chamber
of Commerce's allegations against the experiences of those municipalities.[23]

"Job Killer" Chiefly Targets Democratic/Liberal Policies

During the period under study, the vast majority of "job killer" accusations
were published during Democratic presidential administrations.[24] Almost
all of the allegations were targeted at policies supported by Democratic
politicians and liberal organizations, such as unions, environmental groups,
and consumer advocates. (The sources of those allegations are noted in
figure 6.3.) As figure 6.2 illustrates, more than half (53 percent) of the media's
"job killer" reports dealt with four issues, all proposed federal (and sometimes state) policies: environment/climate change (18 percent), tax policy
(17 percent), health care reform (10 percent), and wage law (8 percent).
Trade policy (7 percent), general industry regulation (4 percent), financial

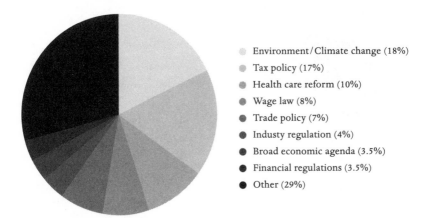

Figure 6.2. Policies alleged to be job killers in the news. Environment/climate change, tax
policy, health care reform, and wage laws accounted for more than half of the allegations.

regulations (3.5 percent), and broadly defined economic policy agendas (3.5 percent) were the next most important issues identified in news reports as job killers. These eight issues accounted for 71 percent of the issues identified as job killers from 1984 to 2011.[25]

A few of the 381 news stories cited multiple issues as "job killers." (For those stories, we counted the most important or first-cited issue in the data above.) Twenty-four of the stories (6 percent) had a second issue, six stories (1.5 percent) cited three issues, two stories (0.5 percent) cited four issues, and one story (0.2 percent) cited five job killer issues. Of these, health care, the environment/climate change, tax policy, energy policy, and welfare/unemployment insurance were cited as an additional issue in more than one instance.

Republicans and Business Organizations Are Main Sources of "Job Killer" Allegations

Figure 6.3 illustrates that, as reported by news organizations, the sources for the phrase "job killer" are mostly Republicans (42 percent) and business organizations (19 percent). Together, they were responsible for 61 percent of the "job killer" charges reported by the four news organizations under study. In 16 percent of the stories, news organizations used the phrase in articles and editorials without attributing the phrase to a source. In other words, the news organization used the "job killer" allegation as conventional wisdom, with no proof or even attribution.

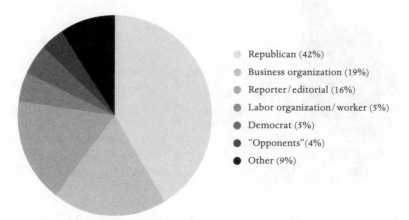

Figure 6.3. Main sources of job killer allegations

Given the history of the use of "job killer" in the past three decades to disparage policies deemed antibusiness, it isn't surprising that business spokespersons and organizations and Republicans are the leading sources for "job killer" charges. But when news organizations use the "job killer" charge without attributing it to any source at all—which accounts for 16 percent of all stories under examination—they are effectively adopting the stance of business groups and Republicans.

Labor union representatives or workers accounted for 5 percent of the "job killer" references, and Democrats accounted for another 5 percent of the charges. Unidentified "opponents" of policies or issues were responsible for about 4 percent of the mentions, and "other" sources (such as academics, advocacy organizations, citizens, and religious organizations) for another 9 percent.

News Organizations Fail to Provide Evidence for "Job Killer" Allegations

Earlier in this chapter, we noted that the "job killer" phrase was embedded in a Republican-sponsored House bill (H.R. 2) in 2011. In this case, at least one journalism organization, the *Tampa Bay Times'* Pulitzer Prize–winning PolitiFact.com, fact-checked the allegation in the bill's name.[26] The writers concluded that the Republican charges about "job killing" misrepresented an analysis of the health care reform law by the nonpartisan Congressional Budget Office report:

> Republicans have used the "job-killing" claim hundreds of times—so often that they used the phrase in the name of the bill. It implies that job losses will be one of the most significant effects of the law. But they have flimsy evidence to back it up.
>
> The phrase suggests a massive decline in employment, but the data doesn't support that. The Republican evidence is extrapolated from a report that was talking about a reduction in the labor supply rather than the loss of jobs, or based on measures that weren't included in the final health care law. We rate the statement False.[27]

Our analysis confirms PolitiFact's study. In 91.6 percent (349 of 381) of the news reports analyzed, news organizations provided no evidence to support the "job killer" claim (see figure 6.4). Even in the 8.4 percent (32 of 381) of the stories in which some evidence was supplied, it's not clear whether or not journalists investigated the veracity of the evidence cited.

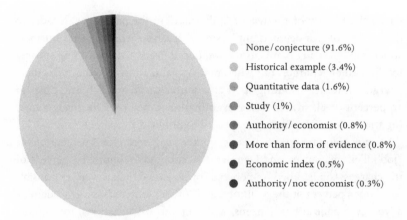

None/conjecture (91.6%)

Historical example (3.4%)

Quantitative data (1.6%)

Study (1%)

Authority/economist (0.8%)

More than form of evidence (0.8%)

Economic index (0.5%)

Authority/not economist (0.3%)

Figure 6.4. The percentage of the news stories that provided evidence to support the "job killer" claims

Similarly, in only 6.8 percent (26) of the 381 stories did reporters provide an alternative claim. In most issues, there are at least two sides to a story. In the case of "job killer" allegations, news organizations typically report only one side. Even in the stories that carried alternative claims—in other words, that reported that some organization or expert challenged the "job killer" allegation—reporters provided evidence to back up challenges to the "job killer" claim in only 8 stories. Thus, in 18 of the 26 alternative claim cases, there was just a competing claim with no supporting evidence.

The net result of presenting the allegations without evidence is a weak "journalism of assertion," rather than a robust "journalism of verification," to use the terms of veteran journalists Bill Kovach and Tom Rosenstiel.[28]

Our data also reveal that in 93.7 percent of the cases, the "job killer" claim had no precise qualifier or estimate of the number of jobs being killed. In 1.0 percent of the cases, it was "thousands" of jobs. In 0.3 percent of the cases, it was "millions." In only 5 percent of the cases were the allegations linked to a specified or estimated number of jobs lost, created, or saved.

Most typical was the assertion of "job killer" without any evidence to quantify. For example, in regard to a 2011 law that limited public employee collective-bargaining rights in Ohio, a spokesperson for Republican Governor John Kasich said that "it is a tool that will enable localities to not have to raise taxes and kill more jobs."[29] Rare was the story that could accurately quantify actual jobs killed. An Associated Press story on March 6, 2009, called the "Recession as Job Killer," cited US Department of Labor data that counted "4.4 million: Net job cuts since recession began in December 2007."[30]

The news media's chronic lack of fact-checking has only encouraged ramped-up use of the "job killer" allegation as a political strategy against the Democrats in recent years. For example, in 2010, Senate Republican Leader Mitch McConnell charged that *everything* the Democrats proposed was a job killer: "Virtually every bill they [Democrats] pass adds more burdens on the very people we need to get us out of the recession and create jobs. If a bill doesn't kill jobs or make it harder to create them, they're not interested."[31]

Newt Gingrich, who started the rhetorical attack with his political memo in the early 1990s, similarly revealed how Republicans should use the "job killer" concept to undermine Democrats' ideas. He told the *Washington Post* in 2010: "To win this fall, win the jobs issue. Job killers will be defeated. Job creators will be elected. When the choice is clear, the outcome will be decisive."[32]

How would the public know who are job killers and job creators? The Associated Press reported the Republican Party's strategy in 2010: "Republican operatives believe the complexity of the [financial industry reform] bill gives them an advantage. 'This bill, in the minds of most Americans, is just a big amoeba,' said John Feehery, a Washington-based GOP strategist. 'Because this bill is so complicated, it makes it easier for Republicans to oppose it, and by opposing it, call it a job killer.'"[33] Even after Republican officials openly admit to cynically deploying charges of "job killer," it did not compel more journalistic scrutiny. In fact, the year 2011 was the biggest year yet for "job killer" allegations.

With no journalistic fact-checking, the job killer meme has become political propaganda that can go through the entire news cycle unscathed and then become even more powerful propaganda as the original allegations get recirculated by political sources as credible "news." For example, House Speaker John Boehner used this strategy in 2011. In an interview with NBC News on January 6, 2011, he called health care reform "the biggest job killer we have in America today." (NBC news anchor Brian Williams ignored Boehner's "job killer" pronouncement about health care, even as he asked Boehner to defend two other allegations he had made.) The next day, Boehner's political blog posted the NBC video with the story headline "On NBC Nightly News, Speaker Boehner Calls 'Obamacare . . . the biggest job killer we have in America today.'" Thus, Boehner's political point emerged intact, with the extra luster of being featured on the national platform of the leading network television newscast.[34]

Newt Gingrich, former Speaker of the House and 2012 Republican presidential hopeful, was a pioneer in using the "job killer" allegations as part of a political strategy. First, he circulated "job killer" allegations about Obama's tax plan on April 13, 2011. The story got picked up by the Associated Press, which reported Gingrich said that "Obama's new proposal to couple spending cuts with tax hikes on the wealthy was 'a job-killing big-government defending avoidance of responsibility.'" The AP story did not question or investigate the veracity of Gingrich's claims.[35] Then Gingrich used the AP story on his own campaign website under the "News" menu, filing the story under the heading "AP: Gingrich Calls Obama's Tax Plan a Job-Killer."[36] Gingrich's unsubstantiated claim now seemed like it must be true, for it was printed as "news."

Thus, the meme continues to spin through the political discourse.

No Correlation between the Frequency of the "Job Killer" Phrase and the Unemployment Rate

When Americans are suffering from a high unemployment rate, it is understandable that they might be wary of proposals from politicians to strengthen regulations on business if they believe that doing so will prolong or worsen the economic hard times. Thus, one might expect the use of the phrase "job killer" to increase during periods of high unemployment. This hypothesis turned out to be wrong, as figure 6.5 reveals.[37] When unemployment was high in the mid-1980s and early 1990s, allegations of "job killers"

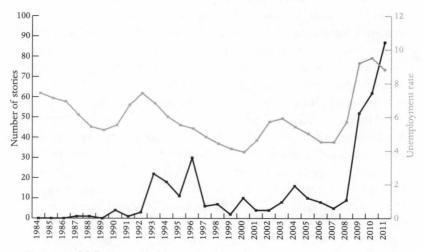

Figure 6.5. Job killer stories (black line) and US unemployment rate (gray line), 1984–2011

were minimal. When the unemployment slid in the mid-1990s, allegations of "job killers" had two significant peaks. As the unemployment rate began to rise in 2000, allegations of "job killers" fell. In 2008, allegations of "job killers" rose faster than the unemployment rate and continued to increase even as the unemployment rate began to decline.

This data suggests that "job killer" allegations correspond much more closely with political cycles. Allegations go up during Democratic administrations and down during Republican administrations (except in years of presidential campaigns). Given that Republicans and business organizations were the leading sources of "job killer" allegations, this political explanation makes sense.

The Ripple Effect of a Single Unverified "Job Killer" Allegation

Although our sample looks at just four leading news organizations, in the instance of "job killer" allegations, a single unverified statement can reverberate thousands of times through the news media. For example, a July 22, 2010, AP story by Matthew Daly reported on the failure of the Senate to pass Obama's energy bill that featured a "cap and trade" plan to reduce carbon emissions. As the article's fifth paragraph stated, "Republicans slammed the bill as a 'national energy tax' and jobs killer, arguing that the costs would be passed on to consumers in the form of higher electricity bills and fuel costs that would lead manufacturers to take their factories overseas."[38] This was one of the stories that provided no evidence to support the conjecture that the energy plan would kill jobs (nor was there any evidence to quantify the number of jobs that would be allegedly harmed). Associated Press stories have great resonance: the organization's news feed serves 1,700 newspapers and 5,000 television and radio news organizations in the United States, and more internationally.[39]

The "job killer" allegation in the July 22, 2010, story was repeated almost verbatim in an AP news brief the same day: "Republicans slammed the bill as a 'national energy tax' and jobs killer, arguing that the costs would be passed on to consumers in the form of higher electricity bills and fuel costs that would lead more manufacturers to take their factories offshore."[40] An AP story on July 23 (by the same author, Matthew Daly) updated activities in US Senate, and included the same original Republican allegation about the bill being a "jobs killer."[41] An AP story on July 27 by another writer, Julie Pace, about Obama and climate change legislation, again used the *same original sentence* from Matthew Daly, repeating the same unverified allegation.[42]

As the thousands of Associated Press clients used these stories, and then websites and blogs (and the AP itself, again) excerpted or repeated them, the original unsubstantiated allegation was further multiplied. A Google search of the sentence's beginning phrase—"Republicans slammed the bill as a 'national energy tax' and jobs killer"—yielded at least 12,800 Web publications.[43]

Such is the power of a single allegation of "job killer," published with no fact-checking.

Yes, Please Fact-Check!

Over time, the untested allegations can gain credibility just by having their claims regularly repeated. As Trudy Lieberman noted in her study of the conservative news media, repetition creates a truth of its own: "If the public hears the same message multiple times, soon people will believe its veracity."[44]

Partisan allegations are to be expected in political discourse. But a press that fails to fact-check partisan allegations does a great disservice to citizens seeking to understand what candidates and elected officials are saying about public policy alternatives. The "routine" nature of harsh political rhetoric and allegations eventually exhausts political journalists, argues George Packer: "Certain forms of deterioration—like writers using 'impact' as a verb, or basketball coaches screaming about every foul—become acceptable by attrition, because critics lose the energy to call them out. Eventually, people even stop remembering that they're wrong."[45] With little or no fact-checking of "job killer" allegations, Americans have no way to know if there is any evidence for these claims or whether they are simply a cynical political ploy used to discredit opponents' policy ideas.

Since the 1990s, and particularly since 2008, "job killer" has been an increasingly frequent allegation hurled by Republican and business sources at Democrats and liberal policies. In recent years, the Internet has magnified the impact of such allegations (which are unverified in 91.6 percent of the cases) as they experience a "ripple effect" through the media environment. When news organizations publish and broadcast such allegations without verification (sometimes making the allegations even in their own editorials and columns, we found), they ultimately contribute to the deterioration of honest political discourse in the United States.

In other words, in the vast majority of news stories the Republican and business sources that use the "job killer" accusation do so with impunity because journalists fail to verify the allegations or give readers a balanced view of the issue. Rather than treat "job killer" as a matter of serious and contentious debate among economists, politicians, interest groups, and others, news organizations primarily serve as transmission belts for those who oppose government regulation of business. As a result, there are rarely consequences in the public record for sources committing misrepresentations, exaggerations, or outright lies. The cavalier nature in which the "job killer" allegations are reported suggests that the term is used loosely by those who oppose government regulations and that they can get away with it because news organizations fail to ask—or at least report—whether they have any evidence for the claims they make and also fail to seek opposing views to counter the "job killer" claims.

Meanwhile, on January 12, 2012, the Public Editor of the *New York Times* wrote a blog entry asking for "reader input on whether and when New York Times news reporters should challenge 'facts' that are asserted by newsmakers they write about."[46] Given the findings of so many unverified claims circulating in political discourse, the obvious answers for the *Times* and all other news organizations is "Yes, they should" and "Start immediately."[47] It is a wonder that the question even had to be asked.

Chapter 7

Rethinking News about US Workers

What if the news media took seriously the notion that US workers haven't received their fair share of the fruits of their labor?

Trillions of dollars in corporate and personal wealth are offshored to tax havens so that corporations and the super-wealthy can withhold their fortunes from being taxed at normal corporate or income tax rates in the United States. "This is the way that the world works," Gary Cohn, then-director of the National Economic Council and chief economic advisor to President Trump, said on CNBC.[1] Cohn's name was listed as an officer for twenty-two tax haven accounts in Bermuda, part of his work for customers at the investment bank Goldman Sachs. Cohn received a $285 million payout in cash and stock in 2017 as he left his position as president and chief operating officer of Goldman Sachs to join the Trump administration.[2]

Yet the only reason that viewers knew about Cohn's involvement in secret Bermuda tax havens is because of leaked legal documents—the Paradise Papers—reported by the International Consortium of Investigative Journalists (ICIJ), the cross-border investigative journalism group. The ICIJ also revealed the Panama Papers in 2016, legal documents for Panamanian-based offshore shell corporations.[3] The Paradise Papers revealed offshore stashes of "more than 120 politicians and world leaders," such as Queen Elizabeth

II, three former Canadian prime ministers, rock star Bono, and "13 advisers, major donors and members" of the Trump administration, including Commerce Secretary Wilbur Ross; Secretary of State Rex Tillerson; fund-raisers Carl Icahn, Paul Singer, Charles and David Koch, Sheldon Adelson, Steve Wynn, and Robert Mercer (patron of Breitbart News and former patron of Steve Bannon); other hedge fund tycoons such as Steven Schwarzman; and more than 100 multinational corporations such as Apple and Nike.[4]

"The way the world works? I don't think anybody's going to have any argument with that," CNBC's John Harwood said in response to Cohn. It's time for the news media to begin to regularly have an argument, a discussion, about the way the world works and to question why it "works" that way.

A Different View on "Job Killers"

Given the increase in economic inequality in the United States since the mid-1970s, is there another way to think about job killers? As more of the profits of US economic activity are captured by the economic elite—i.e., the plutocracy, or the economic royalists, to use Franklin Delano Roosevelt's expression—capital has been captured in enormous amounts for personal gain, with relatively stagnant compensation for ordinary workers and less money available for research, development, innovation, and expansion.[5] Therefore, what if the leaders of industry, through their exorbitant compensation, avoidance of taxes, and accumulation of unprecedented wealth, are what is really troubling the US economy? What if the super-rich, the über-capitalists, are the real job killers?

When the Republicans and conservatives talk about jobs being killed and created, they rarely talk about what *kind* of jobs. (Vaguely calling them "good" jobs often subverts the reality.) First, let's talk compensation. The federal minimum wage in the United States in 2019 is $7.25 per hour, the same rate since 2009. As the Pew Research Center explains, the federal minimum wage's value actually peaked in 1968, when, adjusted for inflation, it equaled $8.68 (in 2016 dollars).[6] At the minimum wage, a worker putting in 40 hours a week for 52 weeks a year would earn $15,080 in annual wages. This includes work every week, with no vacation; in fact, only 39 percent of workers in the bottom 10 percent of wage distribution actually receive a paid vacation.[7] The annual minimum-wage salary is enough to surpass the 2018 poverty guideline for a single-person household of $12,140 but falls short of $16,460, the amount to put a two-person household beyond the poverty threshold.[8] As Barbara Ehrenreich demonstrated in *Nickel and Dimed*, minimum-wage jobs—even if they cross the standard of what officially counts as "poverty" and count as a "job" in the imagination of a politician—don't offer what anyone should think of as a viable situation.[9]

As long as there has been a federal minimum wage (since 1938), workers have argued for a sustainable minimum wage. In recent years, the SEIU (Service Employees International Union) set a new standard for a fair rate—$15—with the Fight for $15 campaign, which began in 2012 and grew nationwide in 2013. The legacy of Occupy Wall Street provided the rationale. "Occupy set the stage for the fast-food protests of 2013 and the broad public support that greeted the demand for higher wages," said David Rolf, then-president of SEIU 775 in Washington state and Montana, and international vice president of SEIU.[10] Rolf led the Fight for $15 campaign in SeaTac and Seattle. A wage of $15 per hour yields $31,200 a year, a modest amount, but one with very beneficial reverberations throughout the economy. The campaign has influenced minimum-wage increases to $12–$15 in several other cities, counties, and states, including New York City; San Francisco; Minneapolis; Montgomery County, Maryland; and the state of Arizona. Target also responded by becoming the nation's first large low-wage retailer to commit to $15 per hour by 2020; Amazon followed in 2018.[11]

A bill introduced in Congress in 2017 that would raise the federal minimum wage to $15 per hour by 2024 "would lift pay for 41 million workers—nearly 30 percent of the U.S. workforce," according to the Economic Policy Institute.[12] The minimum-wage increase would also help to close the broad income gap in the United States and would generate "$144 billion in higher wages for 41 million workers." The bill is a stopgap proposal; by 2024, workers in the nation's most expensive metro areas will require an even higher wage to cover basic living expenses. Yet a higher federal minimum wage remains disparaged by the Right as a job killer. Even in many metro areas that have tried to aid their low-wage workers with higher local minimum wages to meet the cost of living, conservative state legislatures have overturned local rule. At least twenty-five states have passed laws preempting cities and counties from raising their minimum wages above the state minimum.[13]

The Problem of Excess Compensation

Now let's look at executive compensation. For years, the CEO-to-worker compensation ratio was relatively tame. The ratio represents the proportion of executive pay in relation to the salary of the average worker at the same company. In 1965 executives earned 20 times the average worker's salary. By 1973, the ratio was 22.3 to 1. In the 1980s, executive compensation began to escalate in an unprecedented fashion. By 2000, the ratio hit 376.1 times the average annual compensation of workers in the firm.[14] By 2015, with some decline in the stock market valuation, the CEO-to-worker compensation ratio was 276 to 1, still higher than any time from the 1960s through the 1990s. Importantly, as the Economic Policy Institute explains, "CEO pay does not reflect greater productivity of executives but rather the power of CEOs to extract concessions."[15] Thus, reducing CEO compensation would have no effect on productivity. Furthermore, a 2016 study of CEO compensation already found "little evidence to show a link between the large proportion of pay that such awards represent and long-term company stock performance."[16]

As Lawrence Mishel and Jessica Schieder of the Economic Policy Institute note, "From 1978 to 2015, inflation-adjusted CEO compensation increased 940.9 percent, 73 percent faster than stock market growth and substantially greater than the painfully slow 10.3 percent growth in a typical worker's annual compensation over the same period."[17]

The enormous compensation packages for chief executives (which also set standards for compensation of other executives down the corporate ladder) are now a common part of the work economy in the United States. Lawrence Mishel and Alyssa Davis explain that "half (52 percent) of employment and 58 percent of total payroll are in firms with more than 500 or more employees. Firms with at least 10,000 workers provide 27.9 percent of all employment and 31.4 percent of all payroll."[18] It is these big firms where the big CEO pay scales exist. The compensation isn't just a salary paycheck but also includes "bonus, stock and options valued at grant date, any deferred compensation, and other compensation (including benefits and perks)."[19]

Jobs Killed by CEO Compensation

Let's consider executive compensation, with the multiple of 29.9 times the compensation of the average worker. That's what the CEO-to-worker compensation ratio was in 1978, the year before the CEO-to-worker compensation ratio went out of whack. Let's apply this compensation ratio to the nation's best-compensated CEOs today. Anything beyond this salary rate (including bonuses, stock options, and other perks) we will call *excess compensation*.

We'll use the executive compensation data for 341 CEOs from the Equilar/Associated Press S&P 500 CEO Pay Study 2016. These 341 CEOs received a total of $4,298,990,626 in compensation, with an average of $12.6 million each. This amounts to more than $6,000 per hour (based on a 40-hour week, 52 weeks a year). Next, we need the median of the annual total compensation of all employees for each of the 341 executives' companies. Publicly traded corporations began reporting median employee income only in 2018, so it wasn't available for 2016. To simplify, we will use $44,510, the average income for US workers, based on the US Census Bureau's Current Population Survey.[20] Multiplying that average worker salary by 29.9 (the more reasonable 1978 ratio, before CEO salaries skyrocketed) generates an annual CEO compensation of $1,330,849.

Although $1.3 million a year may seem paltry to what CEOs have grown accustomed, it's still enough to make the national 1 percent of top earners (a household income of $389,436 required) and is even enough to break into the 1 percent of those who populate elite enclaves such as Jackson, Wyoming; Summit Park, Utah; and Stamford, Connecticut.[21] Moreover, this level of CEO compensation is closer to what people actually estimate CEOs earn. According to a 2016 Stanford Business School report, "The typical American believes a CEO earns $1 million in pay," when the average is actually $9.3 million.[22]

For illustrative purposes, let's set our fair CEO compensation at $1,330,849 and say that anything above this general 29.9 ratio counts as excess compensation. Collectively, if the 341 executives in the pay study earned $1,330,849 in total annual executive compensation, it would cost $453,819,509. Subtract that from their actual compensation ($4,298,990,626), and $3,845,171,117 in excess compensation remains. Divide that by $31,200 a year, what a $15-per-hour worker makes. The quotient is how many full-time $15-per-hour jobs could be created from the excess compensation of the CEOs. At this rate, CEO excess compensation equals 123,243 jobs. Or, framed in the same way that many in the news frame minimum-wage increases, *excess CEO compensation killed at least 123,243 jobs that could have been funded* (see table 7.1).

Of course, that's the compensation of just the 341 executives in the S&P 500 list of companies. The Standard & Poor's 500 is a stock market index list of 500 leading companies with a "large" market capitalization of $5.3 billion or more.[23] There are many more excessively compensated CEOs in other large-capitalization corporations beyond the top 500 and also in mid- and small-capitalization corporations. Moreover, there are the leaders of private equity firms and hedge funds, who make $12.6 million-a-year corporate CEOs look like chumps.

Table 7.1. Jobs killed by the super-rich

Source of capital	Jobs killed
Excess compensation	
S&P 500 Company Executives (n = 341)	123,243
Top Private Equity Executives (n = 8)	53,776
Top hedge fund managers (n = 25)	381,786
Stockpiled profits	
Corporate profits (publicly traded companies) held offshore	22,275,641
Personal (household) wealth held offshore	1,121,795
Total jobs killed	23,956,241

Note: Jobs killed are defined at 40 hours per week, $15 per hour, $31,200 per year. Excess compensation is defined as anything above $1,330,849, an amount derived by multiplying $44,510, the average income for American workers based on the U.S. Census Bureau's Current Population Survey, by 29.9 (the 1978 CEO-to-worker compensation ratio, before CEO salaries skyrocketed). Lost tax revenue from offshore corporate and personal wealth are estimated by Gabriel Zucman, *The Hidden Wealth of Nations: The Scourge of Tax Havens* (Chicago: University of Chicago Press, 2015).

Jobs Killed by Private Equity Compensation

Because private equity firms don't trade on public stock exchanges, they are able to operate with much less oversight and compensate themselves much more. As Felix Barber and Michael Goold wrote about private equity in the *Harvard Business Review* in 2007 (right before the economic crash), "The fundamental reason behind private equity's growth and high rates of return is something that has received little attention, perhaps because it's so obvious: the firms' standard practice of buying businesses and then, after steering them through a transition of rapid performance improvement, selling them."[24] The notion of "rapid performance improvement" may be a matter of one's perspective, as it might involve improving and growing a business or (as in the case of Hostess Brands, which I will analyze later) firing workers, evading pension obligations, and selling off a company piecemeal, resulting in high rates of return for only some parties. Leading private equity firms include Blackstone Group, Apollo Global Management, KKR & Co., Carlyle Group, Ares Management, and Fortress Investment Group.

We can do the same kind of excess compensation analysis with the eight leading private equity executives, who collectively paid themselves $1,692,813,160 in 2015, with an average compensation of $211.6 million for each of the eight that year.[25] Steven Schwarzman, chairman and CEO of Blackstone, led the list with $799.8 million in compensation in 2015.[26] If these eight executives were instead paid our hypothetical $1,330,849 a year, their excess compensation could fund 53,777 full-time jobs.[27] (See table 7.1.) Of course, we are considering the $1.7 billion in compensation of only *eight* private equity executives. As the *New York Times* explains, there are "thousands" of private equity firms, and its study was able to find executive compensation information for only the roughly half dozen of those firms that are publicly traded: "As such, a private equity executive not captured within this data may make even more."[28]

Jobs Killed by Hedge Fund Manager Compensation

Hedge fund managers sit on top of the pyramid of overly compensated executives. Hedge funds aim to maximize returns for wealthy investors, who usually meet qualification standards of a net worth of $1 million or more. The fund manager gets an annual fee plus a healthy percentage—usually 20 percent—of capital gains, often leading to enormous compensation. The highest-earning hedge fund manager in 2015 was Ken Griffin of Citadel LLC, who made $1.7 billion that year. As *Forbes* magazine noted, "Because they are private investment vehicles that only allow wealthy individuals to invest, hedge funds can pretty much do what they want as long as they disclose the strategy upfront to investors." The funds can invest in a number of financial commodities, including stocks, real estate, land, currencies, and derivatives.[29] Like private equity companies, they can also buy undervalued companies and improve them, or raid a company's assets and sell off parts for greater value.

After examining several cases of insider trading at hedge funds, Lynn Stout, the Paul Hastings Professor of Corporate and Securities Law at the UCLA School of Law, argued that "hedge funds are 'criminogenic' environments that encourage unethical behavior among the entire industry's traders."[30]

We can do the same kind of analysis with the top 25 hedge fund managers and traders, who collectively paid themselves $11,945,000,000 in 2015, with an average compensation of $477.8 million for each of the 25 that year.[31] The excess compensation of the top 25 hedge fund managers and traders equals 381,786 full-time jobs.[32] (See table 7.1.)

What could we do with excess compensation totaling about $17.4 billion (in one year!) from 341 CEOs, 8 top private equity executives, and 25 top hedge fund managers? We could fund 558,805 full-time jobs at $15 per hour. The jobs *not* created because the money instead went to 374 executives is significant; it's enough to create $15-per-hour full-time jobs for all of the unemployed in Ohio, Indiana, Wisconsin, Iowa, West Virginia, and the District of Columbia.[33]

Jobs Killed by Untaxed Wealth Held Offshore

In addition to excess executive compensation as a job killer, we can also consider those corporate profits that have been amassed in offshore accounts to avoid taxes. As Citizens for Tax Justice reported, "At the end of 2015, 303 Fortune 500 companies collectively held $2.4 trillion offshore."[34] These stockpiled profits—created in large part through the labor of hundreds of thousands of workers within those companies—deprive the nation of up to $695 billion in taxes. That money could be spent on a lot of things, including jobs. Apple led the list of corporations in 2015 (the last year data was available), with $200.1 billion in unrepatriated income, skipping out on $60.9 billion in US tax collections. The value of foregone tax revenue— $695 billion—equals almost 22.3 million full-time jobs that pay $15 per hour.[35] (See table 7.1.)

In addition to corporate fortunes, there are also personal fortunes sequestered offshore in tax havens, an enormous cache that does nothing to create jobs. In fact, in 2016 the International Consortium of Investigative Journalists unveiled an extensive investigation of a global tax haven in Panama. The ICIJ described the Panama Papers as "a global investigation into the sprawling, secretive industry of offshore that the world's rich and powerful use to hide assets and skirt rules by setting up front companies in far-flung jurisdictions."[36] The investigation, which focused on a huge leak of documents from Panamanian law firm Mossack Fonseca, led to the recovery of $110 million by a number of national governments in eight months after the first stories were published.[37] And that is the outcome of an investigation of just *one* of the world's shadowy offshore tax haven operations that service the ultra-wealthy. In 2017 the ICIJ revealed even more secret corporate and personal offshore holdings in the Paradise Papers.[38]

Economist Gabriel Zucman has done the difficult work of quantifying offshore wealth and tax evasion. He conservatively estimates that 8 percent of the world's financial personal (household) wealth—totaling $7.6 trillion— is held offshore in places such as the British Virgin Islands, the Cayman Islands, Bermuda, Switzerland, The Netherlands, Ireland, Luxembourg,

Singapore, Hong Kong, the Channel Islands, and Gibraltar.[39] The US portion of that is $1.2 trillion, representing a $35 billion per year loss in corporate tax revenue.[40] (See table 7.1.) That untaxed revenue would pay for about 1.1 million $15-per-hour full-time jobs. (An interesting point: Zucman estimates the offshore wealth of African countries to be 30 percent, and 50 percent for Russia and the oil-rich countries of the Middle East. In many of these oligarchies one can very clearly see the effects of disinvestment in the crumbling infrastructure and the impoverished or substandard living conditions of the workers and citizens.)[41]

The Super-Rich Who Kill Millions of Jobs

The data, again extremely conservative, regarding jobs killed by excess compensation of CEOs, top private equity executives, and top hedge fund managers, and regarding corporate and personal wealth evading taxes in offshore accounts, add up to 23,956,241: *nearly 24 million jobs at $31,200, or full-time at $15 per hour.*

To put this into context, civilian employment in the United States in May 2018 was an estimated 155.4 million. At an unemployment rate of 3.8 percent, 6.065 million were unemployed. Another 4.9 million people worked part-time for economic reasons; that is, they couldn't find a suitable full-time job. And another 1.5 million people were "marginally attached to the labor force," often meaning that they want to have a job but haven't been actively looking, or want a job but have become discouraged by the job market.[42] Including these other people provides the broadest definition of unemployment that the BLS calculates, and that stood at a 7.6 percent rate in May 2018: a total of 12,465,000 citizens out of work.

If we apply all of our excess executive compensation and untaxed offshore wealth to the problem, the problem of *all* unemployment is solved, and then some. (Other workers, including the 1.8 million people working at or below the federal minimum wage, could get the raises, too, and would be very deserving, based on their decades of increasing productivity.[43]) The US economy truly would be great again; it's simply a matter taking more of the capital created by the labor of workers and investing it back into the workers (who would become more able consumers, too) instead of permitting it to be taken and hoarded by a very tiny, elite group of capitalists.

A Taxing Problem

This exploration of an alternative world of elite "job killers" just scratches the surface. There are many other areas in which capital that could be used to create jobs remains with the wealthy. Untaxed or undertaxed personal wealth, particularly by the lower rates of taxation for capital gains and certain dividends, enables the wealthy to enjoy low tax rates and add to their stockpiles of money. (To be clear, *income* is the annual compensation received, usually for work; *wealth* is the capital accumulated over time and held in vehicles such as investments and real estate, which can also generate income.) In short, this means that people who derive all or a significant portion of their income from capital gains or dividends on investments pay a significantly lower taxation rate (15–20 percent) than the income tax rate that typical taxpayers might pay for earnings on their labor (25–28 percent). Billionaire Warren Buffett famously wrote in a 2011 *New York Times* op-ed column (titled "Stop Coddling the Super-Rich") that the federal and payroll tax he was required to pay in the previous year "was only 17.4 percent of my taxable income—and that's actually a lower percentage than was paid by any of the other 20 people in our office. Their tax burdens ranged from 33 percent to 41 percent and averaged 36 percent."[44]

In an analysis of 1950–2015, the independent, nonpartisan Tax Policy Center found that low capital gains taxes do not appear to spur economic growth, an argument often used to justify the policy. Moreover, in a study of capital gains rates in 2016, the Tax Policy Center estimated that "three-quarters of the tax benefit of the lower rates were received by taxpayers with incomes over $1 million," with an average tax saving of $146,050 for that group.[45] For taxpayers in the $40,000–$50,000 cash income level, lower capital gains taxes realize an average tax savings of $30.

Finally, the Tax Policy Center notes that the low tax rates on capital gains also harm potential for economic growth, again a problem of underfunding the public treasury and private development: "Low tax rates on capital gains also play a role in many tax shelters that undermine economic efficiency and growth. These shelters employ sophisticated financial techniques to convert ordinary income (such as wages and salaries) to capital gains. For top-bracket taxpayers, tax sheltering can save 20 cents per dollar of income sheltered. The resources that go into designing, implementing, and managing tax shelters could be used for productive purposes."[46] In other words, the low rates on capital gains are detrimental to the economy and mainly benefit economic elites. In more politically charged language, this favored tax policy of the wealthy is a job killer.

Excessive compensation and low taxation have led to the accumulation of extraordinary wealth by a just a few human beings. In fact, according to Oxfam, the international nongovernmental organization, just eight men have the same wealth as half of the world's population (six of the eight are Americans).[47] The *Forbes* 2016 list of the 400 richest Americans totals $2.4 trillion in wealth, which puts the value of those *just those 400 people* on an equal platform with the gross domestic product (GDP) of France, the world's sixth-largest economy.[48] (One had to have a minimum worth of $1.7 billion to make the *Forbes* 400 list.)[49] The top 20 wealthiest Americans on the *Forbes* 400 list hold more wealth than the bottom half of the US population. The entire *Forbes* 400 holds more wealth than the bottom 61 percent of Americans.[50] Or, put in a slightly different way, by 2017 just three men, Amazon founder Jeff Bezos (worth $95 billion), Microsoft cofounder Bill Gates ($90 billion), and Berkshire Hathaway CEO Warren Buffett ($79 billion), "have collectively more wealth than the 160 million poorest Americans, or half the population of the United States."[51]

That concentration in wealth in the United States (a phenomenon that is also happening globally, especially in other English-speaking countries, such as Great Britain, Canada, and Australia)[52] follows the same general time line of the increase in excessive executive compensation, explain economists Emmanuel Saez and Gabriel Zucman: "We find that wealth concentration was high in the beginning of the twentieth century, fell from 1929 to 1978, and has continuously increased since then. The top 0.1% wealth share has risen from 7% in 1978 to 22% in 2012, a level almost as high as in 1929."[53] Rising executive compensation and the rising concentration of wealth in the United States are not mere coincidence. Saez and Zucman identify the connection: "The increase in wealth inequality in recent decades is due to the upsurge of top incomes combined with an increase in saving rate inequality."

I should now note, because I'm sure some readers are thinking about it, that athletes, actors, and other celebrities may also be part of the compensation problem. But economist Thomas Piketty reminds us that "the vast majority (60 percent to 70 percent, depending on what definition one chooses) of the top 0.1 percent of the income hierarchy in 2000–2010 consists of top managers. By comparison, athletes, actors, and artists of all kinds make up less than 5 percent of this group. In this sense, the new US inequality has much more to do with the advent of 'supermanagers' than with 'superstars.'"[54]

Of course, if you were to ask Americans (and someone did) what they think the compensation for CEOs should be, it would be an amount that would knock CEOs off their "supermanager" perch. The 2016 Stanford Business School report on public perception of CEO compensation found "a majority of all political groups believe CEO pay should be capped in some manner, though Republicans are somewhat less likely to hold this opinion (52 percent) than Democrats (66 percent) or Independents (64 percent). Those who believe in capping CEO pay relative to the average worker would do so at a very low multiple. The typical American would limit CEO pay to no more than 6 times (17.6 times, based on average numbers) that of the average worker."[55]

There is some policy discussion in the United States and Europe of the idea of "maximum income." In one approach, executive compensation would be linked to workers' salaries with a relatively low pay ratio. For example, US Representative Keith Ellison (D-Minnesota) suggested a 20:1 executive-to-worker ratio.[56] In another approach, the government would set an income limit and tax any compensation above it at or near 100 percent. Although this might sound radical to some, the idea of maximum income was foundational for US federal income tax policy for most of the twentieth century. From 1936 to 1980, the top federal income tax bracket was never lower than 70 percent. In the 1950s, during the Eisenhower administration—when America was last great, Trump has said—the top tax bracket ranged from 91 to 92 percent. In 1980 it was 70 percent, but by the last year of the Reagan administration, 1988, the wealthiest paid a federal income tax rate of just 28 percent, accelerating income inequality as labor unions were simultaneously under attack.[57]

Thus, most Americans, regardless of political orientation, would like the CEO-to-worker compensation ratio to be closer to what existed in the 1960s (and lower than what I proposed above). Of course, Americans are not clear on how to resolve the problem, as the Stanford study notes. An indirect way to recover capital is through a financial transaction tax. One such tax, a .03 percent tax on all trades of stocks, bonds, and other financial products, was proposed in Congress in 2013. At that time, Congress's Joint Committee on Taxation estimated it would raise "$352 billion over 10 years."[58] Piketty proposes a progressive global tax on capital, which "would expose wealth to democratic scrutiny, which is a necessary condition for effective regulation of the banking system and international capital flows."[59]

But a solution is not in the offing when there's not even a discussion. Efforts to require disclosure of the worker-to-CEO pay ratio—important data for a national discussion of compensation—have been fraught with hand-wringing by members of the nation's financial elite, and they've fought to block it. In 2010, during the horrible aftermath of the Wall Street financial crisis, President Obama signed the Dodd-Frank Wall Street Reform and Consumer Protection Act, a significant overhaul of the nation's financial regulations. One of the act's requirements is pay-ratio disclosure for publicly traded companies. The goal of the rule, as the Securities and Exchange Commission (SEC) simply stated, is to "provide shareholders with information they can use to evaluate a CEO's compensation."[60]

However, Republicans, Wall Street, and business groups have disdained Dodd-Frank and its provisions from the start. US Representative Jed Hensarling (R-Texas), as chair of the US House of Representatives Financial Services Committee, introduced the Financial CHOICE Act (the CHOICE part stands for Creating Hope and Opportunity for Investors, Consumers and Entrepreneurs). The act unravels the Dodd-Frank provisions, including the relatively minor requirement for pay-ratio disclosure. Amazingly, the House Financial Services Committee proposal for the Financial CHOICE Act argues that the pay-ratio disclosure is (I'm not kidding) a *job killer*: "By hindering the ability of U.S. businesses to grow, compete, and create jobs, the pay ratio rule will directly undermine the SEC's mandate to ensure efficient capital markets and facilitate capital formation."[61] The House of Representatives passed the Financial CHOICE Act in 2017. But by mid-2018, the Senate had not approved it, and the first group of pay-ratio reports under the SEC rule was disclosed in 2018.

Pay-ratio reporting could help to spur a long-overdue, data-informed conversation about CEO compensation as it relates to worker compensation and rising inequality in the United States. For example, the *New York Times* used the data to develop what it called the Marx Ratio, which "captures the relationship between a company's profits—the return to capital, on a per-employee basis—and how much its median employee is compensated, a rough proxy for the return to labor. Companies with high Marx Ratios offer particularly strong rewards to their shareholders relative to workers. . . . Numbers below 1 signal the reverse: a more favorable return to labor."[62] We will see if the *Times* makes the Marx Ratio a regular feature of its coverage, particularly in any stories on executive or worker compensation.

A Labor Story for the United States: The Media Tell the Wrong Story

Part of the problem of reporting news about executive compensation and how workers are being left behind in the economy is finding the situation that has all the elements of a good story. In 2012, that story arrived. A private equity firm had bought a high-profile company, grossly mismanaged it for years, declared bankruptcy, and demanded even more concessions from union workers. The company was nationwide, with 33 production facilities, 565 distribution centers, 570 outlet stores, and 18,500 jobs.

What sent most news media astray is that the company was Hostess Brands, which happened to make cakey consumer confections, including Twinkies, Ding Dongs, Ho Hos, Yodels (the East Coast version of Ho Hos), and Sno Balls. Guess what story most news organizations wanted to serve to their upscale readers and viewers?

Anji Phillips of Bradley University and I analyzed national news media coverage of the 2012 Hostess Brands shutdown. We were both familiar with the Hostess story and its impact: Anji had a Hostess bakery in her hometown of Peoria, Illinois, and my hometown of Cedar Falls/Waterloo, Iowa, had a Hostess bakery plus an outlet store.[63]

Hostess Brands filed for Chapter 11 bankruptcy for its second time in January 2012 and announced its closing in November of that year. This was not a situation of hypothetical job killing; it was the real thing. Unfortunately, we found that the news consistently used narrative frames that prioritized the Hostess management's blaming of unions for the company's shutdown (despite easy-to-find evidence of years of corporate mismanagement) and reporters' own explicit nostalgia for Twinkies and other Hostess treats, sharing their exaggerated consumer pain with their readers and viewers, which far overshadowed discussion of the economic conditions of the company that led to the closing.

Although the management of Hostess consistently blamed the company's labor unions, chiefly the Teamsters Union and the Bakery, Confectionery, Tobacco Workers and Grain Millers' International Union (BCTGM), the unions had already made "substantial concessions," and "annual labor cost savings to the company were about $110 million; thousands of union members lost their jobs," about 10,000 of them since the first bankruptcy filing in 2004.[64]

A private equity company, Ripplewood, gained control of the company during the first bankruptcy by investing millions of dollars, and two hedge funds, Silver Point and Monarch, lent millions more to the company (although the exact amount is private information). As *Fortune* noted, "Both are hedge funds that specialize in investing in distressed companies—whether you call them saviors or vultures depends on whether you're getting fed or getting eaten."[65] When Hostess Brands announced its closing in 2012, CEO Gregory

F. Rayburn wrote that "the BCTGM leadership chose not to negotiate a new labor contract and instead, when presented with a final offer, launched a campaign to cripple the Company's operations and force it to liquidate."[66] Yet, given all of the concessions made by the union, the company's own dismal management record deserved scrutiny: six CEOS in its final decade, no treasury department to manage financial risk, two bankruptcies, and few product innovations.

Michael Hiltzik of the *Los Angeles Times*, one of the best journalists covering the story, argued that Hostess's pension obligations became daunting only because Hostess executives raided the assets and ignored adequately funding them: "The $989 million in pension liabilities Hostess ended up owing various union funds, according to its bankruptcy filing, didn't accumulate in secret, like termite damage. It accrued because Hostess and its sister bakeries judged their retirement obligations to be relatively unimportant in the grand scheme of things. Now that the bill has come due, Hostess blames the workers for demanding what they were promised."[67]

One might expect news organizations to have delved into the very checkered managerial history of Hostess, with leveraged buyouts, a slew of acquisitions, a revolving door to the CEO suite, union concessions, underfunded pensions, two bankruptcies, hedge fund investments, lax accounting, and poor product development. In many ways, Hostess Brands could have been a story that exemplified the excesses and shortcomings of US business over the past several decades, with the added advantage of being a company that most Americans have had some interaction with. Yet the main interpretive frame of the closing of Hostess, and the loss of 18,500 jobs, was primarily a *consumer* story.[68]

From a journalistic perspective, the Hostess story has a great "hook" to bring the audience into a business and labor story. Hostess manufactured a number of products—including spongy snacks and Wonder Bread—that had been familiar consumer products for most of the twentieth century. These familiar processed food products could all serve as hooks to make a labor story immediately relevant to viewers and listeners.

Yet the stories rarely got past the consumer hook. Not unlike many of Hostess's own products, the stories were all sugary, sweet, and empty of substance. The main ingredient of the consumer frame was nostalgia, particularly for Twinkies, which were mentioned by name in 89 percent of the stories. Sixty-seven percent of the stories had some element of consumer nostalgia for Twinkies and Hostess goods. In these cases the reporter or anchor often makes a personal lament or exhortation about Twinkies or

Hostess food in general (e.g., "an end of an era," "say it ain't so," "I remember eating them," "legendary food item," "we're sorry to say," "I love the Twinkies," "Go grab a golden cake while you still can," etc.).

After Hostess Brands announced its bankruptcy filing, news personalities on Fox News' *The Five* (Kimberly Guilfoyle, Eric Bolling, Dana Perino, Bob Beckel, and Greg Gutfeld) discussed the bankruptcy on January 12, 2012. Their conversation lacked the usual political sanctimony for the "forgotten Americans" as they angled to connect with upscale, nostalgic consumers:

> **PERINO:** Yesterday, we had a story about Hostess Brands, which was going bankrupt. And we're all very sad. We sent a young producer, Christa, out and she went all over New York City and couldn't find a Twinkie or a Ho Ho anywhere.
>
> Last night, I went to see (unintelligible) in my hood and look what I found? I got some Ho Hos for Bob. I got Twinkie over. Ho Ho? OK. Twinkie.
>
> **BECKEL:** Anybody out there, send them to me will you because I have to close this down.
>
> **BOLLING:** I don't want a Twinkie. You may want that.
>
> **GUTFELD:** This is the greatest—
>
> **PERINO:** This is like a Bill Schultz (unintelligible)—
>
> **BECKEL:** Be careful with those things, man. Don't eat Twinkies.
>
> **GUILFOYLE:** I better eat this soon. It's only good until February 3rd, which is remarkable.
>
> **PERINO:** The whole shelf was depleted.
>
> **BECKEL:** You know what is in this? This is better than bird droppings.

Bob Beckel's final comment was in reference to the previous story discussion, which involved bird droppings. The following week, the gang from *The Five* put Twinkies in a blender with milk. Greg Gutfeld mused, "When I heard they were liquidating Hostess, I was thinking 'liquidating Twinkies—why haven't I thought of that?'" Bob Beckel chugged a whole glass of Twinkie shake, to everyone's giggles.[69] The idea of uttering "Twinkies," "Ho Hos," or "Ding Dongs" made news anchors lapse into sophomoric humor and complete indifference to the gravity of a situation in which 18,500 people might lose their jobs.

At *CBS Evening News* on November 19, 2012, the usually decorous anchor Scott Pelley announced that "Hostess Brands went into bankruptcy court today to present its plan for going out of business, but the judge had a different idea. He asked Hostess and its striking bakers to take their dispute to mediation to save the company. We're telling you this tonight because the folks here in the newsroom just love to hear me remind you that Hostess makes Twinkies, Ho Hos, and Ding Dongs."

The news media were far more likely (in 61.5 percent of all stories) to attribute the closing to the workers and union, with all other reasons getting 13.2 percent or less (see figure 7.1). Despite multiple communications and postings by the BCTGM through the AFL-CIO's website, few news reports moved beyond the Hostess Brands/consumer position of Twinkie nostalgia and the associated resentment toward the union that apparently halted its production.[70]

The consumer framing of labor news always ends up badly for labor unions, as labor's position gets lost in the emphasis on consumers. For example, even though Hostess workers' labor unions made concessions worth $110 million a year and lost 10,000 jobs in the first bankruptcy of 2004–2009, more than 60 percent of the 2012 news stories blamed the union for the Hostess closing. From the news media framing of the story, only the union's

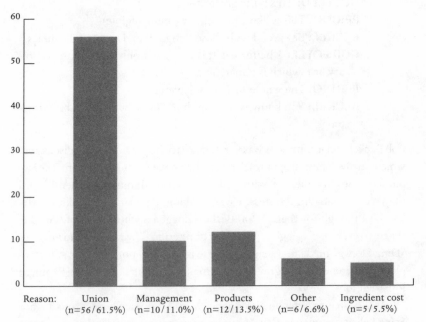

Figure 7.1. Reasons given in reports by seven US radio and television news organizations for the closing of Hostess Brands, 2012; not all stories provided reasons.

resistance to more contract concessions stood between consumers and a continuing supply of Twinkies, Ding Dongs, and Ho Hos.

Of course, there were plenty of happy news stories when Twinkies came back under new management in 2013. CNN's Web story directly addressed consumers: "Good news Twinkies fans, your beloved snack is due back on shelves on July 15."[71]

The Teacher Strike Movement: Carrying the Media with It

In spring 2018 a labor news story emerged that challenged the stereotypical notion of a "worker." These public employees were public school teachers, well-educated, many with graduate degrees. Women—77 percent of public school teachers are women—were the main participants and leaders of the strikes.[72] And then there was the location: the strikes were happening in mostly "red" states in which the majority voted for Trump in 2016: West Virginia, Oklahoma, Kentucky, Arizona, Colorado (the exception), and North Carolina.[73]

The news coverage of the teacher strikes was extensive. The visual image of protesting teachers, numbering in the tens of thousands in each state, often wearing "Red for Ed" shirts, was hard to ignore. Yet the coverage revealed that it had been a long time since public teachers—the most *public* of public workers—have had a voice in the news. In a report on teaching conditions for eleven representative teachers around the country, the *New York Times* documented schools with "25-year-old textbooks and holes in the ceiling" and teachers who annually pay from $300 to $2,000 out of their own pocket to provide supplies to students. The story was eye-opening yet begged a question: why did it take so long for this to be reported? The desire for teachers to tell their story seemed to be pent up. As the *Times* story explained, "We invited America's public school educators to show us the conditions that a decade of budget cuts has wrought in their schools. We heard from 4,200 teachers."

The framing for stories in the upscale news media seemed to presume a disconnect with the lives of the nation's public school teachers and the possibility that people who have master's degrees could be in a precarious financial position. "Public Servants Are Losing Their Foothold in the Middle Class," a *New York Times* headline said.[74] The theme was echoed in the headline in the *New Yorker*: "Can Arizona's Teachers Still Consider Themselves Middle Class?" E. Tammy Kim, who interviewed high school teachers Mitch and Jennie Askew for her report from Arizona for the *New Yorker*, revealed an America where educational accomplishment might not count for much: "Today teachers earn seventeen per cent less than comparably educated workers in other professions. Perhaps on account of their advanced degrees, the Askews, like most teachers I spoke with, identify as workers but not as working-class. 'There are people who are struggling more than we are,' Mitch was careful to say. The distinction, though, seems increasingly thin."[75]

Most of the mainstream news media coverage didn't put the spring 2018 strikes in the context of what happened with earlier strikes, including the successful Chicago teachers strike of 2012, in which 26,000 unionized teachers struck against the city and Democratic Mayor Rahm Emanuel over the direction of public education.[76]

Labor reporter Mike Elk noticed the lack of full-time labor reporters in the South: "Perhaps that explains why so much of the media has initially seemed shocked by the strikes in southern states such as Oklahoma, Kentucky, and West Virginia." Still, Elk, who has spent years covering labor, sees a larger movement: "Something big is happening in America—and it's finally carrying the media with it."[77]

Elk suggests that the bottom-up organizing of journalists themselves might help to reinvigorate labor reporting. Like many of the nation's public school teachers, many journalists are poorly paid and have to work second or third jobs just to sustain themselves. In response to years of job insecurity, journalists recently formed unions at the *Los Angeles Times* and the *Chicago Tribune*, two of the most virulently antiunion newspapers of the twentieth century.[78] Staff at other newspapers have worked to form unions as well, including the *Missoula* (Mont.) *Independent*, the *Casper* (Wyo.) *Star-Tribune*, the *Omaha World-Herald*, the *Southern Illinoisan*, the *Lakeland* (Fla.) *Ledger*, and the *Sarasota* (Fla.) *Herald-Tribune*, plus at the *New Yorker* and *Fast Company*.[79] A number of newsrooms at digital news outlets have also unionized, including *HuffPost*, *The Root*, *Salon*, *Slate*, *Vice*, *MTV News*, *ThinkProgress*, *The Guardian US*, *Jacobin*, *The Intercept*, and *Talking Points Memo*.[80] In 2017 a group including the Chicago Federation of Labor purchased the *Chicago Sun-Times*, promising to make it "a publication that tells stories of the working class and acts as a voice of the people."[81] These are all positive developments for giving a voice to the working class. But they won't make a big difference unless media organizations are willing, persuaded, or pushed to refocus their business model toward a mass audience of workers and to cover news for that entire audience.

A number of news organization owners remain unyielding, and many do not even seem to be focused on journalism at all. The *Lakeland Ledger* and the

Sarasota Herald-Tribune have not yet signed a contract with the owner (the private equity–owned GateHouse) after two years, and billionaire owner Joe Ricketts quickly shut down New York City local news sites *DNAinfo* and *Gothamist* after their staffs voted to join a union.[82] A month earlier, Ricketts (founder of TD Ameritrade and owner of the Chicago Cubs with his family) wrote on his blog that "unions promote a corrosive us-against-them dynamic that destroys the esprit de corps businesses need to succeed. And that corrosive dynamic makes no sense in my mind where an entrepreneur is staking his capital on a business that is providing jobs and promoting innovation."[83] Therefore, Ricketts noncorrosively killed the jobs of 115 people.

Labor Unions Lose Two Countervailing Forces: The Government and Journalism

Since 1935, it has been a legal right of US workers to organize themselves for the purposes of collectively bargaining with their employers over "wages, hours, and other terms and conditions of employment." US workers literally fought for decades—sometimes with the loss of life—to gain the kinds of protections provided by the National Labor Relations Act of 1935 (also called the Wagner Act, after its Senate sponsor).

The value of the Wagner Act was that the federal government threw some of its weight behind the worker in order to balance economic power in the United States. Economist John Kenneth Galbraith called it "countervailing power." In 1956 he wrote that "the support of countervailing power has become in modern times perhaps the major domestic peacetime function of the federal government. Labor sought and received it in the protection and assistance which the Wagner Act provided to union organization. Farmers sought and received it in the form of federal price supports to their markets—a direct subsidy of market power. Unorganized workers have sought and received it in the form of minimum wage legislation."[84]

But just as immediately, there was a fight against the right of workers to collectively organize. There was less brute force of Pinkerton guards pummeling workers, and more antilabor consultants and legalistic maneuvers, each picking away at the NLRA's provisions. And there were efforts to deplete some of the government's countervailing power, first with the Taft-Hartley Act in 1947 (passed by the first Congress with a Republican majority since the Wagner Act was enacted). The laws prohibited most secondary strikes and slowdowns, and permitted states to adopt the badly named "right-to-work" laws, which enable workers to enjoy the benefits of a union contract without having to pay the union dues. Twenty-seven states now have such laws. (Missouri voters rejected their state's year-old right-to-work law in 2018.) Jimmy Carter's weak support for pro-union legislation in the late 1970s and Ronald Reagan's firing of PATCO workers in 1981 made it clear that the federal government could no longer be a reliable countervailing power between workers and businesses.

Fortunately, the press—working in its traditional role as the Fourth Estate—is a countervailing power in US culture, with the weight of the First Amendment. But although journalism continues its heavy public affairs coverage of government and also chronicles (usually not critically) business, its commitment to stories about labor—US workers—is lightweight.

When it was a countervailing force for workers, journalism chronicled the rise of labor and labor unions and their role in the economy for most of the twentieth century. The news was not always fair, but the stories of labor and the working class were a significant part of the news, particularly in newspapers, the leading information medium. The news made workers and their lives visible. In the final third of the twentieth century, newspapers began to shift away from concerns of the working class and, correspondingly, their labor unions. The lifestyle-oriented workplace column sprouted, along with an emphasis on personal finance stories. The labor beat withered. Workers were becoming invisible in the mediated public sphere.

US corporations may have increased their profits by transferring the earnings of worker productivity into their own bank accounts, but they have done a grave disservice to the economy and the political culture. Today, capital has no equal counterbalancing force in the government or journalism. The increasing exclusion of labor unions and workers from the public sphere since the late twentieth century has left them adrift. Simply put, left with little power in an economy rife with inequality, where does one go, and what does one do?

Journalism's Democratic Function

Socioeconomic class is complicated in the United States.

Women and people of color have long been lesser citizens of working life. Below-normal wages, glass ceilings, discrimination, racism, sexism, and unspoken (until just recently) instances of sexual assault and harassment have all been indicators of their lower workplace status.

Through most of the twentieth century, white men were at the top of the heap, with leadership positions, preferential hiring, and easy access to social networks. For white men, especially, the effects of economic inequality hit harder because they haven't been familiar with it and did not expect to be.

If Americans sense that their voices aren't being heard, they may drop out. They may protest, and they may find new allies. Sometimes the voiceless have organized to lead some of America's best moments to expand democracy: abolitionism and the end of slavery, women's suffrage, the civil rights movement, the gay rights movement. Sometimes the voiceless have realigned with ugly currents in US culture and participated in some of the country's worst moments: the Know Nothing Party, the Ku Klux Klan, segregationists, and today's nationalists and white supremacists.

Splintering worker solidarity has long been both a business and a political strategy. What is different in the past fifty years is that it has also been a media strategy. The mainstream news media abandoned the working-class audience. The conservative media took white males, the largest audience of the working class and one already primed by conservative politicians in the 1970s and 1980s, and developed news and commentary to incite and galvanize their grievances. The conservative media became a political institution "which holds considerable and increasing power within the Republican Party" and prioritizes the business point of view.[85] The conservative media is not a countervailing force but another heavy hand in the corner that already packs plenty of power, with business, a major political party, and (from 2016 to 2018) all the branches of the US federal government.

In their prescient 1972 book, *The Hidden Injuries of Class,* Richard Sennett and Jonathan Cobb captured the class divide in their interviews with working-class people in Boston.[86] I've argued earlier in this book for a more expansive view of class, along the lines of the definition provided by economist Michael Zweig: "The working class is made up of people who, when they go to work or when they act as citizens, have comparatively little power or authority."[87] Yet Sennett and Cobb found in their discussions a class inflection point based on education and culture: "People felt that an educated, upper-middle-class person was in the position to judge them, and that the judgment rendered would be that working-class people could not be respected as equals. . . . It might seem, then, that, to borrow a phrase from the most class-conscious politician of our time [Republican Vice President Spiro Agnew], the emotional impact of the class difference here is a matter of 'impudent snobbery,' of shaming, of putdown."[88] These are the same kinds of dismissive charges about the "elite" mainstream media that still come from the Republican Party and, now, conservative media.

Cobb, in an afterword to the book, argued that standards of class, which create feelings of indignity, are set by those in power in society. But he envisions an alternative to a class-based hierarchy: instead of "having 'culture' or not having it, of having 'ability' or not having it," as a class-based social order dictates, we could just appreciate "having different cultures, different values, different developments, different abilities."

Mainstream journalism in the late 1960s could not have possibly suspected exactly where their new business focus on the *right kind* of readers, those who were "well to do," "affluent moderns," and "influentials," would lead (except for the anticipated profits), but it is unfortunate that publishers did not more fully consider what a journalism for only "the upper half" would do to journalism's democratic function.

It may well be that America is in for a reckoning on class. White, working-class males—a group whose political proclivities famously made writer Thomas Frank ask *What's the Matter with Kansas?*—may find that the conservative media, the Republican Party, and corporate overlords really have no interest in helping them more than any other group. The right has stoked their pride and fears because they need their attention for advertisers, their votes every few years, and their misplaced faith that they don't need a labor union at work.

Giving Workers a Voice Again

Many mainstream journalists have been connected to the world of the upscale audience for so long that they are blinded to human experiences beyond their gated community. In a February 2017 opinion piece titled "This Century Is Broken," *New York Times* columnist David Brooks opens by speaking directly to his audience: "Most of us came of age in the last half of the twentieth century and had our perceptions of 'normal' formed in that era. It was, all things considered, an unusually happy period. No world wars, no Great Depressions, fewer civil wars, fewer plagues."[89] In this unusually happy period, apparently no one in Brooks's idea of "us" endured the old or new Jim Crow, lived through sexual harassment or discrimination, died from AIDS, fought in Vietnam or the Gulf wars, got downsized by a private equity firm, lost a pension, or had their union destroyed by lockout or a plant closing. After identifying the "us" of his readers, Brooks moves on to "them": the "American workers." But one can see by his evidence that he really means "men aged 25 to 55 looking for work" or "who have dropped out of the labor force." More specifically, he means the "fifty-seven percent of white males who have dropped out of the labor force" and now "get by on some form of government disability check," and the others who "take pain medication on a daily basis." Brooks, who knows the white, middle-aged, male US worker through the data he cites, sums up: "This is no way for our fellow citizens to live."

Brooks does three things that have represented common sense in US politics and journalism for years: (1) From the "us" of his readers (people who are above the collateral damage of the economy), he splits off the working class as the "them" of his story and kindly pities them as "our fellow citizens." (2) In the great tradition of conservative politicians and journalistic tropes, he identifies only middle-aged white men as US workers and victims of this economy. The absence of women and people of color from the category "American worker" betrays a sexism and racism so commonsense, subtle, and ingrained that it is just as "normal" as the Reagan-era ideologies and policies of Brooks's own coming of age. (3) The complete absence of labor unions from Brooks's narrative cleanly excises the essential contributions that labor unions made to the "happy period" of the second half of the twentieth century. Instead, Brooks participates in the routine practice of making labor unions invisible, for that's not his reading audience anyway.

Brooks identifies the problem of declining growth, but (citing economist Tyler Cowen's book *The Complacent Class*) he blames Americans for being less adventurous, less entrepreneurial, and less innovative as the problem. Then he asks, amazingly, "But where is the social movement that is thinking about the fundamentals of this century's bad start and envisions an alternate path? Who has a compelling plan to boost economic growth?"[90] Because Brooks envisions any solution emerging from highly placed technocrats such as him (and the two conservative economists he cites), he can't imagine any ideas coming from people below him in the class hierarchy. He said as much in October 2011, in his put-down of the Occupy Wall Street movement, describing the "small thinkers" and "milquetoast radicals." In the same article, he identified his choice to lead the economy: "Moderates in suits are much more radical than the pierced anarchists camping out on Wall Street or the Tea Party-types."

Mainstream journalism needs to rethink its conception of audience and to correct its error a half-century ago in deciding to concentrate "on the upper half of the market" and ignore "the less desirable customers."[91]

If journalism is essential to democracy, it should be part of the process: not just selecting a small, desirable audience but also making a public audience out of the entire community, state, and/or nation. Those who worry on the business side would be advised to recall the historically high rates of newspaper readership for those on the lower end of the income spectrum.

Certainly, the news industry is far different from what it was fifty years ago. In recent years, print journalism in particular has taken a hit in its ranks.[92] Beyond a spate of hiring of new reporters at places such as the Jeff Bezos–owned *Washington Post* and the *Los Angeles Times* under the new ownership of Patrick Soon-Shiong, it is certain that newspapers have had serious economic pressures to deal with in the past two decades, including the loss of most classified ads (to Craigslist), the loss of many display ads (to the Internet and the rise of online shopping), their own self-inflicted wounds (taking on far too much debt in mergers), and now a group of private equity firms—including Alden Capital, GateHouse, Citadel, Digital First Media, and Fortress—that are snatching up US newspapers, cutting jobs and journalism, and wringing every last bit of value out of them.[93] Digital start-ups are encouraging but don't come close to filling the gap. According to Alex T. Williams in the *Columbia Journalism Review*, "The number of journalists at digital native publishers has more than tripled [from 2005 to 2015]," but that growth has now leveled off. Moreover, the digital growth "pales in comparison to the number of journalists laid off in the newspaper industry."[94]

Yet newspapers make staff decisions that shape their editorial coverage, and by the looks of newsrooms, newspapers are still in the business of targeting upscale readers, as they began to do in the late 1960s. For example, in 2017:

- The *San Diego Union-Tribune* had six reporters at its business desk (where the labor/workplace beat is most often located) covering technology, real estate, energy, growth and development, e-commerce and digital lifestyle, and tourism and restaurants.
- The *Denver Post* had business reporters assigned to mountains and tourism, technology, commercial real estate, and economy/residential real estate.
- The *Columbus Dispatch* in Ohio had five business reporters covering manufacturing and energy; food and agriculture; retail and technology; aviation, development, and tourism/conventions; banking and insurance; and economics.
- The *Milwaukee Journal Sentinel* had six full-time business reporters, with assignments in manufacturing, motorcycles, and agriculture;

health care and health policy; commercial real estate and development; banking and insurance; retail; and economics.

Of course, as I noted in chapter 1, there are a few newspapers, magazines, and digital news organizations that cover labor and the workplace. Sometimes the beat exists because there is a professional commitment to covering labor or to providing the most comprehensive information to the "most well educated" readers. And some news organizations do outstanding investigative stories outside of a labor/workplace beat that covers those issues. For example, Alexandra Berzon, then a twenty-nine-year-old business reporter for the *Las Vegas Sun* (now a reporter for the *Wall Street Journal*), led a series of reports that won a 2009 Pulitzer Prize in Public Service for revealing "the high death rate among construction workers on the Las Vegas Strip amid lax enforcement of regulations."[95] In 2012 a *New York Times* team investigated the iEconomy, featuring Apple's corporate success built on low-paid outsourced electronics workers in China and low-paid retail employees in glossy stores in the United States.[96] The nine-part series won a Pulitzer Prize in 2013 for explanatory reporting and resulted in several changes in how Apple does its business.[97] In 2017 the *Des Moines Register* revealed the hazardous conditions for workers at the TPI Composites facility in Newton, which makes the enormous blades for giant wind turbines in North America. The factory is a favorite site for visiting politicians, demonstrating the "new economy" of wind energy after appliance maker Maytag left the town in 2008. The *Register* explained that several workers who were required to crawl inside the blades to apply resin are suing the company, alleging that they were fired after being injured by the resin chemicals.[98]

Yet across the nation and in nearly every city and town, no consistent beat covers labor or workplace issues. The occasional stories that do appear lack any sense of continuity or content (Pulitzer Prize–level multipart series investigations are wonderful, but a rare breed). It's not unlike having the sports pages cover the Super Bowl but failing to report the entire season's worth of games leading up to it. How could one appreciate the Super Bowl story's magnitude and significance if there is no understanding of how it relates to what happened during the season and previous years? If only labor and workplace issues were covered with the same scrutiny (an underinflated football?) and comprehensiveness (statistics, salaries, injuries, long-term threats of concussions, and public subsidies to enrich private owners) as professional football.[99]

Unions, the one countervailing power that represents US workers, are not perfect. Their memberships long practiced race and sex discrimination, sometimes in concert with their employers.[100] Since the 1970s, labor unions made significant gains in engaging women and people of color.[101] These days, labor unions do far better than most organizations in representing and championing the diversity of the working class. The facts of labor union membership today defy the common stereotype of the white, male, blue-collar factory employee with a high school education, according to the Economic Policy Institute:

- About two-thirds (65.4 percent) of workers age 18 to 64 and covered by a union contract are women and/or people of color.
- Almost half (46.3 percent) are women.
- More than a third (35.8 percent) are black, Hispanic, Asian, or other nonwhite workers.
- More than half (54.5 percent) of workers age 18 to 64 and covered by a union contract have an associate degree or more education.
- Two out of five (42.4 percent) have a bachelor's degree or more education.

Where union members work defies the stereotype as well:

- Nearly two in five workers (39.8 percent) age 18 to 64 and covered by a union contract work in education or health services.
- One in seven workers (13.9 percent) covered by a union contract work in public administration.
- One in eight workers (12.2 percent) covered by a union contract work in transportation and utilities.
- One in 11 workers (9.1 percent) covered by a union contract work in manufacturing.[102]

The historical effectiveness of unions is hard to deny. Unions have had an enormously positive impact in reducing inequality in the United States since the 1930s. A paper for the National Bureau of Economic Research in 2018 concluded that "when unions expand, whether at the national or the state level, they tend to draw in unskilled workers and raise their relative wages, with significant impacts on inequality."[103]

Yet the question remains: how do Americans learn about the institution of labor unions and the state of the working class (the entire working class, not just the conservative media version of it)? Media critic Michael Massing considered part of the question on the eve of Trump's inauguration in a piece for the *Nation* titled "How to Do Journalism in Trump's America." Massing noted *New York Times* executive editor Dean Baquet's comments to NPR's *Fresh Air* host Terri Gross in December 2016 on how his newspaper would need to improve its coverage: "I want to make sure that we are much more creative about beats out in the country so that we understand the anger and disconnectedness that people feel."[104] Massing's suggestion? "Here's a possible approach: Pry away a journalist from each of the paper's glossy high-end sections—Styles, Travel, Food, Real Estate, Arts & Leisure, and *T* magazine—and reassign them to cover neglected parts of America." For creative beats, Massing suggested "the Bible Belt," "a blue-collar beat," "a small business beat," "a roving culture beat" that concentrates "on how culture—broadly defined—is consumed in and perceived by grassroots communities," and finally a "poverty beat." I agree with Massing, although he goes stereotypical with the "blue-collar beat," defining it as "the world of factory workers, carpenters, plumbers, firefighters, and police officers."[105] A broader labor or "work" beat would avoid the trope that the working class is all white men in stereotypically "male" jobs. (Here is where we would do well to remember the nation's diverse corps of schoolteachers and to return to Baquet's idea that one does not need to be white, male, and working in a particular job to feel "anger or disconnectedness.")

It will not matter if the *New York Times,* or any other news organization, gets the beat right without getting the tone right. Journalism should report the truth. But journalism should also be concerned about to whom they are telling the story. At about the same time that Dean Baquet talked to Terri Gross about how to improve the *Times'* coverage of Trump's America, the *Times'* editorial board (which represents "the voice of the board, its editor and the publisher") wrote a piece lamenting a divided nation that could not even agree on even the plainest of facts.[106]

The editorial noted a Trump supporter from North Carolina who followed phony conservative stories online. But this man nevertheless "missed the days when Walter Cronkite delivered the news to the nation."[107] Cronkite anchored the *CBS Evening News* from 1962 to 1981 and was the nation's leading newscaster at a time when there were just three major television networks, newspapers were mostly still covering a broad audience, national cable TV was in its infancy, and the Internet as a mass medium had not yet been invented. The *Times* editorial pointed out that the man from North Carolina was "not alone; it was different then. Americans knew that whatever they were hearing on the news, their neighbors were hearing, too. Cable TV fractured that shared experience, and then social media made it easier for Americans to curl up in cozy, angry or self-righteous cocoons."

Yet the *New York Times* leaves out its own complicity and that of nearly every other newspaper and news organization. It was different then because Walter Cronkite was talking to a mass audience that included all types of people, not a select group of high-earning, highly educated, upscale people. The loss of that common voice wasn't a predetermined outcome caused by cable TV or social media. It was a choice made by nearly every news organization and one that affected the people whom the news addressed and what stories they were told. If the mainstream news media want to talk to workers, they need to find them, give them a voice, and include them in their audience.

Acknowledgments

This project started with research on the history of labor beat reporters. In the final weeks of my work on the manuscript, we lost one of America's great labor reporters, William Serrin, who wrote for the *Detroit Free Press* and later covered the labor beat for the *New York Times* from 1979 to 1986. I had the pleasure to talk with him a few times, and his stories were invaluable. When I last talked to him in 2017, a year before he died, he said two things that I wish all news media professionals could keep in mind about covering workers: "There's a wealth of stories out there if you get out of the newsroom and talk to them," and "You can sell a lot of papers writing about labor."

There are a number of other journalists I've communicated with over the years regarding this research who have been inspirational and encouraging, including David Moberg, Steven Greenhouse, Stephen Franklin, Connie Schultz, Sarah Jaffe, E. Tammy Kim, Claudia Rowe, Will Yong, Mike Elk, Joan Walsh, David Uberti, Harold Meyerson, Laura Belin, Tom Cullen, and Susan Faludi. The late David Carr ranks as one of the most riveting people I've ever talked to.

My collaborations with Peter Dreier and Anji Phillips have been immensely rewarding and productive, and helped to expand the scope of this book. Peter is indefatigable, and I value his energy in fighting for social justice. Richard Campbell of Miami University provided support from the very beginning of this project, and I appreciate his encouragement and friendship. Jefferson Cowie's work and comments have been extremely valuable in rethinking the labor movement, the 1970s, and Bill O'Reilly. Many others helped with formative comments (even when they might not have been aware of doing so), including Francesco Nespoli, Jim Tobin, Anita Fabos, Robert McChesney, Bonnie Brennan, Steve Macek, Catherine McKercher, Vincent Mosco, Jimmie Reeves, John E. Richardson, and David Rolf.

At the University of Northern Iowa (UNI), thanks go out for the support of John Fritch, Paul Siddens, Catherine Palczewski, Danielle McGeough, Ryan McGeough, Kyle Rudick, Tom Hall, Anelia Dimitrova, Chris Ogbondah, Wally Hettle, Lou Fenech, Barbara Cutter, and Brian Roberts.

My appreciation to Tony Carobine, president of the American Postal Workers Union and National Postal Press Association; Lance Coles, of the Iowa Federation of Labor, AFL-CIO; and Jennifer Sherer and Robin Clark-Bennett of the University of Iowa Labor Center; who all have given me opportunities to talk with workers from across the state and country.

Becky Hawbaker, Carissa Froyum, and Joe Gorton, leaders and fellow workers at United Faculty, UNI's faculty labor union, are extraordinary human beings and give generously of their time to improve university employment conditions, the welfare of our students, and the viability of our public higher education system. I always feel privileged to work with them on United Faculty. Joe always likes to say that "faculty working conditions are student learning conditions." If we could apply a version of that same idea to every other worker and job in the world, we would all be living in a better place. Kira Schuman, Midwest Lead Organizer of the AAUP, has also been a model of effective union organizing. With her help, we built even stronger relationships with our coworkers and won our union's state-imposed recertification election in October 2018. It was a sweet victory, and karmic justice to the anti-worker lobbyists and politicians who tried to destroy public-sector unions in Iowa.

This project was supported, in part, by research support from Miami University, and a Professional Development Assignment and a Summer Fellowship from the University of Northern Iowa. The Western Reserve Historical Society Research Library in Cleveland, the New York Public Library, the Central European University Library in Budapest, the King Library at Miami University, and the Rod Library at University of Northern Iowa all assisted with finding historical materials and research resources.

Dana Potter designed the wonderful time line of the *New York Times* labor beat and markedly improved scans of old *Editor & Publisher* ads. Fran Benson, editorial director of ILR Press at Cornell University Press, has been an exceptional advocate and guiding light, and Meagan Dermody, her assistant at CUP, has been amazingly efficient. Working with Fran, Meagan, and others at CUP (including Karen T. Hwa, Elizabeth Kim, and Carmen Torrado Gonzalez) has been a completely positive experience. Thanks, too, to the manuscript's anonymous reviewers for their close reading and astute comments. I could not imagine better feedback.

Finally, thank you to my siblings: Phil, Mike, and Jennifer. I've learned so much from them sharing their journeys in work and life. And the most thanks to my daughters, Olivia and Sabine, for their love, support, and encouragement, and my partner, Bettina Fabos, for her clear editing, patient listening, creative thinking, and sustaining reserves of love and enthusiasm.

Notes

Introduction

1. Travis Gettys, "'Who Are These People?' Morning Joe Hammers Trump Crowd Calling for McCain's Death," *Rawstory*, August 23, 2017, https://www.rawstory.com/2017/08/who-are-these-people-morning-joe-hammers-trump-crowd-calling-for-mccains-death; Marty Kaplan, "This Is Your Brain on Trump," *HuffPost*, August 28, 2017, https://www.huffingtonpost.com/entry/this-is-your-brain-on-trump_us_59a46689e4b0d6cf7f404f66; Alexander Zaitchik, *The Gilded Rage: A Wild Ride through Donald Trump's America* (New York: Hot Books, 2016); Samhita Mukhopadhyay and Kate Harding, eds., *Nasty Women: Feminism, Resistance, and Revolution in Trump's America* (New York: Picador, 2017); Mike Andrew, "Who Are These People?" *Seattle Gay News*, September 1, 2017, http://www.sgn.org/sgnnews45_35/page9.cfm; George Saunders, "Who Are All These Trump Supporters?" *New Yorker*, July 11 and 18, 2016, https://www.newyorker.com/magazine/2016/07/11/george-saunders-goes-to-trump-rallies; Luke Timmerman, "Who Are Trump's Supporters? Not Who You May Think. Meet My Friend J," *Forbes*, November 9, 2016, https://www.forbes.com/sites/luketimmerman/2016/11/09/who-are-the-trump-supporters-not-who-you-may-think-meet-my-friend-j/#45167ad740ce; Kabir Kanna, "Who Are Trump's Supporters and Opponents?" *CBS News*, August 11, 2017, https://www.cbsnews.com/news/who-are-trumps-supporters-and-opponents; Derek Thompson, "Who Are Donald Trump's Supporters, Really?" *Atlantic*, March 1, 2016, https://www.theatlantic.com/politics/archive/2016/03/who-are-donald-trumps-supporters-really/471714; Drew Magary, "What Kind of Person Would Vote for Donald Trump? These People," *GQ*, August 4, 2015, https://www.gq.com/story/trump-supporters-gop-campaign-iowa; David Masciotra, "Who Are These Idiot Donald Trump Supporters? Trump Loves the Poorly Educated—and They Love Him Right Back," *Salon*, March 20, 2016, http://www.salon.

com/2016/03/20/who_are_these_idiot_donald_trump_supporters_trump_loves_the_poorly_
educated_and_they_love_him_right_back.

2. Amy Chozick, "Middle Class Is Disappearing, at Least from Vocabulary of Possible 2016 Contenders," *New York Times,* May 11, 2015, https://www.nytimes.com/2015/05/12/us/politics/as-middle-class-fades-so-does-use-of-term-on-campaign-trail.html. This article was written a month before Trump entered the presidential race.

3. See Rick Perlstein, *Nixonland: The Rise of a President and the Fracturing of America* (New York: Scribner, 2008); Patrick J. Buchanan, *The New Majority* (Philadelphia: Girard Bank, 1973); Jefferson Cowie, *Stayin' Alive: The 1970s and the Last Days of the Working Class* (New York: New Press, 2010); Christopher R. Martin, *Framed! Labor and the Corporate Media* (Ithaca, NY: Cornell University Press, 2004); Michael Beckel, "How 'Joe the Plumber' Wants Donald Trump to Drain the Swamp," Center for Public Integrity, January 23, 2017, https://www.publicintegrity.org/2017/01/23/20607/how-joe-plumber-wants-donald-trump-drain-swamp.

4. See, for example, Arlie Russell Hochschild, *Strangers in Their Own Land* (New York: New Press, 2016); Katherine J. Cramer, *The Politics of Resentment: Rural Consciousness in Wisconsin and the Rise of Scott Walker* (Chicago: University of Chicago Press, 2016); Joan C. Williams, *White Working Class: Overcoming Class Cluelessness in America* (Brighton, MA: Harvard Business Review Press, 2017); and J. D. Vance, *Hillbilly Elegy: A Memoir of a Family and Culture in Crisis* (New York: Harper, 2016). To be honest, one could just as easily say *white* people elected Trump, or *older* people elected Trump, or *wealthier* people elected Trump. See Matthew Cooper, "How Donald Trump Courted White Americans to Victory," *Newsweek,* November 9, 2016, http://www.newsweek.com/2016/11/18/donald-trump-white-working-class-voters-election-2016-519095.html; Jon Henley, "White and Wealthy Voters Gave Victory to Donald Trump, Exit Polls Show," *Guardian,* November 9, 2016, https://www.theguardian.com/us-news/2016/nov/09/white-voters-victory-donald-trump-exit-polls.

5. Hochschild, *Strangers,* 221–222.

6. Williams, *White Working Class,* chap. 1, Kindle.

7. Cramer, *Politics of Resentment,* 51.

8. Vance, *Hillbilly Elegy,* 4.

9. Nate Cohn, "Why Trump Won: Working-Class Whites," *New York Times,* November 9, 2016, https://www.nytimes.com/2016/11/10/upshot/why-trump-won-working-class-whites.html.

10. See, for example, Timothy Noah, "The Trouble with the Electoral College," *Politico,* November 15, 2016, https://www.politico.com/magazine/story/2016/11/electoral-college-donald-trump-2016-214455; Maya Kosoff, "Comey's Testimony Suggests Bill Clinton May Have Cost Hillary the Election," *Vanity Fair,* June 8, 2017, https://www.vanityfair.com/news/2017/06/comey-testimony-clinton-tarmac-meeting; Sarah Posner, "How Donald Trump's New Campaign Chief Created an Online Haven for White Nationalists," *Mother Jones,* August 22, 2016, http://www.motherjones.com/politics/2016/08/stephen-bannon-donald-trump-alt-right-breitbart-news; Greg Sargent, "Yes, Donald Trump 'Lies.' A Lot. And News Organizations Should Say So," *Washington Post,* January 2, 2017, https://www.washingtonpost.com/blogs/plum-line/wp/2017/01/02/yes-donald-trump-lies-a-lot-and-news-organizations-should-say-so; Abby Phillips, John Wagner, and Anne Gearan, "A Series of Strategic Mistakes Likely Sealed Clinton's Fate," *Washington Post,* November 12, 2016, https://www.washingtonpost.com/politics/a-series-of-strategic-mistakes-likely-sealed-clintons-fate/2016/11/11/82f3fcc0-a840-11e6-ba59-a7d93165c6d4_story.html; Ari Berman, "Rigged: How Voter Suppression Threw Wisconsin to Trump," *Mother Jones,* November/December 2017, http://www.motherjones.com/politics/2017/10/voter-suppression-wisconsin-election-2016/#; Mary Harris, "A Media Post-mortem on the 2016 Presidential Election," *MediaQuant,* November 14, 2016, http://www.mediaquant.net/2016/11/a-media-post-

mortem-on-the-2016-presidential-election; Craig Timberg, "Russian Propaganda Effort Helped Spread 'Fake News' during Election, Experts Say," *Washington Post*, November 24, 2016, https://www.washingtonpost.com/business/economy/russian-propaganda-effort-helped-spread-fake-news-during-election-experts-say/2016/11/24/793903b6–8a40–4ca9-b712–716af66098fe_story.html.

11. Although this book focuses on socioeconomic class, Trump's racist, sexist, and anti-immigrant appeals (and the amplification of those messages in the echo chamber of conservative media) are also part of what binds many of his voters. Trump's appeals have inspired enormous mobilizations of progressive actions in response. See, for example, Ta-Nehisi Coates, "The First White President," *Atlantic*, October 2017, https://www.theatlantic.com/magazine/archive/2017/10/the-first-white-president-ta-nehisi-coates/537909; Jelani Cobb, "The Matter of Black Lives," *New Yorker*, March 14, 2016, https://www.newyorker.com/magazine/2016/03/14/where-is-black-lives-matter-headed; Jia Tolentino, "The Radical Possibility of the Women's March," *New Yorker*, January 22, 2017, https://www.newyorker.com/culture/jia-tolentino/the-radical-possibility-of-the-womens-march; John Bacon and Alan Gomez, "Protests against Trump's Immigration Plan Rolling in More Than 30 Cities," *USA Today*, January 29, 2017, https://www.usatoday.com/story/news/nation/2017/01/29/homeland-security-judges-stay-has-little-impact-travel-ban/97211720.

12. Tina Nguyen, "Trump Admits Taxpayers Will Pay for His 'Great Wall' after All," *Vanity Fair*, January 6, 2017, http://www.vanityfair.com/news/2017/01/donald-trump-border-wall-taxpayer-funded.

13. US Bureau of Labor Statistics, "Employment by Major Industry Sector," October 24, 2017, https://www.bls.gov/emp/ep_table_201.htm.

14. Peter Moore, "Poll Results: Middle Class," *Huffington Post*, May 28, 2015, https://today.yougov.com/news/2015/05/28/poll-results-middle-class. See also Frank Newport, "Fewer Americans Identify as Middle Class in Recent Years," Gallup, April 28, 2015, http://www.gallup.com/poll/182918/fewer-americans-identify-middle-class-recent-years.aspx; Michael Zweig, *The Working Class Majority: America's Best Kept Secret*, 2nd ed. (Ithaca, NY: Cornell University Press, 2011); US Bureau of Labor Statistics, "Employment Situation Summary Table A. Household data, Seasonally Adjusted," January 4, 2019, https://www.bls.gov/news.release/empsit.a.htm; and Michael Zweig, "Introduction: The Challenges of Working Class Studies," in *What's Class Got to Do with It?* (Ithaca, NY: Cornell University Press, 2004), 4.

15. Jesse A. Meyerson, "Trumpism: It's Coming from the Suburbs," *Nation*, May 8, 2017, https://www.thenation.com/article/trumpism-its-coming-from-the-suburbs; Nate Silver, "The Mythology of Trump's 'Working Class' Support," *FiveThirtyEight*, May 3, 2016, https://fivethirtyeight.com/features/the-mythology-of-trumps-working-class-support. Another article made the same argument after the election: Nicholas Carnes and Noam Lupo, "It's Time to Bust the Myth: Most Trump Voters Were Not Working Class," *Washington Post*, June 5, 2017, https://www.washingtonpost.com/news/monkey-cage/wp/2017/06/05/its-time-to-bust-the-myth-most-trump-voters-were-not-working-class. See also Joan C. Williams, "We Need to Redefine What 'Working Class' Means," *Time*, August 14, 2017, http://time.com/4899906/donald-trump-white-working-class.

16. US Census Bureau, "Highest Educational Attainment Levels since 1940," March 30, 2017, https://www.census.gov/library/visualizations/2017/comm/cb17-51_educational_attainment.html. See also Thomas Edsall, "Where Democrats Can Find New Voters," *New York Times*, June 15, 2017, https://www.nytimes.com/2017/06/15/opinion/can-the-democratic-party-find-new-voters.html.

17. See, for example, Reeve Vanneman and Lynn Weber Cannon, *The American Perception of Class* (Philadelphia: Temple University Press, 1987); Erik Olin Wright, *Class Counts: Comparative*

Studies in Class Analysis (Cambridge: Cambridge University Press, 1997); Michèle Lamont, *The Dignity of Working Men: Morality and the Boundaries of Race, Class, and Immigration* (New York: Russell Sage Foundation, 2000); and Stanley Aronowitz and Michael Roberts, eds., *Class: The Anthology* (Hoboken, NJ: Wiley-Blackwell, 2017).

18. In fact, there has even been a shift in self-identification of socioeconomic class in recent years in the United States. Gallup has fielded a national survey question since 2000 that asks people to identify in which social class they think they belong. Gallup uses a hierarchy with five levels: upper class, upper middle class, middle class, working class, and lower class. As Gallup reported, "Americans are considerably less likely now than they were in 2008 and years prior to identify themselves as middle class or upper-middle class, while the percentage putting themselves in the working or lower class has risen. Currently, 51% of Americans say they are middle class or upper-middle class, while 48% say they are lower class or working class." See Frank Newport, "Fewer Americans Identify as Middle Class in Recent Years," Gallup, April 28, 2015, http://news.gallup.com/poll/182918/fewer-americans-identify-middle-class-recent-years.aspx.

19. Bill Kovach and Tom Rosenstiel, *The Elements of Journalism* (New York: Three Rivers, 2001).

20. Leo Bogart, *Preserving the Press: How Daily Newspapers Mobilized to Keep Their Readers* (New York: Columbia University Press, 1991), 157–58.

21. "Now What?" *On the Media*, WNYC, November 9, 2016, www.wnyc.org/story/now-what.

22. Daniel S. Levine, "Over 90 Million Eligible Voters Didn't Vote in the 2016 Presidential Election," *Heavy*, January 11, 2017, https://heavy.com/news/2016/11/eligible-voter-turnout-for-2016-data-hillary-clinton-donald-trump-republican-democrat-popular-vote-registered-results; "If 'Did Not Vote' Had Been a Candidate in the 2016 US Presidential Election, It Would Have Won by a Landslide," *Brilliant Maps*, November 13, 2016, https://brilliantmaps.com/did-not-vote; "Presidential Results," *CNNPolitics*, February 16, 2017, https://www.cnn.com/election/2016/results/president.

23. The annual unemployment rate in 1953 was 2.9 percent. See US Bureau of Labor Statistics, "Annual Unemployment Rate, 1947–2016," Series ID LNU 04000000, July 30, 2017, https://data.bls.gov/pdq/SurveyOutputServlet.

24. US Bureau of the Census, *Historical Abstract of the United States, Colonial Times to 1970* (Washington, DC: Government Printing Office, 1975).

25. US Bureau of Labor Statistics, "Handbook of Labor Statistics 1978," US Department of Labor, June 1979 (Washington, DC: Government Printing Office, 1979). See also BLS Reports, "Labor Force Characteristics by Race and Ethnicity, 2015," US Bureau of Labor Statistics, September 2016, https://www.bls.gov/opub/reports/race-and-ethnicity/2015/home.htm; BLS Reports, "Women in the Labor Force: A Databook," US Bureau of Labor Statistics, May 2014, https://www.bls.gov/opub/reports/womens-databook/archive/womenlaborforce_2013.pdf. See also Elizabeth Waldman, "Labor Force Statistics from a Family Perspective," *Monthly Labor Review*, December 1983, 16–20.

26. Anna Brown and Eileen Patten, "'The Narrowing, but Persistent, Gender Gap in Pay," Pew Research Center, April 3, 2017 http://www.pewresearch.org/fact-tank/2017/04/03/gender-pay-gap-facts. See also Elise Gould and Jessica Schneider, "Black and Hispanic Women Are Paid Substantially Less Than White Men," Economic Policy Institute, March 7, 2017, http://www.epi.org/publication/black-and-hispanic-women-are-hit-particularly-hard-by-the-gender-wage-gap; and Eileen Patten, "Racial, Gender Wage Gaps Persist in U.S. despite Some Progress," Pew Research Center, July 1, 2016, http://www.pewresearch.org/fact-tank/2016/07/01/racial-gender-wage-gaps-persist-in-u-s-despite-some-progress.

27. See, for example, Ira Glasser, "When Exactly Was America Great, Donald?" *HuffPost*, September 28, 2016, http://www.huffingtonpost.com/entry/when-exactly-was-america-great-donald_us_57ec1496e4b024a52d2c58ee.

28. US Census Bureau, "Immigration, by Leading Country or Region of Last Residence: 1901 to 1997," *Statistical Abstract of the United States, 1999*, https://www.census.gov/library/publications/1999/compendia/statab/119ed.html.

29. Gregory Krieg, "Donald Trump Reveals When He Thinks America Was Great," CNN, March 28. 2016, http://www.cnn.com/2016/03/26/politics/donald-trump-when-america-was-great/index.html.

30. J. Lester Feder, "This Is How Steve Bannon Sees the Entire World," *BuzzFeed*, November 15, 2016, https://www.buzzfeed.com/lesterfeder/this-is-how-steve-bannon-sees-the-entire-world. Bannon apparently forgets other history: the Korean War, the Vietnam War, and several other US military interventions between 1946 and 1989.

31. "Donald Trump: 'I Will Be Greatest Jobs President God Ever Created,'" *Guardian*, June 16, 2015, https://www.theguardian.com/us-news/video/2015/jun/16/donald-trump-us-president-republicans-video. See also "I Will Be the Greatest Jobs Producer That God Ever Created," *Washington Post*, January 11, 2017, https://www.washingtonpost.com/video/politics/trump-i-will-be-the-greatest-jobs-creator-that-god-ever-created/2017/01/11/152b5bd6-d827–11e6-a0e6-d502d6751bc8_video.html.

32. Jonathan Capehart, "Trump Asked Blacks, 'What the Hell Do You Have to Lose?' We Now Have Their Response," *Washington Post*, September 27, 2017, https://www.washingtonpost.com/blogs/post-partisan/wp/2017/09/27/trump-asked-blacks-what-the-hell-do-you-have-to-lose-we-now-have-their-response.

33. "Transcript: Donald Trump's Taped Comments about Women," *New York Times*, October 8, 2016, https://www.nytimes.com/2016/10/08/us/donald-trump-tape-transcript.html.

34. For more consideration of working-class roots and middle-class life, see Alfred Lubrano, *Limbo: Blue-Collar Roots, White-Collar Dreams* (Hoboken, NJ: Wiley, 2004).

35. Douglas Martin, "Donald Lukens, Scandal-Tainted Lawmaker, Dies at 79," *New York Times*, May 25, 2010, http://www.nytimes.com/2010/05/25/us/25lukens.html.

36. Anne E. Kornblut, "Spotlight on Lobbying Swings to Little-Known Congressman," *Washington Post*, January 17, 2006, http://www.nytimes.com/2006/01/17/us/front%20page/spotlight-on-lobbying-swings-to-littleknown-congressman.html; Susan Schmidt and James V. Grimaldi, "Ney Sentenced to 30 Months in Prison for Abramoff Deals," *Washington Post*, January 20, 2007, http://www.washingtonpost.com/wp-dyn/content/article/2007/01/19/AR2007011190 0162.html.

37. Stephen Franklin, *Three Strikes: Labor's Heartland Losses and What They Mean for Working Americans* (New York: Guilford, 2001).

38. Steven Greenhouse, "Wisconsin's Legacy for Unions," *New York Times*, February 22, 2014, https://www.nytimes.com/2014/02/23/business/wisconsins-legacy-for-unions.html.

39. Andy Kroll, "Bye Bye, SB 5: Anti-union Law Repealed in Ohio," *Mother Jones*, November 9, 2011, http://www.motherjones.com/politics/2011/11/issue-2-sb-5-ohio-repeal.

40. William Petroski and Brianna Pfannenstiel, "GOP Delivers on Pro-business Bills: Key Issues That Defined Iowa's Legislature 2017 Session," *Des Moines Register*, April 22, 2017, http://www.desmoinesregister.com/story/news/politics/2017/04/22/gop-delivers-pro-business-bills-key-issues-defined-iowas-legislature-2017-session/99010004.

41. William Petroski, "Lobbyist Attending Bargaining Bill Signing Brings Criticism," *Des Moines Register*, February 20, 2017, http://www.desmoinesregister.com/story/news/politics/2017/02/20/lobbyist-attending-bargaining-bill-signing-brings-criticism/98152134.

42. Data from National Low Income Housing Coalition, "Out of Reach 2016," http://nlihc.org/sites/default/files/oor/OOR_2016.pdf.

43. "State Minimum Wages," National Conference of State Legislatures, January 5, 2017, http://www.ncsl.org/research/labor-and-employment/state-minimum-wage-chart.aspx#1.

44. "Fighting Preemption: The Movement for Higher Wages Must Oppose State Efforts to Block Local Minimum Wage Laws," National Employment Law Project, July 6, 2017, http://www.nelp.org/publication/fighting-preemption-local-minimum-wage-laws.

45. Jason Noble, "Despite Lawmakers' Warnings, Few Iowa Farmers Face Estate Tax," *Des Moines Register,* December 2, 2017, https://www.desmoinesregister.com/story/news/2017/12/02/tax-reform-iowa-farmers-estate-tax/906946001; Ashlea Ebeling, "Final Tax Bill Includes Huge Estate Tax Win for the Rich: The $22.4 Million Exemption," *Forbes,* December 21, 2017, https://www.forbes.com/sites/ashleaebeling/2017/12/21/final-tax-bill-includes-huge-estate-tax-win-for-the-rich-the-22-4-million-exemption/#fbc44a81d541.

46. Peter Dreier and Christopher R. Martin, "The News Media, the Conservative Echo Chamber, and the Battle over ACORN: How Two Academics Fought in the Framing Wars," *Humanity & Society* 35, nos. 1–2 (2011): 4–30.

47. Cowie, *Stayin' Alive,* 72.

1. Trump, Carrier, and the Invisible Worker

1. Matthew Boyle, "President-Elect Donald Trump Cuts Deal to Keep Carrier Corporation in United States," Breitbart, November 29, 2016, http://www.breitbart.com/big-government/2016/11/29/president-elect-donald-trump-cuts-deal-to-keep-carrier-corporation-in-united-states.

2. Joe Tacopino, "1K Jobs a Don Deal: A/C Company Flips on Move to Mexico," *New York Post,* November 30, 2016, 5.

3. "Early Start," CNN, November 30, 2016, http://money.cnn.com/2016/11/30/media/carrier-deal-media-divide-on-donald-trump/index.html.

4. Jim Tankersley and Danielle Paquette, "After Trump, Pence Intervene, Carrier Says It'll Keep Workers in U.S.," *Washington Post,* November 30, 2016, A12.

5. Linda Feldman, "How Donald Trump Is Already Remaking the Presidency," *Christian Science Monitor,* December 1, 2016, http://www.csmonitor.com/USA/Politics/2016/1201/How-Donald-Trump-is-already-remaking-the-presidency.

6. Kristen Welker, "Donald Trump Set to Announce Deal to Keep Some Carrier Jobs in Indianapolis," *NBC News,* December 1, 2016, http://www.nbcnews.com/dateline/video/donald-trump-set-to-announce-deal-to-keep-some-carrier-jobs-in-indianapolis-821757507677.

7. "Carrier Air Conditioner (Part of United Technologies) Moving 1,400 Jobs to Mexico," YouTube, https://www.youtube.com/watch?v=Y3ttxGMQOrY. See also Bryan Gruley and Rick Clough, "Remember When Trump Said He Saved 1,100 Jobs at a Carrier Plant? Well, Globalization Doesn't Give a Damn." *Bloomberg Businessweek,* March 29, 2017, https://www.bloomberg.com/news/features/2017-03-29/remember-when-trump-said-he-saved-1-100-jobs-at-a-carrier-plant.

8. Adam Edelman, "Donald Trump—Who Made and Lost Billions with Help of Millions in Loans from Rich Daddy—Claims He Is a 'Blue Collar Worker,'" *New York Daily News,* October 10, 2016, http://www.nydailynews.com/news/politics/billioniare-donald-trump-blue-collar-worker-article-1.2825716.

9. Matthew Boyle, "Exclusive—Donald Trump on Ford, Carrier, Shipping Jobs to Mexico: 'I'm the Only One Who Understands What's Going On,'" Breitbart, February 12, 2016, http://www.breitbart.com/big-government/2016/02/12/exclusive-donald-trump-on-ford-carrier-shipping-jobs-to-mexico-im-the-only-one-who-understands-whats-going-on.

10. "Stomach-Turning Moment 1,400 Workers Lost Their Jobs," *New York Post*, February 12, 2017, http://nypost.com/video/stomach-turning-moment-1400-workers-lost-their-jobs.

11. Ahiza Garcia, "Carrier Workers' Rage over Move to Mexico Caught on Video," *CNNMoney*, February 12, 2016, http://money.cnn.com/2016/02/12/news/companies/carrier-moving-jobs-mexico-youtube.

12. Right Side Broadcasting Network, "Full Speech: Donald Trump Holds Rally in Louisville, KY (3–1–16)," March 1, 2016, https://www.youtube.com/watch?v=0Hzc9yL3_n8. See also Rafael Sanchez, "Trump: If I'm President, Carrier Won't Move to Mexico," WRTV, March 1, 2016, http://www.theindychannel.com/news/call-6-investigators/trump-if-im-president-carrier-wont-move-to-mexico.

13. Syracuse.com, "Donald Trump Emphasizes Bringing Back American Jobs, Boos Carrier Moving Jobs to Mexico," April 16, 2016, https://www.youtube.com/watch?v=6FCaPYWNc2Q; RTV6 The Indy Channel, "Trump: We'll Tax Carrier and They'll Decide to Stay," April 20, 2016, https://www.youtube.com/watch?v=iWSJIqTcwqc.

14. Mike Allen and Jim VanderHei, "Trump 101: What He Reads and Watches," *Axios*, January 24, 2017, https://www.axios.com/trump-101-what-he-reads-and-watches-2210510272.html.

15. Cristina Alesci, "Trump's Message Isn't Wooing Workers Losing Jobs to Mexico," *CNNMoney*, August 23, 2016, http://money.cnn.com/video/news/2016/08/23/carrier-workers-jobs-mexico-trump-trade-indiana-globalization.cnnmoney.

16. "Donald Trump: 'I Will Be Greatest Jobs President God Ever Created'—Video," *Guardian*, June 16, 2015, https://www.theguardian.com/us-news/video/2015/jun/16/donald-trump-us-president-republicans-video.

17. Megyn Kelly, "Carrier Employees Glad Trump 'Lived Up to a Promise,'" Fox News, November 30, 2016, https://www.youtube.com/watch?v=qT1ZaiQp3dI.

18. To fact-check the top of Hannity's head: Hannity usefully forgets Obama's much larger and successful bailout of the US auto industry in the midst of the nation's terrible Great Recession. Hannity opposed the bailout, as did then-US Representative Mike Pence. Trump ultimately opposed it as well. See "True Conservative Mike Pence on the Auto-Bailout," YouTube, December 11, 2008, https://www.youtube.com/watch?v=EjgUPKLQGu0. See also "Hannity on Auto Bailout: The Administration Is on a Mission to Hijack Capitalism in Favor of Collectivism . . . The Bolsheviks Have Already Arrived,'" *Media Matters*, March 30, 2009; and Patrick Caldwell, "Why Trump and Pence Aren't Talking About the Auto Bailout in the Midwest," *Mother Jones*, August 11, 2016, http://www.motherjones.com/politics/2016/08/donald-trump-auto-bailout-mike-pence.

19. Sean Hannity, "Carrier Employee Thanks Trump, Pence for Saving Jobs," Fox News, November 30, 2016, http://www.foxnews.com/transcript/2016/11/30/carrier-employee-thanks-trump-pence-for-saving-jobs-gingrich-on-president-elect.html. Note: Hannity is incorrect; the Indianapolis Carrier plant makes heaters, not air conditioners.

20. Adam Shapiro, "Carrier Employee Thanks President-Elect Trump," Fox Business Network, November 30, 2016, https://www.youtube.com/watch?v=2Nx-41b7A8M.

21. Allen and VanderHei, "Trump 101."

22. "15-Year Carrier Employee Reacts to Jobs Staying in the US," Fox News, December 1, 2016, https://www.youtube.com/watch?v=sWC5HCng3CQ.

23. "Carrier Employee Reacts to Donald Trump Speech," Fox News, December 2, 2016, http://video.foxnews.com/v/5231997526001/?#sp=show-clips.

24. Dean Reynolds, "President-Elect Trump Visits Indiana to Tout Carrier Deal," *CBS This Morning*, December 1, 2016, https://www.youtube.com/watch?v=jIjDllX2M8E; Kristen Welker, "Victory Tour," *NBC Nightly News*, December 1, 2016, http://www.nbcnews.com/nightly-news/video/nightly-news-full-broadcast-december-1st-822412867935; Tom Llamas, "Trump Victory Lap," *ABC World News Tonight*, December 1, 2016, https://www.youtube.com/watch?v=jlgRklRuBe4.

25. Chuck Jones, United Steelworkers Local 1999, telephone conversation with author, April 5, 2017.

26. Nelson D. Schwartz, "Trump Saved Jobs at Carrier, but More Midwest Jobs Are in Jeopardy," *New York Times*, November 30, 2016, https://www.nytimes.com/2016/11/30/business/economy/trump-saved-jobs-at-carrier-but-more-midwest-jobs-are-in-jeopardy.html.

27. Greg Sargent, "Steve Bannon Just Attacked the Media. The Correct Response: Keep Pointing Out the Lies," *Washington Post*, January 27, 2017, https://www.washingtonpost.com/blogs/plum-line/wp/2017/01/27/steve-bannon-just-attacked-the-media-the-correct-response-keep-pointing-out-the-lies/?utm_term=.1131e6447d28.

28. See Jamelle Bouie, "Government by White Nationalism Is upon Us," *Slate*, February 6, 2017, http://www.slate.com/articles/news_and_politics/cover_story/2017/02/government_by_white_nationalism_is_upon_us.html. See also John Hudson, "In Middle Earth, Must All Hobbits Be White?" *Atlantic*, November 30, 2010, https://www.theatlantic.com/national/archive/2010/11/in-middle-earth-must-all-hobbits-be-white/343239.

29. Gruley and Clough, "Remember When."

30. "Timeline: 1,000 Carrier Jobs Saved from Moving to Mexico," WRTV, November 30, 2016, http://www.theindychannel.com/news/local-news/timeline-1000-carrier-jobs-saved-from-moving-to-mexico.

31. "CNBC Transcript: United Technologies Chairman & CEO Greg Hayes on CNBC's 'Mad Money w/ Jim Cramer' Today," CNBC, December 5, 2016, http://www.cnbc.com/2016/12/05/cnbc-transcript-united-technologies-chairman-ceo-greg-hayes-on-cnbcs-mad-money-w-jim-cramer-today.html.

32. Jones, telephone conversation.

33. Kevin Rader, "Trump Cites Carrier Employee's Comments in Preserving Indianapolis Jobs," WTHR, December 2, 2016, http://www.wthr.com/article/trump-cites-carrier-employees-comments-in-preserving-indianapolis-jobs.

34. Donald Trump with Meredith McIver, *Trump: Think Like a Billionaire* (New York: Random House, 2004), 94.

35. "Read Donald Trump's Remarks at Carrier Plant in Indiana," *Time*, December 1, 2016, http://time.com/4588349/donald-trump-carrier-jobs-speech; "CNBC Transcript: United Technologies Chairman & CEO Greg Hayes."

36. Jennie Runevitch, "USW: 730 Union Jobs Saved in Carrier Deal—Not 1,100," WTHR, December 5, 2016, http://www.wthr.com/article/usw-730-union-jobs-saved-in-carrier-deal-not-1100.

37. Jones, telephone conversation.

38. Runevitch, "USW: 730 Union Jobs Saved."

39. One can certainly give Trump and Pence credit for getting UTC to retain some of the positions: 800 (57 percent) of the 1,400 jobs, at huge expense to Indiana. Yet PolitiFact set a very low standard for follow-through on a vow from the president-elect by deeming Trump's promise as "mostly fulfilled," earning its highest rating of "Promise Kept." See Allison Graves, "Promise to Save the Carrier Plant Mostly Fulfilled," PolitiFact, January 20, 2017, http://www.politifact.com/truth-o-meter/promises/trumpometer/promise/1415/save-carrier-plant-indiana.

40. Elizabeth Schulze, "CNBC Survey: Trump's Jobs Offensive Is Scoring Points with Dems and Independents," CNBC, December 10, 2016, http://www.cnbc.com/2016/12/10/cnbc-survey-trumps-jobs-offensive-is-scoring-points-with-dems-and-independents.html. For further data, see also Hart Research Associates/Public Opinion Strategies, "CNBC AAES Fourth Quarter Survey," December 2016, http://hartresearch.com/wp-content/uploads/2016/12/CNBC-4th-Quarter-Toplines.pdf.

41. Bill Hemmer, "RNC Defends Trump's Tweet Attack on Union Boss," Fox News, December 8, 2016, http://video.foxnews.com/v/5240124632001/?#sp=show-clips.

42. Chuck Jones, "I'm the Union Leader Donald Trump Attacked. I'm Tired of Being Lied to about Our Jobs," *Washington Post*, December 8, 2016, https://www.washingtonpost.com/posteverything/wp/2016/12/08/im-the-union-leader-donald-trump-attacked-im-tired-of-being-lied-to-about-our-jobs/?utm_term=.5a37a46775df.

43. Jones, "I'm the Union Leader."

44. Jones, telephone conversation.

45. "2014–2018 Agreement between the Indianapolis Plant of the Carrier Corporation and the United Steel, Paper and Forestry, Rubber, Manufacturing, Energy, Allied Industrial and Service Workers International Union, Local Union 1999," April 28, 2014, http://www.uswlocal1999.org/files/Carrier_2014-2018.pdf.

46. Chuck Jones, "Continue the Fight!" *Steel Voice* 10, no. 1 (2017): 4.

47. "Carrier Workers, Supporters Gathered for Rally at Statehouse Friday," WRTV, April 29, 2016, http://www.theindychannel.com/news/local-news/carrier-workers-supporters-to-gather-for-rally-at-statehouse-Friday. See also Brian Eason and Chelsea Schneider, "Bernie Sanders Rips Carrier Execs: 'They Have No Shame,'" *Indianapolis Star*, April 29, 2016, http://www.indystar.com/story/news/politics/2016/04/29/bernie-sanders-rips-carrier-execs-they-have-no-shame/83667086.

48. Jones, "Continue the Fight!"

49. Gruley and Clough, "Remember When."

50. Rafael Sanchez, "Carrier President: Expecting More Growth This Year," WRTV, March 10 2016, http://www.theindychannel.com/news/call-6-investigators/carrier-president-expecting-more-growth-this-year; "United Technologies Corp," Salary.com, 2016, http://www1.salary.com/UNITED-TECHNOLOGIES-CORP-Executive-Salaries.html.

51. "United Technologies Corp."

52. Tom Huddleston, Jr., "Former CEO of United Technologies Left with $195 Million," *Fortune*, February 6, 2015, http://fortune.com/2015/02/06/united-technologies-exit-pay.

53. "UTC Reports Full Year 2016 Results, Affirms 2017 Outlook," United Technologies Corp., January 25, 2017, http://www.utc.com/News/News-Center/Pages/UTC-Reports-Full-Year-2016-Results-Affirms-2017-Outlook.aspx.

54. "CNBC Transcript: United Technologies Chairman & CEO Greg Hayes."

55. The initial flurry of coverage of Trump and Carrier, and the lack of record-correcting follow-up coverage, were consequential. Although Trump did not fare well on a Gallup survey on six economic areas as he neared his first one hundred days in office, he rated highest (at 35 percent excellent/good) on the item "keeping manufacturing plants from moving overseas." See Frank Newport, "Trump Gets Highest Rating for Keeping Manufacturing in US," Gallup, April 26, 2017, http://www.gallup.com/poll/209258/trump-gets-highest-rating-keeping-manufacturing.aspx.

56. Katie Reilly, "President Trump Likes Taking Credit for Jobs. Here Are the Facts," *Fortune*, March 29, 2017, http://fortune.com/2017/03/29/president-trump-job-claims-fact-check.

57. T. J. Bray, "Carrier Workers Lobby Congress for Help," *Steel Voice* 9, no. 3.

58. See, for example, Tom Davies, "Job Cuts Endure at Indiana Factories despite Trump Pressure," *Indianapolis Star*, March 17, 2017, http://www.indystar.com/story/money/2017/03/17/

job-cuts-endure-indiana-factories-despite-trump-pressure/99315664; and Rafael Sanchez and Katie Cox, "Carrier Deal to Keep 1,069 Jobs in Indy Moves Toward Final Approval," WRTV, March 28, 2017, http://www.theindychannel.com/news/local-news/indiana-board-set-to-endorse-7m-carrier-deal-trump-brokered.

59. Gruley and Clough, "Remember When"; Sean Gregory, "The Jobs That Weren't Saved," *Time*, May 18, 2017, http://time.com/4783921/the-jobs-that-werent-saved; Nelson D. Schwartz, "Trump Saved Carrier Jobs. These Workers Weren't as Lucky," *New York Times*, April 23, 2017, https://www.nytimes.com/2017/04/23/business/economy/indiana-united-technology-factory-layoffs.html; Farah Stockman, "Becoming a Steelworker Liberated Her. Then Her Job Moved to Mexico," *New York Times*, October 14, 2017, https://www.nytimes.com/2017/10/14/us/union-jobs-mexico-rexnord.html; Danielle Paquette, "Trump Tried to Save Their Jobs. These Workers Are Quitting Anyway," *Washington Post*, August 15, 2017, https://www.washingtonpost.com/business/economy/trump-tried-to-save-their-jobs-these-workers-are-quitting-anyway/2017/08/15/6a555f2a-7d50-11e7-a669-b400c5c7e1cc_story.html; Bryce Covert, "Carrier Workers Are Livid after Facing Layoffs despite Trump's Promises," *In These Times*, January 11, 2018, http://inthesetimes.com/working/entry/20830/Donald-Trump-Carrier-workers-layoffs-jobs-broken-promises; Sarah Jaffe, "Back at the Carrier Plant, Workers Are Still Fighting on Their Own," *Nation*, April 20, 2017, https://www.thenation.com/article/back-at-the-carrier-plant-workers-are-still-fighting-on-their-own; Jill Disis, "Trump Couldn't Save These Jobs at Carrier. Today Is the End of the Line," CNN, July 20 2017, http://money.cnn.com/2017/07/19/news/economy/carrier-layoffs-indiana/index.html. A few other media outlets briefly revisited the Carrier story during assessments of Trump's first hundred days as president. See, for example, Rick Hampson, "100 Days into Trump Presidency, Americans Are United on This: They're Divided," *USA Today*, April 28, 2017, https://www.usatoday.com/story/news/politics/2017/04/28/100-days-trump-presidency-americans-united-divided-health-care-twitter-wall-immigration/100925102; and Rebecca Jarvis, "Trump's First 100 Days Promise Tracker: Jobs and the Economy," *Good Morning America*, April 25, 2017, http://abcnews.go.com/GMA/video/trumps-100-days-promise-tracker-jobs-economy-47001919.

60. Stockman, "Becoming a Steelworker."

61. Jaffe, "Back at the Carrier Plant."

62. Gruley and Clough, "Remember When."

63. A brief coda to the story: *NBC Nightly News* reported a follow-up story by Ron Mott on May 7, 2017, about Rexnord's final shutdown and shipping of jobs to Mexico. The report's text banner on the screen said "FACTORY SHIPS JOBS TO MEXICO DESPITE TRUMP TWEET." As Brian Stelter noted in the CNN's *Reliable Sources* newsletter, "Rexnord wasn't mentioned anywhere else in the media over the weekend, so I can pretty confidently say that this wasn't a coincidence: Exactly 20 minutes after the segment, Trump sent out a new tweet that seemed to shift the blame to his predecessor: 'Rexnord of Indiana made a deal during the Obama Administration to move to Mexico. Fired their employees. Tax product big that's sold in U.S.'" See Brian Stelter, "In Case You Missed 'Nightly News' . . . ," *CNNMoney Reliable Sources*, May 7, 2017, http://mailchi.mp/cnn/reliable-may-7-2017?e=1d329005b9.

2. The Rise and Fall of Labor Reporting

1. Troy Rondinone, *The Great Industrial War: Framing Class Conflict in America, 1865–1950* (New Brunswick, NJ: Rutgers University Press, 2010).

2. Some labor writers who didn't have bylines can be identified if their lives merited a published obituary and if their obituary mentioned their role at the newpaper(s) where they worked.

3. Arthur S. Brunswick, "Labor News Shy: Editors Care Little about the Doings of Unions," *Editor & Publisher*, December 21, 1901, 7.

4. This *New York Daily News*, which operated from April 1855 to 1906, according to the Library of Congress, is different from the *New York Daily News* tabloid founded in 1919 by the owners of the *Chicago Tribune* and that has been published by Mortimer Zuckerman since 1993.

5. At that time it was a one-cent newspaper. It had cost four cents in the previous decade.

6. "Death List of a Day; Alexander B. F. Mamreov," *New York Times*, August 16, 1900, 7.

7. "Matters of Import in the Realm of Labor," *New York Sunday News*, January 12, 1902, 23.

8. Brunswick, "Labor News Shy," 7.

9. For the beginnings of the labor press in the United States, see Michael Emery, Edwin Emery, and Nancy L. Roberts, *The Press and America: An Interpretive History of the Mass Media* (Boston: Allyn and Bacon, 1996), 92–93. See also Jon Bekken, "Federated Press: An Independent Labor News Service" (paper presented to the Association for Education in Journalism and Mass Communication meeting, Kansas City, August 2003). For labor radio broadcasting, see Nathan Godfried, *WCFL: Chicago's Voice of Labor, 1926–78* (Urbana: University of Illinois Press, 1997); and Elizabeth Fones-Wolf, *Waves of Opposition: Labor and the Struggle for Democratic Radio* (Urbana: University of Illinois Press, 2006). On the impact of immigration (European and Asian) at the time, see Philip S. Foner, *History of the Labor Movement in the United States*, Volume 2: *From the Founding of the A.F. of L. to the Emergence of American Imperialism* (New York: International Publishers, 1955), 16–19, and Volume 3: *The Policies and Practices of the American Federation of Labor 1900–1909* (New York: International Publishers, 1964), 256–81.

10. Stark was preceded on the labor beat at the *New York Times* by Mamreov, who was a reporter for the *Times* for nearly twenty-five years. Obituaries also mention John H. McLean (d. 1923) and Guy W. Seem (d. 1932) as former labor reporters for the *Times*.

11. "Four Win Awards of Hillman Fund," *New York Times*, December 16, 1951, 46. Murray Kempton, labor reporter for the *New York Post*, was also one of the award winners that evening.

12. *New York Times* journalist and historian Meyer Berger wrote in 1951 that "the Times now uses three to four labor writers regularly." See Berger, *The Story of the New York Times, 1851–1951* (New York: Simon and Schuster, 1951), 545. Berger also confirmed the 1925–1928 labor writer stint of Evans Clark at the *Times*.

13. The *New York Times* sold WQXR-AM to Disney in 2007 and sold WXQR-FM to Univision in 2009.

14. H. W. Ward, "Labor-Management and the Public," *Nieman Reports*, July 1951, 27.

15. Christopher R. Martin, "The Fate of the Labor Beat" (paper presented at the annual meeting of the National Communication Association, Mass Communication Division, Chicago, November 13, 2004).

16. Christopher R. Martin, "Writing Off Workers: The Decline of the U.S. and Canadian Labor Beats," in *Knowledge Workers in the Information Society*, eds. Catherine McKercher and Vincent Mosco (Lanham, MD: Lexington, 2008), 19–35; Project for Excellence in Journalism, "Newspapers," *State of the News Media 2007*, http://www.stateofthemedia.org/2007/newspapers-intro.

17. US Bureau of Labor Statistics, "Employment Situation Summary Table A. Household Data, Seasonally Adjusted," January 4, 2019, https://www.bls.gov/news.release/empsit.a.htm.

18. Michael Barthel, "Newspapers: Fact Sheet," *State of the News Media 2016*, Pew Research Center, June 15, 2016, http://www.journalism.org/2016/06/15/newspapers-fact-sheet.

19. Christopher Martin, "Why Analyzing Labor Coverage Is Important," *Talking Biz News,* April 3, 2013, http://talkingbiznews.com/2/why-analyzing-labor-coverage-is-important.

20. Erin Hennessey, e-mail message to author, May 31, 2017.

21. See Sarah Jaffe, *Necessary Trouble: Americans in Revolt* (New York: Nation, 2016) for the cultural impact of the Occupy movement.

22. "Center Wins First Pulitzer Prize," Center for Public Integrity, May 19, 2014, https://www.publicintegrity.org/2014/04/14/14593/center-wins-first-pulitzer-prize. The Center for Public Integrity has been doing independent, nonprofit, nonpartisan investigative journalism since 1989. Its "Hard Labor" and "Unequal Risk" projects have also been particularly excellent on the hazards faced by many US workers.

23. As a caveat, see the excellent work of *Politico* reporter Marianne Levine, which was praised in Benjamin Mullin, "How a Politico Reporter Helped Bring Down Trump's Labor Secretary Pick," Poynter.org, February 16, 2017, https://www.poynter.org/2017/how-a-politico-reporter-helped-bring-down-trumps-labor-secretary-pick/449199.

24. Michael Schudson, *Discovering the News* (New York: Basic, 1978).

25. Alfred McClung Lee, *The Daily Newspaper in America* (New York: Macmillan, 1937), 259.

26. Willard Grosvenor Bleyer, *Main Currents in the History of American Journalism* (Boston: Houghton Mifflin, 1927), 326.

27. Bleyer, *Main Currents,* 412.

28. Gerald J. Baldasty, "The Economics of Working-Class Journalism: The E. W. Scripps Newspaper Chain, 1878–1908," *Journalism History* 25, no. 1 (1999): 6.

29. Bleyer, *Main Currents,* 412.

30. Baldasty, "The Economics of Working-Class Journalism," 3.

31. Frank Luther Mott, *The News in America* (Cambridge, MA: Harvard University Press, 1952), 184–85.

32. See, for example, Hanno Hardt and Bonnie Brennen, *Newsworkers: Toward a History of the Rank and File* (Minneapolis: University of Minnesota Press, 1995); John Nerone, *Violence against the Press* (New York: Oxford University Press, 1994); Upton Sinclair, *The Brass Check* (Pasadena, CA: 1920).

33. David Halberstam, *The Powers That Be* (New York: Knopf, 1979), 112.

34. Lee, *The Daily Newspaper,* 639.

35. Lee, 638–39 (italics mine).

36. Lee, 633.

37. Lee, 635–36.

38. Leonard Ray Teel, *The Public Press, 1900–1945.* The History of American Journalism, No. 5 (Westport, CT: Praeger, 2006), 172.

39. Richard H. Meeker, *Newspaperman: S. I. Newhouse and the Business of News* (New Haven, CT: Ticknor & Fields, 1983), 101, 106.

40. Daniel Chomsky, " 'An Interested Reader': Measuring Ownership Control at the *New York Times,*" *Critical Studies in Media Communication* 23, no. 1 (2006): 1–18.

41. Chomsky, " 'An Interested Reader,' " 11.

42. Thomas Vail Papers, oral history interview conducted by John P. DeWitt, 1990, Western Reserve Historical Society, MS 4854, container 4, folder 93, 5–13.

43. Paul Bellamy, Anthony J. DiSantis Papers, Western Reserve Historical Society, MS 3790, container 1, folder 2.

44. Thomas Vail Papers, oral history interview conducted by John P. DeWitt, 1990, Western Reserve Historical Society, MS 4854, container 4, folder 92, 2–4.

45. See David Witwer, *Shadow of the Racketeer* (Urbana: University of Illinois Press, 2009), 150. Under Roy Howard's leadership, by the late 1930s "the Scripps-Howard chain abandoned its

identification with progressive causes and moved decisively to the right." Howard also opposed the Newspaper Guild, Witwer notes.

46. See, for example, Halberstam, *The Powers That Be;* and Susan E. Tifft and Alex S. Jones, *The Trust: The Private and Powerful Family behind The New York Times* (Boston: Little, Brown, 1999).

47. Stephen Franklin, "Is Labor Still a Movement? An Appraisal: Looking Back and Moving Forward" (presentation at the ninetieth annual meeting of the National Communication Association, Chicago, November 11–14, 2004).

48. William Serrin, telephone conversation with author, January 11, 2017.

49. Edwin Diamond, *Behind the Times: Inside the New New York Times* (New York: Villard, 1994), 260.

50. Diamond, *Behind the Times,* 260.

51. Ed Bishop, "Dine Talks about Labor and the Press," *St. Louis Journalism Review,* December 2002/January 2003, 26–27.

52. See, for example, Bishop, "Dine Talks about Labor" and David Moberg, "Oversight of Workplace Hazards," *In These Times,* April 25, 1990, http://www.unz.org/Pub/InTheseTimes-1990apr25-00003.

53. Alvin Chang, "The Subtle Ways Colleges Discriminate Against Poor Students, Explained with a Cartoon," *Vox,* April 11, 2018, https://www.vox.com/2017/9/11/16270316/college-mobility-culture; Matthew Stewart, "The Birth of a New American Aristocracy," *Atlantic,* June 2018, 48–63; Richard V. Reeves and Joanna Venator, "The Inheritance of Education," Brookings, October 27, 2014, https://www.brookings.edu/blog/social-mobility-memos/2014/10/27/the-inheritance-of-education; Margaret Sullivan, "Newsroom Diversity: Why We Should Care," *New York Times,* June 17, 2015, https://publiceditor.blogs.nytimes.com/2015/06/17/newsroom-diversity-why-we-should-care; Tal Abbady, "The Modern Newsroom Is Stuck Behind the Gender and Color Line," NPR, May 1, 2017, https://www.npr.org/sections/codeswitch/2017/05/01/492982066/the-modern-newsroom-is-stuck-behind-the-gender-and-color-line.

54. Sarah Smarsh, "Dangerous Idiots: How the Liberal Media Elite Failed Working-Class Americans," *Guardian,* October 13, 2016, https://www.theguardian.com/media/2016/oct/13/liberal-media-bias-working-class-americans; Meg Dalton, "When the Math Doesn't Work," *Columbia Journalism Review,* Spring/Summer 2018, https://www.cjr.org/special_report/journalist-side-hustles.php; Sarah Jones, "The Great Remove," *Columbia Journalism Review,* Spring/Summer 2018, https://www.cjr.org/special_report/journalism-class.php; Gaye Tuchman, *Making News: A Study in the Construction of Reality* (New York: Free Press, 1978).

55. Unadjusted data. See Clara Chang and Constance Sorrentino, "Union Membership Statistics in 12 Countries," *Monthly Labor Review,* December 1991, http://www.bls.gov/fls/mprcs91.pdf.

56. David R. Davies, *The Postwar Decline of American Newspapers, 1945–1965.* The History of American Journalism Series, No. 6 (Westport, CT: Praeger, 2006). See also Emery, Emery, and Roberts, *The Press and America.*

57. Tifft and Jones, *The Trust,* 392–93.

58. Davies, *The Postwar Decline,* 117.

59. The deployment of photocomposition technology in the 1960s also provided newspapers a windfall of labor savings and ultimately led to the demise of unionized typesetter jobs. This savings helped to fund newspaper acquisitions and further consolidation, argues Elizabeth Neiva. See Neiva, "Chain Building: The Consolidation of the American Newspaper Industry, 1955–1980," *Business and Economic History* 24, no. 1 (1995): 22–26.

60. Emery, Emery, and Roberts, *The Press and America.* The growth of newspaper chains at this time occurred because of two main reasons: companies could avoid some taxes in profits

by investing in other newspapers, and independent family owners of newspapers could avoid inheritance taxes (and pay only lower capital gains taxes) by selling them or taking the newspapers public. See also Davies, *The Postwar Decline*, 119.

61. Christopher R. Martin, *Framed! Labor and the Corporate Media* (Ithaca, NY: Cornell University Press, 2004).

62. Doug Underwood, *When MBAs Rule the Newsroom: How the Marketers and Managers Are Reshaping Today's Media* (New York: Columbia University Press, 1993), 40–41.

63. Emery, Emery, and Roberts, *The Press and America*, 538.

64. Emery, Emery, and Roberts, 537.

65. Gilbert Cranberg, Randall Bezanson, and John Soloski, *Taking Stock: Journalism and the Publicly Traded Newspaper Company* (Ames: Iowa State University, 2001).

66. Randal A. Beam, "Size of Corporate Parent Drives Market Orientation," *Newspaper Research Journal* 23 (2002): 46–63.

67. Davies, *The Postwar Decline*, 127.

68. Leo Bogart, *Preserving the Press* (New York: Columbia University Press, 1991), 36; Robert Picard, "U.S. Newspaper Ad Revenue Shows Consistent Growth," *Newspaper Research Journal* 23, no. 4 (2002): 21–33.

69. Richard Campbell, Christopher R. Martin, and Bettina Fabos, *Media & Culture: Mass Communication in a Digital Age*, 10th ed. (New York: Bedford/St. Martin's, 2015), 323.

70. Bogart, *Preserving the Press*, 156.

71. Bogart, 41.

72. Bogart, 43–44.

73. Bogart, 157–58.

74. Davies, *The Postwar Decline*, 64.

75. "Press: Race Daily," *Time*, April 4, 1932, http://content.time.com/time/subscriber/article/0,33009,743467,00.html.

76. Patrick S. Washburn, *The African American Newspaper: Voices of Freedom* (Evanston, IL: Northwestern University Press, 2006). See also Frank Luther Mott, *The News in America* (Cambridge, MA: Harvard University Press, 1952), 15; and Davies, *The Postwar Decline*.

77. Ellis Cose, *The Press* (New York: William Morrow, 1989).

78. Bogart, *Preserving the Press*, 158.

79. Thomas C. Leonard, *News for All: America's Coming-of-Age with the Press* (New York: Oxford University Press, 1995), 175–76.

80. Philip Meyer, *The Vanishing Newspaper: Saving Journalism in the Information Age*, 2nd ed. (Columbia: University of Missouri Press, 2009), 16. In 2017 the *Des Moines Register* published two advertising editions: a Central Iowa edition distributed in twenty-five counties in and surrounding the Des Moines metro area, and a state edition for the other seventy-four Iowa counties.

81. Underwood, *When the MBAs Ruled*, 8.

82. Emery, Emery, and Roberts, *The Press and America*, 544.

83. Conrad C. Fink, *Strategic Newspaper Management* (Boston: Allyn & Bacon, 1996), 251.

84. Leonard, *News for All*, 193.

85. David Shaw, *Journalism Today: A Changing Press for a Changing America* (New York: Harper's College Press, 1977), 219.

86. Leonard, *News for All*, 200.

87. Leonard, 174.

88. Leonard, 174.

89. Lars Willnat and David Weaver, *The American Journalist in the Digital Age: Key Findings*, May 1, 2014, http://news.indiana.edu/releases/iu/2014/05/2013-american-journalist-key-findings.pdf.

90. Meyer, *The Vanishing Newspaper,* 47, 75.

91. David Croteau and William Hoynes, *The Business of Media: Corporate Media and the Public Interest* (Thousand Oaks, CA: Pine Forge, 2001), 205. See also Leonard, *News for All.*

3. The News Media's Shift to Upscale Audiences

1. For example, "upscale" is used by the *Los Angeles Times* media kit. See "Why LA Times," *Los Angeles Times,* 2017, http://mediakit.latimes.com/Media/LosAngelesTimesMediaKit/Toolkit/Why%20LA%20Times.pdf. The terms "influential," "affluent," and "elite" were used by the *New York Times'* media kit. See *New York Times* Media Kit, "Newspaper: Weekday/Sunday Audience," 2017, http://nytmediakit.com/newspaper.

2. Bill Kovach and Tom Rosenstiel, *The Elements of Journalism* (New York: Three Rivers, 2001).

3. Herbert A. Kenny, *Newspaper Row: Journalism in the Pre-television Era* (Chester, CT: Globe Pequot, 1987), 16.

4. Greg Mitchell, "'E&P' Suspends Operations—Good Chance for Return," *Editor & Publisher,* December 31, 2009, http://www.editorandpublisher.com/eandp/news/article_display.jsp?vnu_content_id=1004055964.

5. For this section, I analyzed various early editions of *Editor & Publisher* at the New York Public Library (including 1901, 1910, and 1925) and the 1934 volume (part 2, beginning July 21) at the King Library of Miami University. Starting with the year 1940 (volume 73), I analyzed entire years at 15-year intervals, including 1955 (volume 88) and 1970 (volume 103) at the King Library; and 1985 (volume 118) and 2000 (volume 133) at the Rod Library of the University of Northern Iowa.

6. *Editor & Publisher,* July 21, 1934, 203.

7. Michael Schudson, *Discovering the News* (New York: Basic, 1978).

8. *New York Times,* October 10, 1898, cited in Willard Grosvenor Bleyer, *Main Currents in the History of American Journalism* (Boston: Houghton Mifflin, 1927), 407.

9. Bleyer, *Main Currents,* 408.

10. "The Times Ten Years at One Cent," *New York Times,* October 10, 1908, 8.

11. The *New York Times'* Brown-Smith series first appeared in *Editor & Publisher* on August 17, 1940, and ran intermittently through the October 5, 1940, issue.

12. *Editor & Publisher,* April 13, 1940.

13. Thomas B. Rosenstiel, "Piled Up over Two Decades, Losses Became Insurmountable," *Los Angeles Times,* November 2, 1989, available at "The Wayback Machine: Death of the Herald Examiner," http://herex0.tripod.com/#7.

14. Oviatt Library, "The Last Los Angeles Herald-Examiner Strike," February 3, 2014, http://library.csun.edu/SCA/Peek-in-the-Stacks/Examiner.

15. Ed Keller and Jon Berry, *The Influentials: One American in Ten Tells the Other Nine How to Vote, Where to Eat, and What to Buy* (New York: Free Press, 2003).

16. I retain digital copies of parts of these media kits. These documents are no longer available, for the newspapers update the media kits each year.

17. *Arizona Republic,* "Audience Targeting with Republic Media," November 20, 2017, http://www.republicmedia.com/audience-targeting.

18. *Idaho Statesman,* "Advertising Opportunities," November 21, 2017, http://www.idaho-statesman.com/advertise.

19. *Indianapolis Star,* "2017–2018 Media Guide," November 20, 2017, http://indylb-2135524474. us-east-1.elb.amazonaws.com/marketing/production/b2b/MediaKit2017/sm_StarMedia%20 Guide_09.17.pdf.

20. *News & Record,* "Advertising," November 20, 2017, http://company.news-record.com/advertising/audience-reach.html.

21. *Anchorage Daily News,* "Print Media," November 21, 2017, https://www.adn.com/advertise.

22. *Tulsa World,* "Demographic Profiles," November 21, 2017, http://www.tulsaworld.com/advmediakit/demographics.

23. For a detailed look at all the jobs in Tulsa, see US Bureau of Labor Statistics, "May 2016 Metropolitan and Nonmetropolitan Area Occupational Employment and Wage Estimates, Tulsa, OK," March 31, 2017, https://www.bls.gov/oes/current/oes_46140.htm#00-0000.

24. Ben Bagdikian, *The New Media Monopoly* (Boston: Beacon, 2004), 227.

25. Herbert J. Gans, *Deciding What's News* (New York: Vintage, 1979), 248.

26. Robert McChesney, *Rich Media, Poor Democracy* (New York: New Press, 1999), 55.

27. Tom Cullen, "'The Times Wins the 2017 Pulitzer Prize," *Storm Lake Times,* April 12, 2017, http://www.stormlake.com/articles/2017/04/12/times-wins-2017-pulitzer-prize.

28. JaredStrong, "PulitzerPrizeWasaFather-and-SonEffort,"(Carroll,Iowa)*DailyTimesHerald,*April 11, 2017, http://www.carrollspaper.com/Content/Default/Homepage-Rotating-Articles/Article/ Pulitzer-Prize-was-a-father-and-son-effort/-3/449/24309. The *Pilot-Tribune* publishes three times per week, compared to the *Storm Lake Times'* two times per week.

29. Mark A. Grey, "'Turning the Pork Industry Upside Down: Storm Lake's Hygrade Work Force and the Impact of the 1981 Plant Closure," *Annals of Iowa* 54, no. 3 (1995): 245.

30. US Census Bureau, "American Fact Finder," Buena Vista County, Iowa, 2015 American Community Survey estimates, https://factfinder.census.gov/faces/nav/jsf/pages/community_ facts.xhtml.

31. Daniel P. Finney and Jeffrey C. Kummer, "Iowa to Follow Storm Lake's Lead in Diversity," *Des Moines Register,* October 21, 2014, http://www.desmoinesregister.com/story/ news/2014/10/22/changing-face-iowa-follow-storm-lake-lead/17703097.

32. Strong, "Pulitzer Prize Was a Father-and-Son Effort."

4. The Changing News Narrative about Workers

1. To chart the transformation of labor news, I critically analyzed news reports of all major transit strikes (including metropolitan area transit, such as bus, subway, streetcar, and rail, and national airline travel) at the *New York Times* and *Washington Post* for full years at 15-year intervals: 1940, 1955, 1970, 1985, and 2000.

2. Roger Fowler, *Language in the News* (London: Routledge, 1991).

3. Christopher R. Martin, *Framed! Labor and the Corporate Media* (Ithaca, NY: Cornell University Press, 2004).

4. James W. Carey, *Communication as Culture: Essays on Media and Society* (Boston: Unwin Hyman, 1989), 21.

5. Lance Bennett and Murray Edelman, "Toward a New Political Narrative," *Journal of Communication* 35, no. 4 (1985): 156–71. See also Todd Gitlin, *The Whole World Is Watching* (Berkeley: University of California Press, 1980).

6. Fowler, *Language,* 222.

7. "East Side Bus Line Tied Up by Strike," *New York Times*, July 18, 1940, 18.

8. See Glasgow University Media Group, *Bad News* (London: Routledge and Kegan Paul, 1976); Glasgow University Media Group, *More Bad News* (London: Routledge and Kegan Paul, 1980); and Glasgow University Media Group, *Really Bad News* (London: Readers and Writers, 1982).

9. "Strikers Replaced by Bus Executives," *New York Times*, July 19, 1940, 14.

10. Edward F. Ryan, "Transit Strike Parleys Deadlocked; Wolfson Refuses to Return Next Week; Capital's Worst Traffic Crush Solved," *Washington Post*, July 2, 1955, 1–2. The *Post* was identified in the nameplate as the *Washington Post and Times-Herald* at this time, after the *Post* purchased the *Times-Herald* in 1954.

11. William J. Brady and Richard J. Malloy, "All-Time District Traffic Record Set as Transit Strike Brings Out Cars," *Washington Post*, July 2, 1955, 1–2.

12. "Washington Takes Its Transit Strike in Stride!" *Washington Post*, July 2, 1955, 10.

13. Edward F. Ryan, "Two Parleys Fail in Strike Deadlock; Morse Demands Return of Wolfson," *Washington Post*, July 6, 1955, 1, 29.

14. Edward F. Ryan, "Senators Act on Plea by Ike; Wolfson Shuns Hearing Today," *Washington Post*, July 7, 1955, 1, 2.

15. Edward F. Ryan, "Suggestion Follow Flat Refusal to Arbitrate," *Washington Post*, July 8, 1955, 1, 2.

16. "Strikers Are Grim, Bitter at Wolfson," *Washington Post*, July 5, 1955, 5.

17. Adam Bernstein, "Louis E. Wolfson, 95: Figured in Fortas Scandal," *Washington Post*, January 3, 2008, http://www.washingtonpost.com/wp-dyn/content/article/2008/01/02/AR20 08010203057.html.

18. PATCO was the union that was later infamously destroyed when President Ronald Reagan fired all striking air traffic controllers in 1981.

19. Robert Lindsey, "Some Report Ill," *New York Times*, March 26, 1970, 1, 52.

20. Robert Lindsey, "Traffic Disputes and Wide Storms Snarl Airports," *New York Times*, March 27, 1970, 1, 14.

21. Lindsey, "Traffic Disputes," 14.

22. Lindsey, 14.

23. Robert Lindsey, "Airports Jammed as 'Sick' Stoppage Spreads to West," *New York Times*, March 28, 1970, 1, 19.

24. For more examples, see my account of the 1993 American Airlines flight attendant strike in chapter 5 of *Framed! Labor and the Corporate Media*.

25. Agis Salpukas, "Transport Workers Strike, Halting Pan Am Flights," *New York Times*, March 1, 1985, A10; Kevin Klose, "Busy O'Hare a Beehive of Inactivity," *Washington Post*, May 18, 1985, A6; Steven Greenhouse, "Strike Snarls Flight Plans in Chicago," *New York Times*, May 18, 1985, 32; Joseph P. Fried, "Strike of 4 Bus Lines Disrupts Travel for Thousands in Queens and Bronx," *New York Times*, August 14, 1985, B3.

26. Klose, "Busy O'Hare," A6.

27. See Martin, *Framed!*

28. Ben Bagdikian, *The New Media Monopoly* (Boston: Beacon, 2004), 120–21.

29. Lizabeth Cohen, *A Consumers' Republic: The Politics of Mass Consumption in Postwar America* (New York: Vintage, 2003).

30. Gary Cross, *An All-Consuming Century: Why Commercialism Won in Modern America* (New York: Columbia University Press, 2000), 191.

31. Robert N. Bellah et al., *Habits of the Heart: Individualism and Commitment to American Life* (New York: Harper & Row, 1985).

32. Cohen, *A Consumers' Republic*. See also Jefferson Cowie, *Stayin' Alive: The 1970s and the Last Days of the Working Class* (New York: New Press, 2010).

33. Carey, *Communication as Culture*, 21.

34. Barbara Presley Noble, "At Work; A Job Coach's Sobering Pep Talk," *New York Times*, October 2, 1994, http://www.nytimes.com/1994/10/02/business/at-work-a-job-coach-s-sobering-pep-talk.html.

35. Carol Kleiman, "Working, Writing Woman Looks Back, Ahead," *Chicago Tribune*, January 31, 2006, http://articles.chicagotribune.com/2006-01-31/business/0601310115_1_working-woman-minorities-and-women-african-american-women.

36. Kleiman, "Working, Writing Woman."

37. Carol Kleiman, *Winning the Job Game: The New Rules for Finding and Keeping the Job You Want* (Hoboken, NJ: Wiley & Sons, 2002), xx.

38. Chris Roush, "Carol Kleiman Q&A," *History of Business Journalism*, http://www.bizjournalismhistory.org/history_kleiman.htm.

39. Penelope Trunk, "Working for a Living: The Workplace Beat," Publicity Club of New York, May 19, 2006, accessed September 23, 2006, http://www.publicityclub.org/DOCS/051906_Trunk.pdf.

40. Mackenzie Dawson, "Working for a Living: The Workplace Beat," accessed September 23, 2006, May 19, 2006, accessed September 23, 2006, http://www.publicityclub.org/DOCS/051906_Dawson.pdf.

41. Michael Miner, "The Tribune Casualty List," *Chicago Reader*, August 18, 2008, http://www.chicagoreader.com/Bleader/archives/2008/08/17/the-tribune-casualty-list.

42. Phil Rosenthal, "28 Newsroom Jobs, New City News Cut by Tribune," *Chicago Tribune*, December 2, 2005, http://articles.chicagotribune.com/2005-12-02/business/0512020102_1_newsroom-tax-court-ruling-chicago-tribune. The *Chicago Tribune* filled the labor reporter position with Alexia Elejalde-Ruiz in 2014.

43. Rex Huppke, "I Just Work Here" archive, *Chicago Tribune*, http://www.chicagotribune.com/business/careers/ijustworkhere.

44. Rex Huppke, "Bosses Must Become Vacation Evangelists," *Chicago Tribune*, May 19, 2017, http://www.chicagotribune.com/business/careers/ijustworkhere/ct-need-for-vacations-huppke-work-advice-0521-biz-20170518-column.html; and "It's Time for CEOs to Address Stagnant Worker Pay," *Chicago Tribune*, May 16, 2017, http://www.chicagotribune.com/business/careers/ijustworkhere/ct-stagnant-wages-huppke-work-advice-0514-biz-20170512-column.html.

45. Thomas Frank, *One Market under God* (New York: Doubleday, 2000), 120.

46. Philip H. Dougherty, "Advertising: Time Inc. Will Offer New Magazine, Money, in Fall," *New York Times*, April 21, 1972, 60. Prior to the launching of *Money* magazine, one could get some Wall Street news on PBS, where the program *Wall Street Week with Louis Rukeyser* began its long run in 1970.

47. Adam Bernstein, "Henry Brown; Sire of Money Market Fund Investment," *Washington Post*, August 15, 2008, http://www.washingtonpost.com/wp-dyn/content/article/2008/08/14/AR2008081403509.html. See also Joseph Nocera, *A Piece of the Action: How the Middle Class Joined the Money Class* (New York: Simon & Schuster, 1994).

48. Jenny Strasberg, "The Genesis of Discount Brokerage / 1975 SEC Deregulation Offered an Opening; Schwab Stepped In," *SFGate*, May 1, 2005, http://www.sfgate.com/business/article/The-genesis-of-discount-brokerage-1975-SEC-2637815.php.

49. Dean Starkman, *The Watchdog That Didn't Bark: The Financial Crisis and the Disappearance of Investigative Journalism* (New York: Columbia University Press, 2014), Ebook edition, chapter 5.

50. Diana B. Henriques, "Business Reporting: Behind the Curve," *Columbia Journalism Review*, November/December 2000, 18–21.

51. Starkman, *The Watchdog,* chapter 5.

52. Starkman. Interestingly, Roger Ailes hired Bartiromo at CBNC before he left to establish Fox News. In 2009 CNBC kick-started the Tea Party movement.

53. Frank, *One Market,* 120.

54. Judith Stein, *Pivotal Decade: How the United States Traded Factories for Finance in the Seventies* (New Haven, CT: Yale University Press, 2011), 296.

55. Edward N. Wolff, "Household Wealth Trends in the United States, 1962 to 2013: What Happened over the Great Recession?" *RSF: The Russell Sage Foundation Journal of the Social Sciences* 2, no. 6 (2016): 24–43.

56. Wolff, "Household Wealth Trends." Wolff's numbers are rounded, so they don't add up to precisely 100 percent here.

57. Wolff. If we include passive investments such as retirement plans, 41 percent of the middle 60 percent of US households own stocks. But they are not able to be active traders of those investments.

58. Henriques, "Business Reporting," 21.

59. Henriques.

60. The National Rifle Association (NRA) also published magazines, which became more oriented to conservative politics with the appointment of Ashley Halsey, Jr., a former associate editor of the *Saturday Evening Post,* to edit *American Rifleman* in 1966. Members today can choose from four magazines: *American Rifleman* (established 1923), *American Hunter* (1973), *America's First Freedom* (1993), and *Shooting Illustrated* (added as an official NRA member magazine in 2016). See Thomas J. Brown, "Civil War Memory and American Gun Culture," NCPH History @ Work, November 10, 2015, http://ncph.org/history-at-work/civil-war-and-american-gun. Brown explains that Halsey was a Civil War buff and Confederacy sympathizer, and he "fought to defeat efforts to enact new gun control legislation following the assassination of John F. Kennedy."

61. Richard A. Viguerie and David Franke, *America's Right Turn: How Conservatives Used New and Alternative Media to Take Power* (Chicago: Bonus, 2004), 91.

62. Viguerie and Franke, *America's Right Turn,* 12.

63. Sarah Ellison, *War at the* Wall Street Journal (Boston: Houghton Mifflin Harcourt, 2010), xix.

64. David Brock, *The Republican Noise Machine* (New York: Crown, 2004).

65. Richard A. Viguerie, "We're Coming for You, John Boehner," *Politico,* April 17, 2014, https://www.politico.com/magazine/story/2014/04/were-coming-for-you-john-boehner-105781_Page2.html. Viguerie was also part of the Moral Majority, a conservative religious lobbying organization started by televangelist Jerry Falwell in 1979.

66. Robert L. Hilliard and Michael C. Keith, *Waves of Rancor: Tuning in the Radical Right* (Armonk, NY: M. E. Sharpe, 1999), 15.

67. Hilliard and Keith, *Waves of Rancor,* 17.

68. Rush Limbaugh, *See I Told You So* (New York: Pocket Star, 1993), 372.

69. "The Top Talk Radio Audiences," *Talkers,* April 2018, http://www.talkers.com/top-talk-audiences. The only national talk radio host in the top 10 for April 2018 who did not specialize in conservative political talk radio was Dave Ramsay, who hosts a personal finance talk show.

70. David Foster Wallace, "Host," *Atlantic,* April 2005, https://www.theatlantic.com/magazine/archive/2005/04/host/303812.

71. Kathleen Hall Jamieson and Joseph N. Cappella, *Echo Chamber: Rush Limbaugh and the Conservative Media Establishment* (Oxford: Oxford University Press, 2008), 46.

72. Jane Meyer, "The Reclusive Hedge-Fund Tycoon behind the Trump Presidency," *New Yorker,* March 27, 2017, https://www.newyorker.com/magazine/2017/03/27/the-reclusive-hedge-fund-tycoon-behind-the-trump-presidency.

73. Patrick J. Buchanan, *The New Majority: President Nixon at Mid-passage* (Philadelphia: Girard Bank, 1973), 21–22.

74. David Folkenflik, "Roger Ailes' Unparalleled Impact on the Public Sphere," NPR, July 23, 2016, http://www.npr.org/2016/07/23/487181154/the-rise-fall-and-lasting-influence-of-roger-ailes.

75. Marisa Guthrie, "Roger Ailes Resigns as Fox News Chief after Sexual Harassment Accusations," *Hollywood Reporter*, July 21, 2016, https://www.hollywoodreporter.com/news/roger-ailes-resigns-as-fox-913206. Murdoch maintained control of Fox News after Ailes's departure and moved into Ailes's old office to personally run Fox News. Even after Murdoch made a deal to sell 21st Century Fox to Disney for $52.4 billion in late 2017, Murdoch planned to retain some properties, including Fox News.

76. Trump's number of followers in January 2019.

77. Mathew Ingram, "The 140-Character President," *Columbia Journalism Review*, Fall 2017, https://www.cjr.org/special_report/trump-twitter-tweets-president.php.

78. Dan Glaister, "Recordings Reveal Richard Nixon's Paranoia," *Guardian*, December 3, 2008, https://www.theguardian.com/world/2008/dec/03/richard-nixon-tapes.

79. Michael M. Grynbaum, "Trump Calls the News Media the 'Enemy of the American People,'" *New York Times*, February 17, 2017, https://www.nytimes.com/2017/02/17/business/trump-calls-the-news-media-the-enemy-of-the-people.html.

80. Rush Limbaugh, *The Way Things Ought to Be* (New York: Pocket Books, 1992), 268–69.

81. Wallace, "Host."

82. Susan Douglas, "Letting the Boys Be Boys: Talk Radio, Male Hysteria, and Political Discourse in the 1980s," in *Radio Reader: Essays in the Cultural History of Radio*, eds. Michele Hilmes and Jason Loviglio (New York: Routledge, 2002), 487.

83. Bill O'Reilly, *Who's Looking Out for You?* (New York: Broadway, 2003), 78.

84. For a deeper dive into "backlash conservativism," see chapter 6 of Thomas Frank, *What's the Matter with Kansas? How Conservatives Won the Heart of America* (New York: Metropolitan, 2004).

85. Joshua Green, *Devil's Bargain* (New York: Penguin, 2017), 86.

86. StarMedia Media Guide 2017–2018, "Our Content Engages High Value Consumers," http://indylb-2135524474.us-east-1.elb.amazonaws.com/marketing/production/b2b/Media Kit2017/sm_StarMedia%20Guide_09.17.pdf, 5. Gannett acquired the *Indianapolis Star* in 2000.

5. Workers and Political Voice

1. "Roosevelt Weighs War Labor Parley," *New York Times*, December 10, 1941, 28.

2. S. Thomma, "Bush Marks Pearl Harbor Day," *San Jose Mercury News*, December 8, 2001, 6A.

3. George W. Bush, "Remarks by the President to Airline Employees, O'Hare International Airport," Chicago, Illinois, September 27, 2001, http://www.whitehouse.gov/news/releases/2001/09/20010927-1.html.

4. D. Finney, "'Let's Roll': Unlike the World War II Generation, Today's Americans Are Being Exhorted to Spend, Not Save," *Omaha World Herald*, November 22, 2001, 1D.

5. Steven Greenhouse, "Labor Issue May Stall Security Bill," *New York Times*, July 28, 2002, 22.

6. Bill Kovach and Tom Rosenstiel, *The Elements of Journalism* (New York: Three Rivers, 2001), 139.

7. Thomas Frank, *Listen, Liberal, or What Ever Happened to the Party of the People?* (New York: Metropolitan, 2016).

8. See Christopher R. Martin, *Framed! Labor and the Corporate Media* (Ithaca, NY: Cornell University Press, 2004).

9. Christopher R. Martin, "'Upscale' News Audiences and the Transformation of Labor News," *Journalism Studies* 9, no. 2 (2008): 178–94.

10. Philip Rucker, "Mitt Romney Says 'Corporations Are People' at Iowa State Fair," *Washington Post*, August 11, 2011, http://www.washingtonpost.com/politics/mitt-romney-says-corporations-are-people/2011/08/11/gIQABwZ38I_story.html. To see to which people the corporate money actually goes, see Michael Barbaro, "After a Romney Deal, Profits and Then Layoffs," *New York Times*, November 12, 2011, http://www.nytimes.com/2011/11/13/us/politics/after-mitt-romney-deal-company-showed-profits-and-then-layoffs.html.

11. Union rates hit 34.7 percent in 1954. See US Bureau of the Census, *Statistical Abstract of the United States* (Lanham, MD: Bernan, 1993). See also US Bureau of Labor Statistics, *Union Members—2017*, January 19, 2018, http://www.bls.gov/news.release/pdf/union2.pdf.

12. Dwight D. Eisenhower, "Address at the Cow Palace on Accepting the Nomination of the Republican National Convention," August 23, 1956, http://www.presidency.ucsb.edu/ws/?pid=10583.

13. John F. Kennedy, "Address of Senator John F. Kennedy, Accepting the Democratic Party Nomination for the Presidency of the United States," Democratic National Convention, July 15, 1960, http://www.4president.org/speeches/1960/jfk1960acceptance.htm.

14. Lyndon Johnson, "President Lyndon B. Johnson's Remarks before the National Convention upon Accepting the Nomination," Democratic National Convention, August 27, 1964, http://www.4president.org/speeches/1964/lbj1964acceptance.htm.

15. Erin Hatton, *The Temp Economy: From Kelly Girls to Permatemps in Postwar America* (Philadelphia: Temple University Press, 2011).

16. Richard M. Nixon, "Nomination Acceptance Speech," Republican National Convention, August 8, 1968, http://www.4president.org/speeches/1968/nixon1968acceptance.htm.

17. See, for example, George Lakoff, *Don't Think of an Elephant! Know Your Values and Frame the Debate* (White River Junction, VT: Chelsea Green, 2004); Thomas Frank, *What's the Matter with Kansas? How Conservatives Won the Heart of America* (New York: Metropolitan, 2004); Paul Krugman, *The Conscience of a Liberal* (New York: W.W. Norton, 2007).

18. Jefferson Cowie, *Stayin' Alive: The 1970s and the Last Days of the Working Class* (New York: New Press, 2010), 130.

19. Richard M. Nixon, "Nomination Acceptance Speech," Republican National Convention, August 23, 1972, http://www.4president.org/speeches/1972/nixon1972acceptance.htm.

20. Jimmy Carter, "Nomination Acceptance Speech," Democratic National Convention, July 15, 1976, http://www.4president.org/speeches/1976/carter1976acceptance.htm.

21. Robert H. Zeiger and Gilbert J. Gall, *American Workers, American Unions*, 3rd ed. (Baltimore, MD: Johns Hopkins University Press, 2002), 247–48. See also Cowie, *Stayin' Alive*.

22. Mary Russell and Spencer Rich, "Carter's Fiscal Conservativism Irks Party Leaders," *Washington Post*, May 8, 1977, https://www.washingtonpost.com/archive/politics/1977/05/08/carters-fiscal-conservatism-irks-party-leaders/adcf3142-e4ad-4b90-a3fe-f954c2986b30/?utm_term=.60e4846e9fc0. US Representative Gus Hawkins was cosponsor of the Humphrey-Hawkins full employment legislation that was enacted in 1978 but made impotent in the legislative process and because of Carter's tepid support.

23. Ronald Reagan, "Nomination Acceptance Speech," Republican National Convention, July 17, 1980, http://www.4president.org/speeches/1980/reagan1980acceptance.htm.

24. David Harvey, *The Condition of Postmodernity* (Cambridge, MA: Blackwell, 1990).

25. Ronald Reagan, "Nomination Acceptance Speech," Republican National Convention, August 23, 1984, http://www.4president.org/speeches/1984/reagan1984acceptance.htm.

26. George H. W. Bush, "Nomination Acceptance Speech," Republican National Convention, August 18, 1988, http://www.4president.org/speeches/1988/georgebush1988acceptance.htm.

27. Bill Clinton, "Nomination Acceptance Speech," Democratic National Convention, July 16, 1992, http://www.4president.org/speeches/1992/clintongore1992convention.htm.

28. Critical geography scholar David Harvey defines neoliberalism as "a theory of economic practices that proposes that human well-being can best be advanced by liberating individual entrepreneurial freedoms and skills within an institutional framework characterized by strong private property rights, free markets, and free trade. The role of the state is to create and preserve an institutional framework appropriate to such practices." See David Harvey, *A Brief History of Neoliberalism* (New York: Oxford University Press, 2005), 2.

29. Bill Clinton, "Nomination Acceptance Speech," Democratic National Convention, August 29, 1996, http://www.4president.org/speeches/1996/clintongore1996convention.htm.

30. George W. Bush, "Nomination Acceptance Speech," Republican National Convention, August 3, 2000, http://www.4president.org/speeches/2000/bushcheney2000convention.htm.

31. George W. Bush, "Nomination Acceptance Speech," Republican National Convention, September 2, 2004, http://www.4president.org/speeches/2004/bushcheney2004convention.htm.

32. Annie Lowrey, "Happy 10th Birthday, Bush Tax Cuts! You've Been a Failure in Every Conceivable Way," *Slate*, June 8, 2011, http://www.slate.com/articles/business/moneybox/2011/06/happy_10th_birthday_bush_tax_cuts.html.

33. Barack Obama, "Nomination Acceptance Speech," Democratic National Convention, August 28, 2008, http://www.4president.org/speeches/2008/barackobama2008acceptance.htm.

34. Barack Obama, "Nomination Acceptance Speech," Democratic National Convention, September 6, 2012, http://www.4president.org/speeches/2012/barackobama2012conventionacceptance.htm.

35. Glenn Kessler and Ye Hee Lee, "Fact-Checking Donald Trump's Acceptance Speech at the 2016 RNC," *Washington Post*, July 22, 2016, https://www.washingtonpost.com/news/fact-checker/wp/2016/07/22/fact-checking-donald-trumps-acceptance-speech-at-the-2016-rnc/?utm_term=.dcc126e72365; Lori Robertson, "FactChecking Trump's Big Speech," FactCheck.org, July 22, 2016, http://www.factcheck.org/2016/07/factchecking-trumps-big-speech.

36. John Gramlich, "5 Facts about Crime in the U.S.," Pew Research Center, February 21, 2017, http://www.pewresearch.org/fact-tank/2017/02/21/5-facts-about-crime-in-the-u-s.

37. "Full Text: Donald Trump 2016 RNC Draft Speech Transcript," *Politico*, July 21, 2016, https://www.politico.com/story/2016/07/full-transcript-donald-trump-nomination-acceptance-speech-at-rnc-225974.

38. Eisenhower, "Address at the Cow Palace."

39. Maxwell McCombs and Donald Shaw, "The Agenda-Setting Function of Mass Media," *Public Opinion Quarterly* 36 (1972): 176–87; Dennis Chong and James N. Druckman, "Dynamic Public Opinion: Framing Effects over Time," *American Political Science Association* 104, no. 4 (2008): 663–80.

40. Elizabeth Weingarten, "The Language Time Machine," *Slate*, September 9, 2013, http://www.slate.com/articles/technology/future_tense/2013/09/google_ngram_viewer_a_language_time_machine.html. See also Google Books Ngram Viewer, 2013, https://books.google.com/ngrams/info. (The name "Ngram" refers to the variable number of words one can use in a search.)

41. Jean-Baptiste Michel et al., "Quantitative Analysis of Culture Using Millions of Digitized Books," *Science*, December 16, 2010, www.sciencemag.org/content/early/2010/12/15/science.1199644.

42. Gary Andrew Poole, "'Wealth Porn,' and Beyond." *Columbia Journalism Review*, November/December 2000, 22–23.

43. US Census Bureau, *Statistics of U.S. Businesses (SUSB)—U.S., All Industries*, 2008, http://www.census.gov/econ/susb.

44. US Bureau of Labor Statistics, *Characteristics of Minimum Wage Workers: 2010*, http://www.bls.gov/cps/minwage2010.htm.

45. Jack Shafer, "Who Said It First?" *Slate*, August 30, 2010, http://www.slate.com/articles/news_and_politics/press_box/2010/08/who_said_it_first.html.

46. Congressional Budget Office, "Trends in the Distribution of Household Income between 1979 and 2007," October 2011, http://cbo.gov/ftpdocs/124xx/doc12485/10-25-HouseholdIncome.pdf.

47. Thomas Piketty and Emmanuel Saez, "Income Inequality in the United States, 1913–1998," *Quarterly Journal of Economics* 118, no. 1 (2003): 1–39.

48. Sylvia Allegretto, "The State of Working America's Wealth, 2011: Through Volatility and Turmoil, the Gap Widens," Economic Policy Institute, March 23, 2011, Briefing Paper 292, http://epi.3cdn.net/2a7ccb3e9e618f0bbc_3nm6idnax.pdf.

49. Michael C. McGee, "In Search of 'The People': A Rhetorical Alternative," *Quarterly Journal of Speech* 61, no. 3 (1975): 246.

50. "Rick Santelli Calls for Tea Party on Floor of Chicago Board of Trade," CNBC, February 19, 2009, https://www.youtube.com/watch?v=wcvSjKCU_Zo.

51. Sarah Jaffe, *Necessary Trouble: America in Revolt* (New York: Nation, 2016), 23, 25.

52. Angie Maxwell and T. Wayne Parent, "A 'Subterranean Agenda'? Racial Attitudes, Presidential Evaluations, and Tea Party Membership," *Race and Social Problems* 5, no. 3 (2013): 226–37.

53. Jaffe, *Necessary Trouble*, 34.

54. "#OccupyWallStreet," *Adbusters*, July 13, 2011, http://www.adbusters.org/blogs/adbusters-blog/occupywallstreet.html.

55. Jaffe, *Necessary Trouble;* see also Esther Addley, "Occupy Movement: From Local Action to a Global Howl of Protest," *Guardian*, October 17, 2011, https://www.theguardian.com/world/2011/oct/17/occupy-movement-global-protest. My hometown of Cedar Falls, Iowa, had its own encampment in the park across from City Hall along with protest marches that attracted hundreds. Cedar Falls also has its share of Tea Party members involved in Republican politics.

56. Jaffe, *Necessary Trouble*, 37.

57. Dave Gilson, "It's the Inequality, Stupid," *Mother Jones*, March/April 2011, http://motherjones.com/politics/2011/02/income-inequality-in-america-chart-graph; Robert Borosage and Katrina vanden Heuvel, "The American Dream: Can a Movement Save It?" *Nation*, October 10, 2011, 11–15.

58. Theodore Schliefer, "King Doubles Down on Controversial 'Babies' Tweet," CNN, March 14, 2017, http://www.cnn.com/2017/03/13/politics/steve-king-babies-tweet-cnntv/index.html.

59. Adam Nagourney, "Obama Takes Iowa in a Big Turnout as Clinton Falters; Huckabee Victor," *New York Times*, January 4, 2008, https://www.nytimes.com/2008/01/04/us/politics/04elect.html.

60. "Pivot Counties in Iowa," Ballotpedia, March 31, 2017, https://ballotpedia.org/Pivot_Counties_in_Iowa.

61. Nate Cohn, "Why Trump Won: Working-Class Whites," *New York Times*, November 9, 2016, https://www.nytimes.com/2016/11/10/upshot/why-trump-won-working-class-whites.html.

62. "Election Results and Statistics," Iowa Secretary of State, https://sos.iowa.gov/elections/results/#11.

63. Carl Bialik, "No, Voter Turnout Wasn't Way Down from 2012," *FiveThirtyEight*, November 15, 2016, https://fivethirtyeight.com/features/no-voter-turnout-wasnt-way-down-from-2012.

64. See "Iowa Counties by Population," Iowa Demographics, March 2018, https://www.iowa-demographics.com/counties_by_population.

65. Dubuque County, Iowa's eighth-largest county, with a population close to 100,000, and on the state's eastern border of the Mississippi River, is the exception. Trump won with 46.71 percent of the vote, just 612 more votes than Clinton, who received 45.5 percent of the county's vote. Third-party candidates made up the balance.

66. Katherine J. Cramer, *The Politics of Resentment* (Chicago: University of Chicago Press, 2016).

67. Iowa Community Indicators Program, "Educational Attainment of the Adult Population," Iowa State University, December 2014, https://www.icip.iastate.edu/tables/education/attainment.

68. Matthew Stewart, "The Birth of a New American Aristocracy," *Atlantic*, June 2018, 48–63. See also Nate Silver, "Education, Not Income, Predicted Who Would Vote for Trump," *FiveThirtyEight*, November 22, 2016, http://fivethirtyeight.com/features/education-not-income-predicted-who-would-vote-for-trump.

69. One of the counties that Clinton won, Black Hawk, is just below the state percentage, with 25.3 percent of citizens twenty-five years of age or older with a bachelor's degree or higher.

70. Cramer, *The Politics*, 51.

71. Chris Kolmar, "These Are the 10 Fastest Growing Cities in Iowa for 2018," HomeSnacks, December 17, 2017, https://www.homesnacks.net/fastest-growing-cities-in-iowa-127076.

72. For an excellent deeper analysis of pivot counties across several states, see Jeff Guo, "Yes, Working Class Whites Really Did Make Trump Win. No, It Wasn't Simply Economic Anxiety," *Washington Post*, November 11, 2016, https://www.washingtonpost.com/news/wonk/wp/2016/11/11/yes-working-class-whites-really-did-make-trump-win-no-it-wasnt-simply-economic-anxiety.

73. "Iowa Caucus Results," *New York Times*, September 29, 2016, https://www.nytimes.com/elections/2016/results/primaries/iowa.

74. Jeff Stein, "Hillary Clinton: I'm Breathing a 'Big Sigh of Relief' after Iowa Caucus," *Vox*, February 2, 2016, https://www.vox.com/2016/2/2/10892714/hillary-clinton-iowa-reaction.

75. Jeff Stein, "Here's the Full Text of Bernie Sanders's Iowa Speech," *Vox*, February 2, 2016, https://www.vox.com/2016/2/2/10892752/bernie-sanders-iowa-speech.

76. "Iowa Caucus Results."

77. "Full Text: Donald Trump 2016."

78. United States Census Bureau, "Quick Facts—Iowa," July 1, 2017, https://www.census.gov/quickfacts/IA. On Trump voters and throwing out the old rules of politics, see David Leonhardt, "A Time for Big Economic Ideas," *New York Times*, April 22, 2018, https://www.nytimes.com/2018/04/22/opinion/big-economic-ideas.html.

79. Jeff Stein, "The Bernie Voters Who Defected to Trump, Explained by a Political Scientist," *Vox*, August 24, 2017, https://www.vox.com/policy-and-politics/2017/8/24/16194086/bernie-trump-voters-study.

80. Diana C. Mutz, "Status Threat, Not Economic Hardship, Explains the 2016 Presidential Vote," *Proceedings of the National Academy of Sciences*, May 8, 2018, https://doi.org/10.1073/pnas.1718155115. See also Andrew J. Cherlin, "You Can't Separate Money from Culture," *New York Times*, May 6, 2018, https://www.nytimes.com/2018/05/06/opinion/trump-supporters-economy-racism.html.

81. "What the Media Missed: Fear of Losing Status, Not Economic Anxiety, Moved 2016 Voters," *Reliable Sources with Brian Stelter Podcast*, April 26, 2018, https://tunein.com/podcasts/Noticias-y-Poltica/Reliable-Sources-with-Brian-Stelter-p111627/?topicId=121115831.

82. Leonard Pitts, Jr., "This Time, the Joke Was on Roseanne Barr," *Miami Herald,* May 29, 2018, http://www.miamiherald.com/opinion/opn-columns-blogs/leonard-pitts-jr/article212149519.html.

83. "2016 General Election Editorial Endorsements by Major Newspapers," American Presidency Project, November 8, 2016, http://www.presidency.ucsb.edu/data/2016_newspaper_endorsements.php. Other newspapers did not endorse.

84. Register Media, *Des Moines Register,* 2017, https://www.registermedia.com/advertising/the-des-moines-register.

85. Iowa has twenty-two stations owned by the Educational Media Foundation, the largest Christian radio broadcaster in the country, and five stations owned by American Family Radio, the next-largest Christian radio group.

86. Darren Samuelsohn, "The Soccer Moms of 2016," *Politico,* July/August 2016, https://www.politico.com/magazine/story/2016/07/2016-election-battleground-swing-states-soccer-moms-nascar-dads-demographics-trump-clinton-214047.

6. "Job Killers" in the News

1. Maxwell McCombs and Donald Shaw, "The Agenda-Setting Function of Mass Media," *Public Opinion Quarterly* 36 (1972): 176–87.

2. See T. Michael Maher, "Framing: An Emerging Paradigm or a Phase of Agenda Setting?" In *Framing Public Life,* eds. Stephen D. Reese, Oscar H. Gandy, and August E. Grant (Mahweh, NJ: Erlbaum, 2001), 83–94. See also Joseph N. Cappella and Kathleen Hall Jamieson, "News Frames, Political Cynicism, and Media Cynicism," *Annals of the American Academy of Political and Social Science* 546, no. 1 (1996): 71–84.

3. Frank Luntz, "The Persuaders," PBS, November 9, 2004, http://www.pbs.org/wgbh/pages/frontline/shows/persuaders/interviews/luntz.html.

4. Dennis Chong and James N. Druckman, "Dynamic Public Opinion: Framing Effects over Time," *American Political Science Association* 104, no. 4 (2008): 663–80.

5. Dennis Chong and James N. Druckman, "A Theory of Framing and Opinion Formation in Competitive Elite Environments," *Journal of Communication* 57 (2007): 99–118.

6. Bill Kovach and Tom Rosenstiel, *The Elements of Journalism* (New York: Three Rivers, 2007), 79.

7. Society of Professional Journalists, "SPJ Code of Ethics," September 6, 2014, https://www.spj.org/ethicscode.asp.

8. Valid search terms included *job killer, kill jobs* (including phrases with intervening descriptors, such as *kill many jobs* or *kill more jobs,* and *kill manufacturing jobs*).

9. Institute for Policy Integrity, "The Regulatory Red Herring: The Role of Job Impact Analyses in Environmental Policy Debates," New York University School of Law, April 2012, http://policyintegrity.org/files/publications/Regulatory_Red_Herring.pdf.

10. Job Creators Alliance, "Communications Team/Media Placement," http://jobcreatorsalliance.org/About.aspx. For additional critical background, see the Center for Media and Democracy, "Job Creators Network," https://www.sourcewatch.org/index.php/Job_Creators_Network.

11. On the increasing inequality in wealth and income over that period, see "Trends in the Distribution of Household Income between 1979 and 2007," Congressional Budget Office, October 2011, http://cbo.gov/ftpdocs/124xx/doc12485/10-25-HouseholdIncome.pdf; Thomas Piketty and

Emmanuel Saez, "Income Inequality in the United States, 1913–1998," *Quarterly Journal of Economics* 118, no. 1 (2003): 1–39; Sylvia Allegretto, "The State of Working America's Wealth, 2011: Through Volatility and Turmoil, the Gap Widens," Economic Policy Institute, Briefing Paper 292, March 23, 2011, http://epi.3cdn.net/2a7ccb3e9e618f0bbc_3nm6idnax.pdf.

12. Luntz, "The Persuaders."

13. Tim Murphy and David Corn, "Newt in His Own Words: 33 Years of Bomb-Throwing," *Mother Jones*, April 6, 2011, http://motherjones.com/politics/2011/04/newt-gingrich-greatest-rhetorical-hits.

14. Michael Oreskes, "Political Memo; For G.O.P. Arsenal, 133 Words to Fire," *New York Times*, September 9, 1990, http://www.nytimes.com/1990/09/09/us/political-memo-for-gop-arsenal-133-words-to-fire.html. See also "Language: A Key Mechanism of Control," February 1995, http://www.fair.org/index.php?page=1276.

15. Associated Press, "FAQs," http://www.ap.org/pages/about/faq.html#7.

16. Because the focus of our study was longitudinal (i.e., to track the term "job killer" over time), we limited the study to these four major news organizations, which have available public archives for the twenty-eight-year period.

17. After limiting our search to the news outlets below, we conducted a Lexis-Nexis search with the following terms: *job killer OR jobs killer OR job killers OR kill jobs OR kills jobs OR kill more jobs AND NOT top kill jobs AND NOT authority job kill! AND NOT kill you AND NOT job is killing AND NOT job killed AND NOT job of killing AND NOT jobs they are killing AND NOT (job w/5 killed)*. Most of these search terms were used for our search through ProQuest for relevant *Wall Street Journal* stories (the search engine is not as robust, so the last term could not be added). We limited our stories to uses of "job killer" by domestic (US) sources because our focus was on how the term is deployed in US culture. The data was gathered by five coders, each of whom was trained multiple times throughout the study in order to maximize inter-coder reliability of more than 80 percent.

18. The enormous rise in usage of the "job killer" term since 2008 is consistent with the conclusions of a similar study by the Institute for Policy Integrity at the New York University School of Law, which found that "between 2007 and 2011, use of the phrase 'job-killing regulations' in U.S. newspapers increased by 17,550 percent." See Michael A. Livermore, "Use of Phrase 'Job Killing Regulations' Increases 17,550 Percent in Newspapers Since 2007," ThinkProgress.org, April 24, 2012, http://thinkprogress.org/climate/2012/04/24/469582/phrase-job-killing-regulations-increases-17000-in-newspapers-since-2007.

19. Jamieson and Cappella define an "echo chamber" as a "bounded, enclosed media space that has the potential to both magnify the messages delivered within it and insulate them from rebuttal." It "creates a common frame of reference and positive feedback loops for those who listen to, read, and watch these media outlets." See Kathleen Hall Jamieson and Joseph N. Cappella, *Echo Chamber: Rush Limbaugh and the Conservative Media Establishment* (New York: Oxford University Press, 2008), 76. See also Peter Dreier and Christopher R. Martin, "How ACORN Was Framed: Political Controversy and Media Agenda Setting," *Perspectives on Politics* 8, no. 3 (2010): 761–92.

20. David Espo, "Obama Budget Gives Dems a Roadmap, GOP a Target," Associated Press, February 27, 2009.

21. Michael D. Shear and Paul Kane, "For Parties, the Soul-Searching Begins; 'Do People Think We're Tending to the Things They Care About?' " *Washington Post*, November 5, 2009, A01.

22. CalChamber, "Job Killers," http://www.calchamber.com/governmentrelations/pages/jobkillers.aspx. See also Mitchel Benson, "The 'Job Killer' Scare: Can It Work Once More?" *Wall Street Journal*, July 2, 1997, C2.

23. Sheila Kumar, "Calif. Would Be the First State to Ban Foam Containers," Associated Press, August 28, 2011.

24. On rare occasions, however, labor unions leveled the phrase "job killer" at corporations for laying off workers or exporting jobs overseas. In 1996, for example, the Associated Press reported that the United Auto Workers viewed General Motors' move to outsource production of auto parts to lower-wage suppliers as a "job killer." (Actually, no labor source was quoted saying those words; the AP reporter used the term to characterize the union's position: "The strike has focused primarily on outsourcing, the practice of buying parts from outside manufacturers to reduce labor and production costs. The union sees it as a job-killer, while GM says it needs that option to remain competitive.") See James Hannah, "Experts Say Marathon GM Talks Indicate Many Differences," Associated Press, March 19, 1996. Similarly, labor union sources sometimes tagged trade pacts (such as the North American Free Trade Agreement [NAFTA], which passed Congress with bipartisan support in November 1993) as job killers. For example, in the month before NAFTA's passage, the Associate Press noted that "Teamsters President Ron Carey said this week the administration efforts on behalf of the training program is an admission that NAFTA is a 'job killer.'" See John D. McClain, "Reich Says Government Won't Spend All Available Retraining Funds," Associated Press, October 21, 1993.

25. Issues cited as "job killers" in news stories and included in the "Other" category, in order of frequency, are ballot issue (2.4 percent), outsourcing (2.4 percent), political slur (calling someone a job killer disconnected from any issue) (2.1 percent), energy policy (not related to climate change) (1.8 percent), management practices (1.6 percent), new technology (1.6 percent), pro-labor policy (not union issue or wage law) (1.3 percent), corporations (1.3 percent), financial industry (1.0 percent), recession (1.0 percent), immigration (1.0 percent), intellectual property rights (0.8 percent), economic stimulus (0.8 percent), currency/monetary policy (0.5 percent), insurance policy/workers compensation (0.5 percent), jobs bill/job creation policy (0.5 percent), union issue (0.5 percent), government healthy food policy (0.5 percent), employee behavior (0.5 percent), and "all" (0.3 percent, one story): agriculture, consumer protection, corporate malfeasance, credit/debt policy or issue, family leave, market changes, natural resources, workplace fairness, increased productivity, background checks, bureaucracy, budget deficit, group of people, uncertainty, airline regulations, litigation, Internet regulation, unspecified regulation, corporate merger, environmental disaster, workplace safety rules, and private equity business.

26. The *St. Petersburg Times* changed its name to the *Tampa Bay Times* effective January 1, 2012. See http://www.tampabay.com/newname/st-petersburg-times-becomes-tampa-bay-times.

27. PolitiFact.com, *Tampa Bay Times*, January 20, 2011, http://www.politifact.com/truth-o-meter/statements/2011/jan/20/eric-cantor/health-care-law-job-killer-evidence-falls-short. The investigation by PolitiFact represents the best kind of work by journalists. There has been pushback by some conservative opinion journalists who charge that fact-checking units like PolitiFact are "the liberal media's latest attempt to control the discourse." See Mark Hemingway, "Lies, Damned Lies, and 'Fact Checking': The Liberal Media's Latest Attempt to Control the Discourse," *Weekly Standard*, December 19, 2011, http://www.weeklystandard.com/articles/lies-damned-lies-and-fact-checking_611854.html.

28. Kovach and Rosenstiel, *The Elements of Journalism,* 86.

29. Kris Maher, "U.S. News: Unions Push to Undo Ohio Law—Showdown Looms over Referendum to Repeal Public-Employee Bargaining Limits," *Wall Street Journal,* June 3, 2011, A5.

30. Christopher S. Rugaber, "Meltdown 101: Unemployment by the Numbers," Associated Press, March 6, 2009.

31. David Wessel, "U.S. News—CAPITAL: Parsing an Ascendant GOP's Economic Prescriptions," *Wall Street Journal,* September 2, 2010, A2.

32. "Topic A," *Washington Post,* August 15, 2010, A11.

33. Jim Kuhnhenn and Ann Sanner, "GOP Sees Political Advantage Opposing Banking Bill," Associated Press, July 15, 2010.

34. Boehner's Blog, "On NBC Nightly News, Speaker Boehner Calls 'Obamacare . . . the Biggest Job Killer We Have in America Today,'" January 7, 2011, http://www.johnboehner.com/blog/nbc-nightly-news-speaker-boehner-calls-percentE2 percent80 percent9Cobamacare percentE2 percent80 percentA6-biggest-job-killer-we-have-america-today percentE2 percent80 percent9D.

35. This is one of the many places the story appeared: Shannon McCaffrey, "Gingrich Calls Obama's Tax Plan a Job-Killer," Associated Press, April 14, 2011, http://abcnews.go.com/Politics/wireStory?id=13369574#.T2Kt08xiu7s.

36. Newt2012, "AP: Gingrich Calls Obama's Tax Plan a Job-Killer," April 13, 2011, http://m.newt.org/news/ap-gingrich-calls-obama percentE2 percent80 percent99s-tax-plan-job-killer.

37. Unemployment data from US Bureau of Labor Statistics, "Annual Average Unemployment Rate, Civilian Labor Force 16 Years and Over (Percent)," February 3, 2011, http://www.bls.gov/cps/prev_yrs.htm.

38. Matthew Daly, "Senate Democrats Abandon Comprehensive Energy Bill," Associated Press, July 22, 2010.

39. Associated Press, "FAQs," http://www.ap.org/pages/about/faq.html.

40. Associated Press, "AP News in Brief," July 22, 2010.

41. Matthew Daly, "Senate Democrats Turn Focus to Gulf Spill Response," Associated Press, July 23, 2010.

42. Julie Pace, "Obama Says He Still Supports Climate Legislation," Associated Press, July 27, 2010.

43. Google search for "Republicans slammed the bill as a 'national energy tax' and jobs killer," conducted January 2, 2012.

44. Trudy Lieberman, Slanting the Story: The Forces That Shape the News (New York: New Press, 2000).

45. George Packer, "Un-American Activities," New Yorker, January 3, 2012, http://www.newyorker.com/online/blogs/comment/2012/01/santorum-and-the-republicans.html.

46. Arthur S. Brisbane, "Should the Times Be a Truth Vigilante?" New York Times, January 12, 2012, http://publiceditor.blogs.nytimes.com/2012/01/12/should-the-times-be-a-truth-vigilante.

47. At the Cleveland Plain Dealer, political reporters were vigilantly checking political statements for veracity in the 2012 election season. The Columbia Journalism Review praised the Plain Dealer's work: "Even if fact-check stories don't persuade every reader, the research and digging that go into them—and that take the coverage past he-said, she-said—should be de rigueur." See T. C. Brown, "The Plain Dealer on a Potential Senator's 'Estrangement' from Truth," Columbia Journalism Review, March 29, 2012, http://www.cjr.org/swing_states_project/the_plain_dealer_on_a_potentia.php.

7. Rethinking News about US Workers

1. John Harwood, "Gary Cohn Says the 'Paradise Papers' Don't Worry Him at All," CNBC, November 7, 2017, https://www.cnbc.com/2017/11/07/gary-cohn-says-the-paradise-papers-dont-worry-him-at-all.html.

2. Kate Kelly, "Goldman's $285 Million Package for Gary Cohn Is Questioned," New York Times, January 25, 2017, https://www.nytimes.com/2017/01/25/business/dealbook/goldman-sachs-gary-cohn-285-million-departure-package.html.

3. International Consortium of Investigative Journalists, *The Panama Papers*, https://panama-papers.icij.org.

4. International Consortium of Investigative Journalists, *Paradise Papers*, https://www.icij.org/investigations/paradise-papers. See also Aimee Picchi, "Paradise Papers: Names of the Rich Linked to Offshore Accounts," *MoneyWatch*, November 6, 2017, https://www.cbsnews.com/news/paradise-papers-names-of-the-rich-lined-to-offshore-accounts.

5. Several excellent books, over many years, have chronicled America's increasing inequality, including *The Downsizing of America* (New York: Times Books, 1996); David K. Shipler, *The Working Poor: Invisible in America* (New York: Vintage, 2004); David Cay Johnson, *Free Lunch: How the Wealthiest Americans Enrich Themselves at Government Expense (and Stick You with the Bill)* (New York: Portfolio, 2007); Jared Bernstein, *Crunch: Why Do I Feel So Squeezed* (San Francisco: Berrett-Koehler, 2008); Peter Gosselin, *High Wire: The Precarious Financial Lives of American Families* (New York: Basic, 2008); Steven Greenhouse, *The Big Squeeze: Tough Times for the American Worker* (New York: Knopf, 2008); Steven Hill, *Raw Deal: How the "Uber Economy" and Runaway Capitalism Are Screwing American Workers* (New York: St. Martin's, 2015); and Robert B. Reich, *Saving Capitalism: For the Many, Not the Few* (New York: Knopf, 2015).

6. Drew DeSilver, "5 Facts about the Minimum Wage," Pew Research Center, January 4, 2017, http://www.pewresearch.org/fact-tank/2017/01/04/5-facts-about-the-minimum-wage.

7. Elise Gould, "Millions of Working People Don't Get Paid Time Off for Holidays or Vacation," Economic Policy Institute, September 1, 2015, http://www.epi.org/publication/millions-of-working-people-dont-get-paid-time-off-for-holidays-or-vacation.

8. Office of the Assistant Secretary for Planning and Evaluation, "HHS Poverty Guidelines for 2018," https://aspe.hhs.gov/poverty-guidelines. The guidelines are for the forty-eight contiguous states and the District of Columbia. Poverty thresholds are higher for Alaska and Hawaii.

9. Barbara Ehrenreich, *Nickel and Dimed: On (Not) Getting by in America* (New York: Henry Holt, 2001), 214.

10. David Rolf, *The Fight for $15: The Right Wage for a Working America* (New York: New Press, 2016).

11. Jill Disis, "Target Raises Minimum Wage to $11 an Hour, $15 by 2020," *CNNMoney*, September 25, 2017, http://money.cnn.com/2017/09/25/news/companies/target-minimum-wage/index.html; Laura Stevens, "Amazon to Raise Its Minimum US Wage to $15 an Hour," *Wall Street Journal*, October 2, 2018, https://www.wsj.com/articles/amazon-to-raise-its-minimum-u-s-wage-to-15-an-hour-1538476027; also see Karen Weise, "Why Some Amazon Workers Are Fuming about Their Raise," *New York Times*, October 9, 2018, https://www.nytimes.com/2018/10/09/technology/amazon-workers-pay-raise.html.

12. "Why America Needs a $15 Minimum Wage," Economic Policy Institute, April 26, 2017, http://www.epi.org/publication/why-america-needs-a-15-minimum-wage.

13. National Employment Law Project, "Fighting Preemption: The Movement for Higher Wages Must Oppose State Efforts to Block Local Minimum Wage Laws," July 6, 2017, http://www.nelp.org/publication/fighting-preemption-local-minimum-wage-laws.

14. Lawrence Mishel and Alyssa Davis, "Top CEOs Make 300 Times More Than Typical Workers," Economic Policy Institute, June 21, 2015, http://www.epi.org/publication/top-ceos-make-300-times-more-than-workers-pay-growth-surpasses-market-gains-and-the-rest-of-the-0–1-percent.

15. Lawrence Mishel and Jessica Schieder, "Stock Market Headwinds Meant Less Generous Year for Some CEOs," Economic Policy Institute, July 12, 2016, http://www.epi.org/publication/ceo-and-worker-pay-in-2015.

16. Ric Marshall and Linda-Eling Lee, "Are CEOS Paid for Performance? Evaluating the Effectiveness of Equity Incentives," MSCI ESG Research, July 2016, https://www.msci.com/documents/10199/91a7f92b-d4ba-4d29-ae5f-8022f9bb944d.

17. Mishel and Schieder, "Stock Market Headwinds."

18. Mishel and Davis, "Top CEOs Make 300 Times More."

19. Equilar/Associated Press, "Equilar/Associated Press S&P 500 CEO Pay Study 2016," May 25, 2016, http://www.equilar.com/reports/37-associated-press-pay-study-2016.html. As Equilar explains, "This study includes 341 CEOs who served in that role at an S&P 500 company for at least two years as of fiscal year-end. The companies must have filed a proxy between January 1st and April 30th of this year to be included in this study." In the 2016 pay study, only three CEOs—all multibillionaires with vast stock holdings—accepted less than $1 million for their annual compensation: Larry Page (Google cofounder) and John Mackey (Whole Foods Market cofounder) paid themselves $1, while Warren Buffett (head of the Berkshire Hathaway holding company and the third-richest man in America) received $470,244.

20. US Census Bureau, "PINC-01. Selected Characteristics of People 15 Years and over, by Total Money Income, Work Experience, Race, Hispanic Origin, and Sex," Current Population Survey (CPS) Annual Social and Economic (ASEC) Supplement, 2016, http://www.census.gov/data/tables/time-series/demo/income-poverty/cps-pinc/pinc-01.html.

21. Estelle Sommeiller, Mark Price, and Ellis Wazeter, "Income Inequality in the U.S. by State, Metropolitan Area, and County," Economic Policy Institute, June 16, 2016, http://www.epi.org/publication/income-inequality-in-the-us/#epi-toc-3.

22. David Larcker, Nicholas Donatiello, and Brian Tayan, "Americans and CEO Pay: 2016 Public Perception Survey on CEO Compensation," Stanford Graduate School of Business, 2016, https://www.gsb.stanford.edu/faculty-research/publications/americans-ceo-pay-2016-public-perception-survey-ceo-compensation.

23. S&P Dow Jones Indices, http://us.spindices.com/indices/equity/sp-500.

24. Felix Barber and Michael Goold, "The Strategic Secret of Private Equity," *Harvard Business Review*, September 2007, https://hbr.org/2007/09/the-strategic-secret-of-private-equity.

25. Nathan Vardi, "The Highest-Earning Hedge Fund Managers & Traders," *Forbes*, February 24, 2016, http://www.forbes.com/hedge-fund-managers.

26. Schwarzman's compensation enabled him in 2017 to throw himself a "a multimillion-dollar 70th birthday party in Palm Beach, Fla.—complete with camels, Mongolian greeters, a custom-built temple and a performance by Gwen Stefani. Schwarzman, who is President Trump's economic adviser, was fêted by 400 guests at the epic Silk Road-themed bash, rumored to have cost over $10 million." See Emily Smith, "Blackstone CEO Throws Himself 'the Party of the Century,'" *Page Six*, February 3, 2017, http://pagesix.com/2017/02/13/blackstone-ceo-throws-himself-the-party-of-the-century.

27. Paying these eight executives our hypothetical $1,330,849 a year, they would collectively earn $14,976,000, with the remaining $1,677,837,160 deemed excess compensation. This excess compensation equals 53,777 full-time jobs at $15 per hour/$31,200 per year.

28. Ben Protess and Michael Corkery, "Just How Much Do the Top Private Equity Earners Make?" *New York Times*, December 10, 2016, https://www.nytimes.com/2016/12/10/business/dealbook/just-how-much-do-the-top-private-equity-earners-make.html.

29. Sham Gad, "What Are Hedge Funds?" *Forbes*, October 22, 2013, http://www.forbes.com/sites/investopedia/2013/10/22/what-are-hedge-funds/#51c7ed032782.

30. Lynn Stout, "How Hedge Funds Create Criminals," *Harvard Business Review*, December 13, 2010, https://hbr.org/2010/12/how-hedge-funds-create-crimina.

31. Vardi, "The Highest-Earning Hedge Fund Managers."

32. If we paid the top 25 hedge fund managers and traders our hypothetical CEO compensation of $1,330,849 per year, they would collectively earn $33,271,225, with the remaining $11,911,728,775 deemed excess compensation. This excess compensation equals 381,786 full-time jobs that pay $15 per hour/$31,200 per year.

33. Based on unemployment counts for April 2018. See "Table 3. Civilian labor force and unemployment by state and selected area, seasonally adjusted" in US Bureau of Labor Statistics, "Table 1. Civilian labor force and unemployment by state and selected area, seasonally adjusted," April 2018, https://www.bls.gov/news.release/laus.t01.htm. There are also privately owned corporations. These are companies that do not have publicly traded stock. As such, they aren't subject to federal reporting requirements, including executive compensation. But we would be fair to assume that the CEO-to-worker compensation ratio is also out of whack in this sector. *Forbes* magazine's 2016 ranking of America's largest private companies includes 225 companies with at least $2 billion in annual revenues. The companies "have combined revenues of $1.57 trillion . . . and employ 4.7 million people." See Andrea Murphy, "America's Largest Private Companies," *Forbes*, August 9, 2017, https://www.forbes.com/sites/andreamurphy/2017/08/09/americas-largest-private-companies-2/#2ae83361247c. The top ten private corporations are a list of familiar names: Cargill, Koch Industries, Albertsons, Deloitte, PricewaterhouseCoopers, Mars, Publix Super Markets, Bechtel, Ernst & Young, and C&S Wholesale Grocers.

34. Citizens for Tax Justice, "Fortune 500 Companies Hold a Record $2.4 Trillion Offshore," March 3, 2016, http://ctj.org/pdf/pre0316.pdf.

35. Citizens for Tax Justice, "Fortune 500 Companies." Under a new tax law, Apple repatriated most of its holdings but used the largest chunk to buy back its own stock, thus raising the share price for the mostly wealthy individuals who own Apple's stock. Most other affected companies also used repatriated money to buy back stock. See Jack Nicas, "Apple Says It Will Buy Back $100 Billion in Stock," *New York Times*, May 1, 2018, https://www.nytimes.com/2018/05/01/technology/apple-stock-buyback-earnings.html; and Matt Phillips, "Trump's Tax Cuts in Hand, Companies Spend More on Themselves Than on Wages," *New York Times*, February 26, 2018, https://www.nytimes.com/2018/02/26/business/tax-cuts-share-buybacks-corporate.html.

36. International Consortium of Investigative Journalists, *The Panama Papers*, April 3, 2016, https://panamapapers.icij.org/video.

37. Will Fitzgibbon and Emilia Díaz-Struck, "By the Numbers: Eight Months of Panama Papers Global Impact," International Consortium of Investigative Journalists, December 1, 2016, https://panamapapers.icij.org/blog/20161201-impact-graphic.html.

38. International Consortium of Investigative Journalists, *Paradise Papers*.

39. Gabriel Zucman, *The Hidden Wealth of Nations: The Scourge of Tax Havens* (Chicago: University of Chicago Press, 2015), 35. See also Ronen Palan, Richard Murphy, and Christian Chavagneux, *Tax Havens: How Globalization Really Works* (Ithaca, NY: Cornell University Press, 2010).

40. Zucman, *Hidden Wealth*, 53.

41. Zucman, ix.

42. US Bureau of Labor Statistics, "Employment Situation Summary," June 1, 2018, https://www.bls.gov/news.release/empsit.nr0.htm. For more on "discouraged workers," see Adam Davidson, "Trump and the Truth: The Unemployment-Rate Hoax," *New Yorker*, September 10. 2016, http://www.newyorker.com/news/news-desk/trump-and-the-truth-the-unemployment-rate-hoax.

43. BLS Reports, "Characteristics of Minimum Wage Workers, 2017," US Bureau of Labor Statistics, March 2018, https://www.bls.gov/opub/reports/minimum-wage/2017/home.htm.

44. Warren E. Buffett, "Stop Coddling the Super-Rich," *New York Times*, August 14, 2011, http://www.nytimes.com/2011/08/15/opinion/stop-coddling-the-super-rich.html.

45. Tax Policy Center, "What Is the Effect of a Lower Tax Rate for Capital Gains?" Tax Policy Center's Briefing Book, 2016, http://www.taxpolicycenter.org/briefing-book/what-effect-lower-tax-rate-capital-gains.

46. Tax Policy Center, "What Is the Effect of a Lower Tax Rate?"

47. "Just 8 Men Own Same Wealth as Half the World," Oxfam, January 16, 2017, https://www.oxfam.org/en/pressroom/pressreleases/2017-01-16/just-8-men-own-same-wealth-half-world.

48. World Bank, "Gross Domestic Product 2015," http://databank.worldbank.org/data/download/GDP.pdf.

49 "Forbes Releases 35th Annual Forbes 400 Ranking of the Richest Americans," *Forbes*, October 4, 2016, https://www.forbes.com/sites/forbespr/2016/10/04/forbes-releases-35th-annual-forbes-400-ranking-of-the-richest-americans/#6a41d18c502f. See also Chase Peterson-Withorn, "Forbes 400: The Full List of the Richest People in America 2016," *Forbes*, October 4, 2016, https://www.forbes.com/sites/chasewithorn/2016/10/04/forbes-400-the-full-list-of-the-richest-people-in-america-2016/#28fb123b22f4.

50. Chuck Collins and Josh Hoxie, "Billionaire Bonanza Report: The Forbes 400 and the Rest of Us," Institute for Policy Studies, December 2015, http://www.ips-dc.org/wp-content/uploads/2015/12/Billionaire-Bonanza-The-Forbes-400-and-the-Rest-of-Us-Dec1.pdf.

51. Catherine Clifford, "Bill Gates, Jeff Bezos and Warren Buffett Have More Wealth Than Half the Population of the US Combined," CNBC, November 9, 2017, https://www.cnbc.com/2017/11/09/gates-bezos-buffett-have-more-wealth-than-half-the-us-combined.html.

52. Thomas Piketty, *Capital in the Twenty-First Century* (Cambridge, MA: Belknap Press, 2014), 315.

53. Emmanuel Saez and Gabriel Zucman, "Wealth Inequality in the United States since 1913: Evidence from Capitalized Income Tax Data," *Quarterly Journal of Economics* 131, no. 2 (2016): 519–78, https://doi.org/10.1093/qje/qjw004. Saez and Zucman further note that "in 2012, the top .1% included about 160,000 families with a net wealth above $20.6 million."

54. Piketty, *Capital*, 302–03.

55. Larcker, Donatiello, and Tayan, "Americans and CEO Pay."

56. Dayton Martindale, "Why Keith Ellison and Jeremy Corbyn Think We Should Cap CEO Pay," *In These Times*, May 29, 2018, http://inthesetimes.com/article/21114/maximum-wage-keith-ellison-jeremy-corbyn-income-ceo-pay.

57. "Historical Highest Marginal Income Tax Rates," Tax Policy Center, 2017, https://www.taxpolicycenter.org/statistics/historical-highest-marginal-income-tax-rates. In 2018 the Trump administration's tax law lowered the top rate from 39.6 percent to 37 percent and increased the threshold for that rate to those making $500,000 or more. See Paul Katzell, "How Tax Reform Impacts Your Tax Bracket and Rate," *Investor's Business Daily*, May 16, 2018, https://www.investors.com/etfs-and-funds/personal-finance/how-tax-reform-impacts-your-tax-bracket-and-rate.

58. Jesse Eisinger, "The .03% Solution," *ProPublica*, February 6, 2013, https://www.propublica.org/article/the-03-solution.

59. Piketty, *Capital*, 471.

60. US Securities and Exchange Commission, "SEC Adopts Rule for Pay Ratio Disclosure," August 5, 2015, https://www.sec.gov/news/pressrelease/2015-160.html.

61. US House Financial Services Committee, "The Financial CHOICE Act," June 23, 2016, http://financialservices.house.gov/uploadedfiles/financial_choice_act_comprehensive_outline.pdf, 113.

62. Neil Irwin, "Is Capital or Labor Winning at Your Favorite Company? Introducing the Marx Ratio," *New York Times*, May 21, 2018, https://www.nytimes.com/interactive/2018/05/21/

upshot/marx-ratio-median-pay.html. As Irwin explained in the note accompanying the story, "A better number for the idea we're really trying to get at would be average compensation for nonexecutive employees, but companies aren't required to report that publicly." I agree: reporting the median compensation means high executive compensation stretches the median upward, which doesn't capture the experience of the vast majority of employees.

63. Christopher R. Martin and Anji L. Phillips, "The 99% Want Twinkies: Systematic Information Exclusion and the Shutdown of Hostess Brands" (paper presented at the Union for Democratic Communications/Project Censored joint conference, San Francisco, November 2013). We analyzed the narratives of seven national television and radio news sources (ABC News, CBS News, CNN, Fox News Network, MSNBC, NPR, and NBC News) and tracked these news stories of Hostess Brands over the entire year of 2012. The analysis covered a total of ninety-one stories.

64. David A. Kaplan, "Hostess Is Bankrupt . . . Again," *CNNMoney*, July 26, 2012, http://management.fortune.cnn.com/2012/07/26/hostess-twinkies-bankrupt. See also Steven F. Davidoff, "Corporate Forces Endangered the Twinkie, but May Save It," *New York Times*, February 5, 2013, http://dealbook.nytimes.com/2013/02/05/corporate-forces-endangered-the-twinkie-but-may-save-it.

65. Kaplan, "Hostess Is Bankrupt."

66. Hostess Brands, "Hostess Brands Is Closed," http://hostessbrands.com/Closed.aspx.

67. Michael Hiltzik, "Poor Management, Not Union Intransigence, Killed Hostess," *Los Angeles Times*, November 25, 2012, http://articles.latimes.com/2012/nov/25/business/la-fi-hiltzik-20121125.

68. David Crary, "AP Poll: Mass Shootings Voted Top 2012 News Story," Associated Press, December 20, 2012, http://www.ap.org/Content/AP-In-The-News/2012/AP-poll-Mass-shootings-voted-top-2012-news-story.

69. "Got Twinkies?" *The Five*, November 19, 2012, http://video.foxnews.com/v/1978418503001.

70. For union communications, see http://www.aflcio.org/Blog/%28tag%29/1668 (blog posts tagged with Hostess); http://www.aflcio.org/Blog/%28offset%29/10/%28tag%29/14521 (blog posts tagged with Hostess Brands); and http://www.aflcio.org/Blog/%28tag%29/1669 (blog posts tagged with Twinkies).

71. Chris Isadore, "Start the Countdown! Twinkies Return to Shelves July 15," CNN, June 24, 2013, http://money.cnn.com/2013/06/24/news/companies/twinkies-return/index.html.

72. Alia Dastagir, "West Virginia Teachers' Victory Shows 'Power of Women' as More Battles Loom," *USA Today*, March 8, 2018, https://www.usatoday.com/story/news/2018/03/08/west-virginia-teachers-victory-shows-power-women-more-battles-loom/403474002. See also National Center for Education Statistics, "Characteristics of Public Elementary and Secondary School Teachers in the United States," US Department of Education, August 2017, https://nces.ed.gov/pubs2017/2017072.pdf.

73. Leah Varjacques, Taige Jensen, and Japhet Weeks, "We Are Republican Teachers Striking in Arizona. It's Time to Raise Taxes," *New York Times* video, 3:53, April 26, 2018, https://www.nytimes.com/2018/04/26/opinion/red-arizona-republican-teacher-strike.html.

74. Patricia Cohen and Robert Gebeloff, "Public Servants Are Losing Their Foothold in the Middle Class," *New York Times*, April 22, 2018, https://www.nytimes.com/2018/04/22/business/economy/public-employees.html.

75. E. Tammy Kim, "Can Arizona's Teachers Still Consider Themselves Middle Class?" *New Yorker*, May 2, 2018, https://www.newyorker.com/news/dispatch/can-arizonas-teachers-still-consider-themselves-middle-class.

76. Steven K. Ashby and Robert Bruno, *A Fight for the Soul of Public Education: The Story of the Chicago Teachers Strike* (Ithaca, NY: Cornell University Press, 2016).

77. Mike Elk, "The Teachers' Strikes Prove It: The Media Is Finally Seeing America's New Labor Landscape," *Guardian*, April 28, 2018, https://www.theguardian.com/us-news/2018/apr/28/us-teachers-strikes-workers-labor-unions.

78. Stephen Franklin, "The Chicago Tribune Is Finally Union as the Media Organizing Wave Intensifies," *In These Times*, June 4, 2018, http://inthesetimes.com/working/entry/21182/chicago_tribune_union_labor_media_tronc_newsguild.

79. Sharon Knolle, "Newsrooms Are Forming Unions to Create Better Pay, Better Benefits and Better Journalism," *Editor & Publisher*, May 1, 2018, http://www.editorandpublisher.com/feature/newsrooms-are-forming-unions-to-create-better-pay-better-benefits-and-better-journalism; Tom Kludt, "Staffers at *The New Yorker* Organize a Union," CNN, June 6, 2018, http://money.cnn.com/2018/06/06/media/new-yorker-union/index.html; Dave McNary, "Fast Company Unionizes with Writers Guild of America East," *Variety*, June 6, 2018, https://variety.com/2018/digital/news/fast-company-unionizes-writers-guild-of-america-1202833901.

80. Gary Weiss, "An Unlikely Big Player in Digital Media: Unions," *Columbia Journalism Review*, June 21, 2017, https://www.cjr.org/business_of_news/digital-media-unions.php.

81. Julie Bosman and Sydney Ember, "At Chicago Sun-Times, New Owners Vow Return to Paper's Working-Class Roots," *New York Times*, July 23, 2017, https://www.nytimes.com/2017/07/23/business/media/chicago-sun-times-ownership.html.

82. Andy Newman and John Leland, "DNAinfo and Gothamist Are Shut Down after Vote to Unionize," *New York Times*, November 2, 2017, https://www.nytimes.com/2017/11/02/nyregion/dnainfo-gothamist-shutting-down.html.

83. Joe Ricketts, "Why I'm Against Unions at Businesses I Create," *Joe Ricketts Blog*, September 12, 2017, http://blog.joericketts.com/?p=557.

84. John Kenneth Galbraith, *American Capitalism: The Concept of Countervailing Power* (Boston: Houghton Mifflin, 1956), 136.

85. Matt Grossman and David A. Hopkins, *Asymmetric Politics: Ideological Republicans and Group Interest Democrats* (New York: Oxford University Press, 2016), 11.

86. Richard Sennett and Jonathan Cobb, *The Hidden Injuries of Class* (New York: Knopf, 1972).

87. Michael Zweig, "Introduction: The Challenges of Working Class Studies," in *What's Class Got to Do with It?* ed. Michael Zweig (Ithaca, NY: Cornell University Press, 2004), 4.

88. Sennett and Cobb, *Hidden Injuries*, 38.

89. David Brooks, "This Century Is Broken," *New York Times*, February 21, 2017, https://www.nytimes.com/2017/02/21/opinion/this-century-is-broken.html.

90. Brooks, "This Century."

91. Leo Bogart, *Preserving the Press* (New York: Columbia University Press, 1991), 157–58.

92. Robert W. McChesney and John Nichols, *The Death and Life of American Journalism* (New York: Nation, 2010).

93. Robert Kuttner and Hildy Zenger, "Saving the Free Press from Private Equity," *American Prospect*, December 27, 2017, http://prospect.org/article/saving-free-press-private-equity.

94. Alex T. Williams, "Employment Picture Darkens for Journalists at Digital Outlets," *Columbia Journalism Review*, September 27, 2016, https://www.cjr.org/business_of_news/journalism_jobs_digital_decline.php.

95. "The 2013 Pulitzer Prize Winner in Public Service," Pulitzer Prizes, http://www.pulitzer.org/winners/las-vegas-sun-and-notably-courageous-reporting-alexandra-berzon.

96. "The iEconomy," 2012 series, *New York Times*, http://www.nytimes.com/interactive/business/ieconomy.html?_r=0.

97. "The 2013 Pulitzer Prize Winner in Explanatory Reporting," Pulitzer Prizes, http://www.pulitzer.org/winners/staff-74.

98. Kevin Hardy and Grant Rodgers, "Chemical Exposure Results in Injuries, Pink Slips at Iowa Wind Blade Maker, Lawsuits Claim," *Des Moines Register,* December 16, 2017, https://www.desmoinesregister.com/story/money/business/2017/12/16/former-tpi-iowa-workers-claim-they-were-fired-after-chemical-exposure/844600001.

99. "Deflategate Timeline: After 544 days, Tom Brady Gives In," ESPN, July 15, 2016, http://www.espn.com/blog/new-england-patriots/post/_/id/4782561/timeline-of-events-for-deflategate-tom-brady.

100. Robert Zeiger, *For Jobs and Freedom: Race and Labor in America since 1865* (Lexington: University Press of Kentucky, 2010); Ruth Milkman, ed., *Women, Work and Protest: A Century of US Women's Labor History* (New York: Routledge, 2013).

101. Lane Windham, *Knocking on Labor's Door: Union Organizing in the 1970s, and the Roots of a New Economic Divide* (Chapel Hill: University of North Carolina Press, 2017).

102. Josh Bivins et al., *How Today's Unions Help Working People* (Washington, DC: Economic Policy Institute, 2017), http://www.epi.org/publication/how-todays-unions-help-working-people-giving-workers-the-power-to-improve-their-jobs-and-unrig-the-economy.

103. Henry S. Farber, Daniel Herbst, Ilyana Kuziemko, and Suresh Naidu, "Unions and Inequality over the Twentieth Century: New Evidence from Survey Data," Working Paper 24587, National Bureau of Economic Research, May 2018, http://www.nber.org/papers/w24587.

104. Terri Gross, "'New York Times' Executive Editor on the New Terrain of Covering Trump," NPR *Fresh Air,* December 8, 2016, https://www.npr.org/2016/12/08/504806512/new-york-times-executive-editor-on-the-new-terrain-of-covering-trump.

105. Michael Massing, "How to Do Journalism in Trump's America," *Nation,* January 18, 2017, https://www.thenation.com/article/how-to-do-journalism-in-trumps-america.

106. New York Times Editorial Board, June 12, 2017, http://www.nytimes.com/interactive/opinion/editorialboard.html.

107. "Truth and Lies in the Age of Trump," *New York Times,* December 10, 2016, https://www.nytimes.com/2016/12/10/opinion/truth-and-lies-in-the-age-of-trump.html.

Index

ABC, 31

ABC Radio, 128

Abramoff, Jack, 13

accountability journalism, 24

Adbusters magazine, 153

Advance Publications, 58, 59–60

advertising, 49, 119, 132, 226n80; influence on labor reporting, 53; magazines and, 63; marketing executives, 65–66; race and, 64, 71; revenue and circulation coverage, 63, 67–68, 71, 74–77, 83–85, 88, 90; suburban migration and, 63–64. *See also* audience shift, mass to upscale

advertising in *Editor & Publisher*, mass-to-upscale emphasis shift, 18, 70–106, 227n5; *Anchorage Daily News*, 105; *Arizona Republic*, 105; *Baltimore News American*, 91, 92; *Baltimore Sun*, 72, 74, 75, 92; *Chicago Tribune*, 74, 76, 98–100; *Cincinnati Enquirer*, 71, 73; *Cleveland Plain Dealer*, 92–96, 100, 105; college and preparatory school readership, 78–79, 81; *Columbus Dispatch*, 71, 73; *Democrat and Chronicle*, 97–98; *Detroit Free Press*, 71–72; gross market size, 85–88; *Idaho Statesman*, 105; *Indianapolis News*, 71, 74; *Indianapolis Star*, 105; local economy and, 72–73; *Los Angeles Herald-Examiner*, 88–90; *Los Angeles Times*, 83–85, 85, 86; native-born Americans, 71; *News & Record*, 105; *New York Herald Tribune*, 78, 81; *New York Post*, 105; *New York Sun*, 78, 81, 99; *New York Times*, 76–80, 82, 99, 100–104, 227n11; *New York World-Telegram*, 79, 82–83; *Oregonian*, 105; *Philadelphia Inquirer*, 85–88; *Pittsburgh Sun-Telegraph*, 74, 75; "quality" audiences sought, 77, 84, 88, 92, 96–97, 100, 105–6; race and, 71; *Seattle Post-Intelligencer*, 96–97; *St. Louis Globe-Democrat*, 85, 87; *Tulsa World*, 105–6; *Washington Post*, 100, 103–5. *See also* audience shift, mass to upscale

African Americans, 7, 8, 13, 31–33, 64

agenda-setting effect of media, 147, 164

Agnew, Spiro, 201

Ailes, Roger, 129, 131, 231n52, 232n75

Air Lines Pilot Association, 113

air traffic controllers strike (1970), 116–17

Albuquerque Tribune, 56

Alesci, Cristina, 32

Althusser, Louis, 135

American Association of University Professors (AAUP), 15

American Bankers Association, 153

American Dream, 152

40, 41, 43–44; follow-up investigation, 43–44, 45; news coverage, 20–21, 28–30, 40. *See also* jobs and employment, outsourcing
Carrier plant, Trump and, 18; campaign promises to save jobs, 4, 20, 21, 23–24, 42, 43; ignores outsourcing in other locations, 38; mistakes as air conditioner assembly plant, 23, 35, 36, 37; news coverage, 20–21, 24, 39, 40; speech at, 21, 26, 33–39; Trump supporters in, 26, 28, 30–31, 40, 43, 45; tweets on, 20, 23, 26–27, 40–41; union activity opinion, 38, 40–41; visit, 20–21, 33–40. *See also* Trump, Donald J.
Carrier plant closure announcement: Local 1999 and, 33, 38, 39, 40–42, 45; news coverage, 22–23, 27, 34; profit and, 42–43; Trump's attention to, 23–25, 34, 36, 37–38; viral video, 22–23, 27, 31–32, 42–43. *See also* jobs and employment, outsourced
Carrier plant coverage: closure announcement, 22–23, 27, 34; follow-up investigation, 24, 39, 41; jobs agreement, 20–21, 28–30, 40; legislation and economic angle ignored, 44–45; local, 33, 38, 42, 43, 45; mistaken as air conditioning assembly plant, 29, 40; national, 31, 32, 39, 42, 43, 45; quality of, 32–33; reported as win for Trump and jobs, 21–22, 28–31, 39, 221n55; Trump as focus, 20–21, 24–26, 28, 39, 42; white, male workers as focus, 18, 26, 27–31, 32, 39, 43
Carter, Jimmy, 139, 200, 233n22
Casper Star-Tribune, 198
CBN, 129
CBS, 23, 31
CBS Evening News, 195–96, 207
CBS News, 1
Center for Public Integrity, 54, 224n22
CEO-to-worker compensation ratio, 182–84, 190–92, 242n19, 244n62. *See also* income inequality
Charles Schwab & Company, 123
Chenevert, Louis, 42
Chicago Federation of Labor, 198
Chicago Sun-Times, 198
Chicago Tribune: advertising in *E & P,* 74, 76, 98–100; Franklin at, 51, 60, 122; lifestyle-oriented workplace column in, 120–22; subscription cuts, 65; unions at, 198
Chomsky, Daniel, 58–59
Chong, Dennis, 164
Christian Broadcasting Network (CBN), 127
Christian Coalition, 127
Christian Science Monitor, 21
Cincinnati Enquirer, 71, 73
Cincinnati Post/Kentucky Post, 56

CIO (Congress of Industrial Organizations), 50
circulation, 44, 106–7, 167; advertising and, 63, 67–68, 69, 71, 74–77, 83–85, 88, 90; audience shift and, 63–64, 65–66, 88, 90, 92–93, 106; decline, 63–68, 90, 106; increase, 55–56; newspaper cost and, 55, 76–77; race and, 65; readership research, 66–67, 69–70; urban/suburban migration and, 63–64. *See also* audience shift, mass to upscale
Citadel LLC, 186
citizen, presidential rhetoric on, 147–48, 151
Citizens for Tax Justice, 187
citizenship, as value, 114, 116, 145
civic beats, 48
civil rights, 7–8
Clark, Evans, 52
Cleland, Nancy, 51
Cleveland Plain Dealer, 9–10; advertising in *E & P,* 92–96, 100, 105; business staff, 124; fact-checking at, 240n47; labor reporting and, 51, 59; Newhouse and, 58, 59–60
Cleveland Press, 56, 59
Clinton, Bill, 128, 135, 142–43, 160
Clinton, Hillary, 3, 24; Iowa and, 155, 156, 157, 158–61, 236n65
Clinton administration, 166–67, 168–69
Close Tax Loopholes That Outsource American Jobs Act (H.R. 5145), 44
Clough, Rick, 33
CNBC, 42, 124, 126, 152, 180, 181, 231n52
CNN, 21, 45, 197
CNNMoney, 23, 26, 32
Cobb, Jonathan, 201–2
Cohn, Gary, 180
Cohn, Nate, 155
Columbia Journalism Review, 124, 125, 130, 148, 204, 240n47
Columbus Dispatch, 71, 73, 204
Comey, James, 3
Complacent Class, The (Cowen), 203
conglomeration. *See* newspaper industry conglomeration
Congressional Budget Office, 151
conservative media, 237n85; grievance-highlighting coverage of liberal media, 11–12; NRA magazines, 231n60; political rhetoric and, 147; rise of, 6, 11–12, 126–31, 231n60; talk radio, 128, 231n69; Trump campaign and, 161–62; working class audience and, 6, 18–19, 126–31, 152, 162, 201–2
consumer-focused coverage, 9–12, 111–12; data analysis, 134, 147–51; harms labor interests, 119; in Hostess Brands story, 193–97, 245n63; photo of exhausted

Kilborn, Peter T., 52
Kim, E. Tammy, 197–98
King, Steve, 154
Kleiman, Carol, 120–22
Klein, Drew, 15, 16
Knight Ridder newspapers, 62, 65
KNKX (Seattle-Tacoma station), 53–54
Koch brothers, 15, 181
Kovach, Bill, 5–6, 69, 134, 164–65
Kroc, Joan, 53

Labor Notes, 54
labor reporting (labor beat), 6, 47–68, 106, 205; audience shift and, 60–61; in broadcast television, 53; bylines, 47, 49, 223n2; corporate news, 55–61; current state of, 51–55; decline, 49, 51, 59, 61; editorial and ownership limitations on, 49, 58–59, 61–65; historical overview, 47–51; identifying reporters, 47, 223n2; lifestyle-oriented workplace column replaces, 120–23, 200; *New York Times,* 18, 48, 50, 51, 52, 58–59, 60; online, 54; personal finance journalism replaces, 125; on radio, 53–54
labor unions, 5, 15, 121–22, 134, 199–200, 205–6; audience shift and, 59–60; in consumer-focused coverage, 10–11; coverage about, editorial limitations, 57–60; Hostess Brands shutdown and, 193; invisibility of, 6, 203; "job killer" term used by, 173, 239n24; Local 1999, 33, 38, 39, 40–42, 45; membership numbers, 9, 61, 136, 166; negotiation language, 112; in news industry, 58, 59, 60, 198; presidential rhetoric on, 141, 145, 146; Reagan's anti-union policies, 12, 140, 200; Trump's opinions, 38, 40–41. *See also* strikes; transit strikes coverage; worker-focused coverage
LaGuardia, Fiorello, 109
Lakeland Ledger, 198–99
Langfitt, Frank, 53
Las Vegas Sun, 205
Lazio, Rick, 169
Leary, John J., Jr., 50
Lee, Alfred McClung, 55–56, 57–58
legislation, outsourced jobs and, 44
Leonard, Thomas C., 64, 66
Levey, Stanley, 52
Levine, Marianne, 224n23
Levy, Harry, 48
liberal bias, 129, 130–31
Lieberman, Trudy, 178
Life magazine, 63
lifestyle-oriented workplace column, 120–23, 200
Limbaugh, Rush, 128, 130–31, 161

Link, Rick, 30–31
Llamas, Tom, 31
Lloyd, Matthew, 39
Local 1999 (United Steelworkers, Carrier plant), 33, 38, 39, 40–42, 45
local newspapers: acquisition of, 61–62; community focus, 106–8
Loftus, Joseph A., 52
Look magazine, 63
Los Angeles Examiner, 57–58
Los Angeles Herald-Examiner, 88–90
Los Angeles Newspaper Guild union, 90
Los Angeles Times, 65, 124, 194, 198; advertising in *E & P,* 83–85, 86; labor reporting and, 51, 53, 57
Lukens, Donald "Buz," 12–13, 14
Luntz, Frank, 164, 167

Mackey, John, 242n19
magazine industry, 63, 124, 231n60
Mahoney, C. A., 48
mainstream media: "liberal bias," 129, 130–31; political rhetoric and, 146–47; Trump campaign and, 161–62; use of term "job killer" in, 168
Make America Great Again slogan, 7, 160
Mamreov, Alexander Benjamin Finkelstein, 48, 52
Marcus, Bernie, 166
market democracy, 124
marketing executives, 65–66. *See also* advertising
Martin, Christopher R., 12–15, 16–17
Marx Ratio, 192, 244n62
mass audience. *See* audience, working class; audience shift, mass to upscale
Massing, Michael, 206–7
"maximum income" policy discussion, 191
Mayer, Jane, 129
Maynard, Robin, 28–30
McCain, John, 2, 144, 155
McChesney, Robert, 106
McConnell, Mitch, 169, 175
McDonough, Bob, 20, 42
McGee, Michael C., 152
McKechnie, John T., 48
McLean, John H., 52
McNerney, Jerry, 44
media corporations. *See* corporations
Memphis Press-Scimitar, 56
men. *See* white, male working class
Mercer, Robert, 128, 181
Metropolitan Transit Authority strike, 110
Mexico, jobs outsourced to. *See* jobs and employment
Meyer, Philip, 65, 68

North American Free Trade Agreement (NAFTA), 239n24
NPR, 53, 129, 207

Obama, Barack, 144–45, 152, 192, 223n63; Iowa and, 155, 156, 158; "job killer" accusations against, 166–67, 168–69, 170, 176; US auto industry bailout by, 219n18
obituaries, labor reporters identified through, 52, 223n2, 223n10
#OccupyWallStreet, 153
Occupy Wall Street (OWS) movement, 19, 153–54, 159, 182, 203, 235n55
Ochs, Adolph, 76–77
offshore untaxed wealth, 187–88
Omaha World-Herald, 198
online journalism, 54, 128–29, 198
On the Media (WNYC program), 6
op-ed page, introduction of, 100
Orange County Register, 53
Oregonian, 105
O'Reilly, Bill, 131
Otis and Chandler families *(Los Angeles Times)*, 57
outsourcing jobs. *See* Carrier plant; jobs and employment
Overseas Outsourcing Accountability Act (H.R. 357), 44
Oxfam, 190

Pace, Julie, 177
Packer, George, 178
Page, Larry, 242n19
Panama Papers, 180, 187
Paquette, Danielle, 51
Paradise Papers, 180–81, 187
PATCO (the Professional Air Traffic Controllers Organization), 116, 117, 200, 229n18
Payday Report, 54
Pearl Harbor attack, 133–34
Pelley, Scott, 195–96
Pence, Mike, 20–21, 33, 34, 41, 219n18
penny press, 47, 55
people of color, 2, 206; African Americans, 7, 8, 13, 31–33, 64
Perino, Dana, 195
Perot, Ross, 2
personal finance journalism, 123–26, 231n69
Philadelphia Bulletin, 86
Philadelphia Inquirer, 51, 85–88
Phillips, Anji, 193, 245n63
Piketty, Thomas, 190, 191
Pilot-Tribune (Storm Lake, Iowa), 106–7
Pisani, Bob, 126
Pitts, Leonard, Jr., 161

Pittsburgh Press, 56, 74
Pittsburgh Sun-Telegraph, 74, 75
pivot counties, 155–56, 157
political voice. *See* conservative media; Democrats; Iowa, political voice and; Republicans
Politico, 54
PoliticoPro, 54
Politics of Resentment, The: Rural Consciousness in Wisconsin and the Rise of Scott Walker (Cramer), 3
PolitiFact.com, 173–74, 220n39, 239n27
Pomfret, John D., 52
Poole, Gary Andrew, 148
Portland Oregonian, 58
poverty line, 181–82, 241n8. *See also* income; wealth
presidential campaigns, 135–36; "job killers" term and, 165–66. *See also* Trump campaign; working class invisibility, presidential rhetoric and
presidential elections, Iowa and, 154–61. *See also* Trump, election of
Price, William G. F., 48
private equity compensation, 185–86
ProPublica, 54
public employees, union bargaining rights for, 15. *See also* labor unions
publicly traded newspaper companies, 55, 62, 88
Pulitzer, Joseph, 48, 56, 58, 76

"quality" demographics, 77, 84, 88, 92, 96–97, 100, 105–6. *See also* advertising in *Editor & Publisher*, mass-to-upscale emphasis shift; audience shift, mass to upscale
Quayle, Dan, 141–42

race, 58, 120–21; advertising and, 64, 71; African Americans, 7, 8, 13, 31–33, 64; Carrier worker demographics, 31–32; newspapers' audiences and, 64, 65; people of color, 2, 7, 8, 13, 31–33, 64, 206; wage gap, 7. *See also* white, male working class
radio journalism, 53–54; conservative talk radio, 128, 237n85
Ramsay, Dave, 231n69
rapid performance improvement, 185
Raskin, A. H., 50, 52
Rayburn, Gregory F., 193–94
readership. *See* circulation: decline
readership, advertisers' focus on, 69–70
Reagan, Ronald, 2, 119, 140–41, 142–43, 229n18; anti-union stance, 12, 140, 200; conservative media and, 128
Reagan administration, 168, 169, 191